Aftermath

Aftermath

Editors of FLYING® *Magazine*

TAB Books
Division of McGraw-Hill, Inc.
New York   San Francisco   Washington, D.C.   Auckland   Bogotá
Caracas   Lisbon   London   Madrid   Mexico City   Milan
Montreal   New Delhi   San Juan   Singapore
Sydney   Tokyo   Toronto

Notices
Aftermath   Hachette Filipacchi Magazines, Inc.
Flying®

© 1994 by *Flying* **magazine**.
Published by TAB Books, a division of McGraw-Hill, Inc.

pbk 2 3 4 5 6 7 8 9 0 DOH/DOH 9 9 8 7 6 5 4
hc   1 2 3 4 5 6 7 8 9 DOH/DOH 9 9 8 7 6 5 4

Library of Congress Cataloging-in-Publication Data
Aftermath / by the editors of FLYING magazine.
      p. cm.
    ISBN 0-8306-4283-8 ISBN 0-8306-4282-X (pbk.)
    1. Aeronautics—Accidents—Human factors. 2. Aeronautics—Safety
measures. I. Flying (Los Angeles, Calif.)
TL553.5.A44 1993
629.132'52'0289—dc20   93-27575
                                                             CIP

Acquisitions editor: Jeff Worsinger
Editorial team: Joanne Slike, Executive Editor
                Susan W. Kagey, Managing Editor
Production team: Katherine G. Brown, Director
                Ollie Harmon, Coding
                Wanda S. Ditch, Layout
                Linda L. King, Proofreading
Design team: Jaclyn J. Boone, Designer
                Brian Allison, Associate Designer   GEN1
Cover design: Holberg Design, York, Pa.   4312

Contents

Introduction *ix*

1 Decision-Making *1*

Avianca 052: How Did It Happen? *by Peter Garrison* *1*
Following Orders *by Peter Garrison* *7*
Bad Bet *by Peter Garrison* *11*
Late for Work *by Peter Garrison* *15*
Angel of Mercy *by Peter Garrison* *19*
Too Late to Turn Back *by Peter Garrison* *23*
Hidden Pressure *by Peter Garrison* *27*
The Road Warrior *by Peter Garrison* *30*
Uncontrolled Experiment *by Peter Garrison* *33*
Pride Before the Fall *by Peter Garrison* *36*
Dropping the Reins *by Peter Garrison* *40*
Deferred Maintenance *by Peter Garrison* *45*
Point of Know Return *by Peter Garrison* *49*

2 Attitude *54*

Patterns of Destruction *by Peter Garrison* *54*
End of a Rule-Breaker *by Peter Garrison* *59*
Flying Squirrel *by Peter Garrison* *63*
Flying Above the Law *by J. Mac McClellan* *69*
Hot Head *by Peter Garrison* *72*
Heart Trouble *by Peter Garrison* *76*

3 Ice *80*

Too Long in the Ice *by J. Mac McClellan* *80*
Ice Box *by J. Mac McClellan* *83*

Ice is Where You Find It *by Peter Garrison*   86
Frost Bite *by Peter Garrison*   90
Just a Little Ice *by Peter Garrison*   95
Ice Stalled the Tail *by Peter Garrison*   99

4 Thunderstorms   *103*
By Jove *by Peter Garrison*   *103*
Inexplicable Breakup *by Peter Garrison*   *108*
Radar Trap *by J. Mac McClellan*   *111*
Blind Alley *by J. Mac McClellan*   *115*

5 Mechanical Problems   *120*
Door Open to Disaster *by Nigel Moll*   *120*
Loose Needle *by Peter Garrison*   *124*
You Can Go Home Again *by Peter Garrison*   *126*
Misrigged and Rolling *by Peter Garrison*   *130*
Unsolved Mysteries *by J. Mac McClellan*   *134*

6 Human Error   *138*
Danger Zone: IFR to VFR *by Peter Garrison*   *138*
Low and Slow *by Peter Garrison*   *142*
Formation Disaster *by Peter Garrison*   *145*
"See and Avoid" or Blind Faith? *by J. Mac McClellan*   *149*
Flight of the Intruder *by J. Mac McClellan*   *152*
Don't Blame Us *by Peter Garrison*   *156*
Snow Storm *by Peter Garrison*   *159*
Mistaken Identity *by Peter Garrison*   *164*
Tuned for Disaster *by Peter Garrison*   *167*
Flap Trap *by Peter Garrison*   *171*
Sins of Omission *by J. Mac McClellan*   *176*
Control Conundrum *by Peter Garrison*   *180*
Pushed to the Limit *by Peter Garrison*   *183*
Too Hot to Handle *by J. Mac McClellan*   *187*
What Failed, Gyro or Pilot? *by Peter Garrison*   *191*
Just Say No-Go *by Peter Garrison*   *195*
The Perils of Perseverance *by Nigel Moll*   *198*
Reverse Psychology *by J. Mac McClellan*   *203*
Falling Stars *by Peter Garrison*   *206*

7 Mixed Bags   *210*

Waiting to Happen *by Peter Garrison*   210
Exploring the Down-to-Earth *by J. Mac McClellan*   214
Twice-Told Tale *by J. Mac McClellan*   219
The Good, Bad and Ugly *by Peter Garrison*   222

Introduction

A monthly analysis of a National Transportation Safety Board (NTSB) accident report began appearing in *Flying* magazine 20 years ago under the title "Pilot Error." We soon realized that accidents were caused by a combination of factors, not just piloting mistakes, and changed the name to "Aftermath."

All pilots have an intense interest in accident reports. We want to know what went wrong so we can avoid putting ourselves in similar situations. Most of the important improvements in aircraft design and pilot training have resulted, sadly, from accident investigations. Aviation safety continues to improve as we learn from the mistakes of pilots, mechanics, aircraft designers, and air traffic controllers.

The NTSB is the official source of all aviation accident reports in the United States and is independent of all other transportation regulatory groups, such as the Federal Aviation Administration (FAA) or the Department of Transportation (DOT). This independence allows the NTSB to arrive at unbiased "probable cause" findings for each accident and to recommend changes in regulations or procedures that will help prevent future accidents.

Many of our Aftermath accident report analyses concern larger aircraft, because they carry the infamous "black box" recorders. The recorders have never been black—they are actually painted fluorescent orange to help investigators find them in the wreckage—but the "black box" name applied by television and newspaper reporters has stuck. One box records all cockpit conversations for 30 minutes prior to the accident, and the other records the flight profile of the aircraft, noting such facts as altitude, airspeed, heading, and so on. Data on the recorders allows the NTSB to perform a much more thorough investigation, thus providing us with more information for the "Aftermath" column. Light-airplane accident investigations can be revealing and conclusive, but they are often short-circuited by a dearth of information about the last moments of the flight, leaving both the NTSB and *Flying* with an inconclusive answer to the inevitable question: What went wrong?

We hope you learn from the mistakes and misfortune of other pilots presented in this book. If you do, Aftermath will have been a success.

J. Mac McClellan
Editor-in-Chief, *Flying*

1

Decision-Making

The accidents that find their way into *Flying* magazine's Aftermath column are not chosen at random. For the purposes of the column, there are "good" and "bad" accidents, the "good" ones being those from which pilots can learn something. Accidents that involve the unforeseeable failure of a well-maintained machine aren't "good," because pilots could not have done anything to avoid them. In contrast, accidents that arise purely from the pilot's actions usually reveal patterns that other pilots might recognize and avoid. Not surprisingly, therefore, many of the accidents in this collection fall into the broad category of "improper inflight decision-making."

Decision-making includes not only the particular choices a pilot makes—to go ahead into bad weather rather than to land, for instance—but also the pilot's style. Is the pilot's sense of options clear or muddled? Does the pilot take the initiative or turn it over to a controller? Does the pilot act promptly or procrastinate?

Often, a pilot defers making a decision—even the right one—until it's too late. Procrastination can have several causes, including reluctance to expose a previous error or misjudgment. The first accident in this group is a famous case of fatal procrastination: the crash of an Avianca 707 a few miles from JFK airport in New York.

Avianca 052: How Did it Happen?
by Peter Garrison

General aviation airplanes run out of fuel regularly. Okay, a lot of these guys are amateurs. But when an airliner runs out of fuel, the layman's first reaction is disbelief. Airline fuel loads are checked and rechecked by professional dispatchers; their routes and fuel burns are carefully documented; their onboard metering equipment is presumably of a high order; and in many cases, a third crewmember—the second officer or flight engineer—has little to do in flight other than monitor the engine conditions and the fuel state. How can air-carrier jets possibly run out of fuel?

And yet they do.

A DC-8 did it at Portland a decade or so ago; a 767 ran dry and landed (safely!) on a drag strip; and most recently, an Avianca 707, Flight 052, crashed on a night approach to John F. Kennedy Airport (JFK) on January 25, 1990, after all four engines flamed out for lack of fuel.

The weather at JFK that evening was bad, fluctuating just around minimums. A tangle of occluded and cold fronts lay over the Eastern seaboard from Illinois to Cape Cod. At 2100 Eastern Standard Time (EST), half an hour before the accident, JFK was reporting an indefinite ceiling 200 feet, sky obscured, visibility one-quarter mile in drizzle and fog, with a 21-knot surface wind. Conditions were somewhat variable; at the time of the accident, 2134 EST, the sky was only partially obscured, and the visibility was up to three-quarters of a mile. The runway visual range was 5,500 feet on Runway 4R.

Flight 052 had filed Boston Logan as an alternate, but weather there was worse than at JFK: A 2050 observation called it zero ceiling with sky obscured, one-eighth-mile visibility, with an RVR of 1,400 to 1,600 feet.

The flight had originated in Bogotá and made an intermediate stop at Medellin, Colombia, where it refueled before setting out for JFK. The distance from Medellin is 2,100 nm, about the same as the distance from Los Angeles to New York. The airplane, a −321B variant of the venerable 707, was designed to fly 6,000-mile intercontinental legs at Mach .9.

The flight plan for the trip was generated by a computer in Paris and reached the Avianca dispatchers in Bogotá and Medellin via teleprinter. (One world!) It provided for 4 + 40 en route, 30 minutes to the alternate, 30 minutes for holding, and a 28-minute additional reserve. With an allowance for taxi, the total fuel requirement came to 73,930 pounds.

The dispatcher at Medellin had the airplane fueled with 78,000 pounds; the additional 4,070 pounds brought the airplane up to the maximum allowable weight for the planned departure runway. The captain subsequently decided to use another runway and ordered an additional 2,000 pounds of fuel, making the total 80,000 pounds. The flight engineer's records of fuel quantity indicated a still higher figure—about 82,000 pounds—based on the readings of the fuel gauges. The 2,000-pound discrepancy is within the plus/minus three-percent limits of accuracy of the fuel-gauging system.

In addition to the various pads and reserves built into the fuel calculations, the en route fuel consumption of the airplane was assumed to be 10 percent over book because of the airplane's age—built in 1967, it had almost 62,000 airframe hours—and because of noise-reduction equipment added to the engines. Based on these conservative assumptions about fuel burn, the airplane should have used 11,541 pounds climbing to Flight Level 370, and then burned about 11,500 pounds per hour in cruise. Holding at around 200 KIAS, it would burn about 9,000 pph, regardless of altitude.

The computed fuel for diversion to an alternate included en route fuel, plus a 30-minute hold at 1,500 feet and one missed approach at the alternate. For a handful of possible alternates the computed fuel requirement ranged from 12,600 to 15,300 pounds.

Initial weather forecasts for the JFK area had called for one- to one-and-a-half-mile visibilities and ceilings of 400 to 800 feet around the time of their arrival and gave the crew of Flight 052 no reason to expect trouble. Although various flight-following services were available en route, the crew did not contact them for weather updates. As the flight progressed, however, conditions at many of the major airports along the Northeastern Corridor were deteriorating. JFK would eventually dip below minimums, and increasing numbers of flights were missing approaches.

The first indications of potential difficulties for Flight 052 came in the form of a series of holds as the flight ascended the Atlantic seaboard, first for 19 minutes at Norfolk and then for 29 minutes at Atlantic City. By the time the flight left the holding pattern at Atlantic City, nearly all of its "extra" fuel was gone.

At 2018 EST, ATC placed the flight in a third holding pattern at Camrn Intersection, 39 nm south of the airport, at 14,000 feet. That hold lasted another 29 minutes.

Although the cockpit voice recorder tapes were of excellent quality, the recordings cover only the 45-minute period before the crash. Consequently, we know nothing about the level of the crew's concerns about fuel earlier in the flight. But at 2044:50, in the holding pattern at Camrn and without an expected further clearance time, the first officer of Flight 052, who handled all radio communications, advised center that "we need priority." He told the controller that the flight was no longer able to reach its alternate and that it could hold for no more than another five minutes. This was the first that center knew of the flight's critical fuel state; but because of a breakdown in communication, the fact that Flight 052 no longer had sufficient fuel to reach its alternate did not register with controllers.

At 2046, New York Tracon authorized the hand-off controller to insert Flight 052 into the traffic stream for JFK's ILS 22L approach, and the flight left the holding pattern. Ten minutes later, center relayed a wind-shear advisory of "increases" of 10 knots at 500 and 1,500 feet.

The flight had to make one more 360-degree turn for spacing and began its approach at 2111. Aware that its fuel supply was extremely low, the crew briefed for possible go-around with minimum acceleration and a limited nose-up attitude. The captain was impatient to lower the landing gear, but the first officer advised waiting, because a lower speed would mean a higher deck angle and a greater chance of starving a fuel pump.

The next few minutes were crucial. Despite the rather mild wind-shear advisory, the headwind at 1,000 feet was at least 60 knots, decreasing to 50 knots at 500 feet and to 20 knots at the surface. This meant that unusually high power was required to maintain a three-degree glideslope. Nevertheless, the captain called for flaps 40 before the outer marker and for flaps 50 less than a minute later, even though the operations manual for the airplane prohibited using those flap settings for reasons of noise abatement. In this case noise was the least of the captain's worries, but he seems not to have realized that the drag of a high flap deflection was increasing his fuel consumption and would also slow the airplane's response to power when it had to accelerate through the impending wind shears.

The captain flew the ILS roughly, with full glideslope needle deflections at several points and without ever achieving a stabilized rate of descent. At a distance of 2.6 nm from the threshold and a height of about 640 feet the airplane sank drastically below the glideslope, dropping 440 feet in three-tenths of a mile.

Amid the insistent whoops of the ground proximity warning system, the captain repeatedly asked, "Where is the runway? I don't see it! I don't see it!" Two miles from the threshold he called for gear up and initiated a missed approach. None of the crewmembers had seen the runway; they were still too far away.

The crews' hearts must have been in their throats. "Tell them we are in emergency," the captain twice told the first officer, who replied, "I already told him." Actually, the first officer had emphasized the low fuel state to tracon, but he had never used the word "emergency." The most emphatic statement the first officer had made—that they would run out of fuel if they had to divert to Boston—had gone unheeded by the controller.

The following dialogue ensued, conversation between the captain and the first officer being in Spanish:

APPROACH CONTROL: Climb and maintain 3,000.

CAPTAIN: Tell him we don't have fuel.

FIRST OFFICER: Maintain 3,000 and we're running out of fuel, sir.

APPROACH: Okay, fly heading 080.

CAPTAIN: Did you already tell him that we don't have fuel?

FIRST OFFICER: Yes sir, I already told him . . .

APPROACH: Avianca 052 heavy, I'm gonna bring you about 15 miles northeast and then turn you back onto the approach. Is that fine with you and your fuel?

At this instant there remained a slight chance that if the crew had declared an emergency, and the captain, exercising his emergency authority, had requested a turn directly to the outer marker or even inside it and had flown a successful ILS, the flight might have run out of fuel on the runway. But the first officer said, "I guess so, thank you very much."

Flight crews have a peculiar penchant for minimizing their difficulties. Is it just good manners, as when we ask the man who has been diagnosed with cancer how he is, and he replies, "Fine"? Perhaps the first officer was intimidated by the controller; New York controllers can have that effect. "What did he say?" asked the captain. "The guy is mad," said the second officer (*"El man se calentó"*).

A few moments later the captain said, "I'm going to follow this [ILS] as if my life depended on it (*a morir*)."

At 2130:36 the first officer told approach, in reply to a clearance to climb to 3,000, "Negative, sir, we just running out of fuel, we . . . okay, 3,000 now, okay." At 2131 the approach controller said, "You're number two for the approach. I just have to give you enough room so you make it without having to come out again."

Flight 052 was turning left to intercept the localizer 15 miles from the runway at 2132 when the engines began one by one to flame out. "We just lost two engines, we need priority please," radioed the first officer, at this point, however, priority was meaningless. Tracon replied with eerie banality, "Avianca 052, turn left heading 250, you're 15 miles from the outer marker, maintain 2,000 until established on the localizer, cleared for ILS 22L . . ." The jet struck a wooded embankment shortly afterwards. Of 158 persons aboard, 73 died, including all members of the flight crew.

The National Transportation Safety Board divided responsibility for the accident among several parties. It felt that the conduct of the flight by the flight crew had been in some part responsible; they had not kept abreast of weather at JFK (so far as was known) and had not communicated their deteriorating fuel state to ATC in a timely way. Their alternate, Boston, did not meet criteria for an alternate; the weather there was worse than at JFK. The Board noted, too, that although after the missed approach fuel exhaustion and a dead-stick landing became a distinct possibility, the flight crew did not advise the cabin attendants to prepare for it.

The Board criticized the FAA for its flow-control procedures, which "did not adequately account for overseas arrivals [which are not subject to ground holding procedures] and missed approaches at JFK"; but it did not find fault with the actions of controllers.

Insistence upon precise terminology often seems pedantic, but in this case much hinged upon the failure to declare an emergency or to make a forceful case for expedited handling with ATC. Phrases like "we are running out of fuel" can mean almost anything, and "priority" has no formal significance in ATC procedures. Only a specific declaration of an emergency and a solid estimate of time remaining, such as "five minutes to flameout," would have alerted the harried New York controllers to the true situation.

The crux of the drama, however, was the failure of the captain to complete the first ILS approach. Investigators found that the autopilot and flight director on the airplane had been plagued by trouble and speculated that the crew might have hand-flown the airplane all the way from Colombia and then executed the difficult ILS approach on raw data—that is, the ILS indicator needles—rather than flight director commands.

Actually, it took remarkable self-control on the part of the pilot to fly the missed approach, given the fuel emergency; many a pilot has persisted beyond the MDA—as often as not with disastrous results—after getting a full fly-up indication on the glideslope. The captain's anguished "Where is the runway?" suggests, however, that he was not aware that he was still two miles from the threshold when he started the missed approach.

Undoubtedly, the occasional air-carrier flight that runs out of fuel is only the luckless straggler of a much larger troop that run low on fuel for one reason or another, but manage to land safely. All crews are reluctant to declare emergencies, and a developing fuel emergency usually takes the form, as this one did, of a series of advances and pauses that make estimating the actual time of arrival almost impossible. Nonpilots who read on January 26 that a Colombian airliner had run out of fuel on the way into JFK probably made jokes about snowmobiles and secretly suspected that foreign crews aren't really up to snuff; but many pilots—air-carrier pilots among them—probably said to themselves, "There but for the grace of God go I."

In many respects, particularly that of the initial delay in reporting a low fuel state, the next accident is similar. Whereas the Avianca captain had taken on every bit of fuel he could for the trip, however, this pilot bowed to company pressure to travel light and took a little less than he needed.

Following Orders
by Peter Garrison

On a foggy January morning in 1989, a cargo-carrying Navajo was nearing the end of a one-hour IFR flight from Indianapolis to Columbus. The 22-year-old, 1,000-hour pilot had requested and gotten a series of descents from tracon to keep him out of icing; he had been cleared out of 6,000 for 4,000 when, at 8:04:22 a.m., he called the controller working him and said, "I've got a little fuel problem, I need to make sure I can get into Columbus as soon as possible."

A fuel problem is rarely "little," but the transmission did not convey the precise dimensions of this one. The controller did what he could.

(34Y = the Navajo; DAY = Dayton Arrival/Departure Control; COL = Columbus Approach. Landline communications between controllers are in italics. Times are local time.)

TIME: 0804:28

DAY: Okay, verify you're landing at OSU.

34Y: At OSU.

DAY: Stand by.

DAY: *Columbus north side, Dayton 87, reference 34Y . . . flashing at you there on Victor 12.*

COL: *Yeah, I see him just starting to come on there.*

DAY: *Okay, he says he has a little fuel problem and he's gonna need to be sure that he can get into OSU with minimum delay.*

COL: *Okay, he'll be straight in . . . they're IFR with estimated 600 overcast, three miles and fog.*

DAY: 34Y, I talked to Columbus Approach. They said you can expect straight in over at OSU with no delay.

34Y: 34Y.

TIME: 0805:43

34Y: And Dayton, what do you show the closest airport to 34Y?

DAY: 34Y, Urbana northwest of your position or Springfield is about 15 miles southwest. They have an ILS approach you could be turned right onto at the present time.

34Y: Stand by . . . 34Y'll take vectors to the nearest airport.

DAY: 34Y, turn right to a heading of 210, expect the ILS 24 approach at Springfield. No weather available there, Patterson is showing measured ceiling 500 overcast visibility two, fog, wind calm, altimeter 2983.

34Y: 2983 and 210 on the heading . . . You say the name of the airport is Springfield?

DAY: Yes sir, Springfield Beckley Airport, stand by, I'll get the localizer frequency for you . . . 34Y, the localizer frequency is 111.3 and amend your heading, make it 180 heading now, that'll be for a 10-mile final, you're 15 miles flying from the airport.

34Y: 111.3 and 180 on the heading . . . Do you show inbound course?

DAY: I'm sorry, say again.

34Y: Do you show the inbound course for that?

DAY: Stand by, I'll check it . . . 238.

34Y: 238 . . . As soon as you can do it I need it.

DAY: Okay, I'll tell you what, if you'd like a close turn on fly heading of 200, it'll be a turn on closer to the marker.

34Y: 200 . . . that's the ILS Runway 24.

DAY: ILS 24 at Springfield, that's correct.

34Y: Thanks.

COL; *Dayton, Columbus, 34Y.*

DAY: *He's gonna have to come in to Springfield.*

COL: *Okay, we'll forget about him then.*

TIME: 0808:54

DAY: 34Y, Hawker traffic just went into Springfield reported the ceiling at 300.

34Y: 34Y, thanks.

DAY: And amend that make it 200 on the ceiling, you can descend to 3,000.

34Y: Thank you . . . how many miles out do you have me?

DAY: Eight miles.

34Y: Thank you.

TIME: 0810:12

DAY: 34Y, you're seven miles from the airport maintain 2,600 until established, cleared ILS 24 approach, you're just about two miles outside of the marker, you'll be intercepting right at the marker.

34Y: 34Y's lost an engine, I need to get in now, give me a heading.

DAY: 34Y fly heading of 220.

34Y: 220.

DAY: 34Y the airport is 11:30 and seven miles.

34Y: 34Y.

DAY: 34Y, turn left 10 degrees.

34Y: Left 10 degrees.

TIME: 0811:16

34Y: 34 . . . 34Y's lost both engines, give me a heading.

DAY: 34Y, turn left 10 degrees, the airport is at 11:30 and five miles . . . 34Y, left 10 degrees, you're about five miles northeast of the airport, I show you going to the right, make a left turn . . . 34Y you're about five miles northeast of the airport it's 11 o'clock and five miles . . . 34Y is low altitude, the altimeter 2983.

34Y: Dayton, do you have 34Y?

DAY: 34Y, affirmative, turn left 15 degrees if you're able, you're headed away from the airport.

TIME: 0812:39

DAY: 34Y radar contact lost four miles northeast of the Springfield airport.

The airplane struck a garage in a residential area; the pilot was killed in the impact. The propellers had not been feathered. There was no fire, because there was no fuel aboard.

It was the policy of the company operating the Navajo to carry no more fuel than that required for the current flight plus legally required reserves, in order to ensure maximum payload capacity. The president of the company stated to an accident investigator that "he did not encourage carrying a lot of extra fuel."

The father of the pilot corroborated this statement though he put it somewhat differently. He stated that "his son reported that he had been 'chewed out' by the company for taking on 'too much fuel' for some flights . . . another pilot [working for the same company] had told him that he had been pressured to fly with minimum fuel on board . . . [His son] had told him that both he and [the other pilot] were consistently running with minimum fuel on board."

Other pilots also reported to investigators that the company was "very hard" on pilots who took extra fuel in lieu of freight. Something of the flavor of the operation can be inferred from the accident pilot's statement to a friend that when he complained about maintenance "the company would hand him a screwdriver and tell him to fix it."

Records of the fueling of the Navajo during the 30 days prior to the accident revealed that "consistently less fuel was added than was used on the previous flight or needed for the upcoming flight."

The company fuel policy must have been a topic of frequent discussion with the pilot's family, because, according to the father, the pilot's sister liked to tease him about "taking on too much fuel." But despite his dislike of the policy, the pilot adhered to it. According to the pilot's father, his son "would not have done anything that would have jeopardized his obtaining multiengine time for his planned career of flying for a major airline."

The policy of the company was to flight-plan 47 gph in the Navajo. This is generous; you would expect the airplane's two 310-hp engines to burn about 16 or 17 gph each when properly leaned at high cruise. Short leg lengths and IFR ground holds would push the block figure up somewhat, and the seemingly conservative figure of 47 gph may have been based on operating experience. (Ferrying fuel around exacts a small penalty in additional fuel burn—about one gph per 50 gallons of fuel carried at Navajo speeds—but there is no indication that this fact entered into company calculations.)

In principle there should be no objection to carrying the legally required fuel for the trip, a deviation to an alternate, and a reserve. In practice, however, there are pitfalls when trips are short. The Navajo's four fuel tanks carry a total of 190 usable gallons. Because of the company policy on fuel, however, pilots added fuel in quantities of 10, 20 or 30 gallons at a time. Fuelers at an Indianapolis FBO that frequently serviced the Navajo stated that "they had never seen the airplane tanks full, either prior to or subsequent to refueling." Sometimes no fuel could be seen in the tanks even after fueling.

If you never fill tanks and presumably never empty them, you never know exactly how much fuel you have aboard. Fuel gauges tell you something; but they are not reliable at the extreme bottom end of the dial, and when an airframe has accumulated nearly 6,000 hours, as this one had, its gauges and transmitters are even more than normally suspect.

On the morning of the accident, the pilot had been sufficiently concerned about the ticklish balance between fuel and payload—or between safety and unemployment—to have the cargo removed from the airplane and weighed. The load came to 992 pounds, and he decided not to add any fuel for the one-hour flight to Columbus. This decision is puzzling, since the Navajo's cargo capacity even with full tanks should have been about 1,000 pounds. But the pressure not to carry extra fuel evidently transcended mere numbers.

Exactly what the fuel gauges indicated as he took off would depend on the distribution of fuel among the four tanks; perhaps there was something about the indications that led him to believe that he was closer to half tanks than to the quarter he actually had. But at some point during the flight—perhaps immediately after takeoff—the pilot must have sensed that his fuel state would be marginal. There are plenty of airports between Indianapolis and Columbus. Why did he wait until eight minutes before dry tanks to announce his problem to ATC?

Ambition, pressure from above, a youthful belief in one's luck, a deep reluctance to expose an error—it's not hard to put together the elements. A precautionary landing to refuel would have shown good judgment, but it would have revealed a misjudgment in not taking on more fuel in the first place. And so the young man who "would not have done anything that would have jeopardized his planned career" did instead the one thing that would end it altogether.

A special subset of fuel-exhaustion accidents comprises those in which the pilot doesn't actually get around to running out of fuel before making some other fatal error to which concern about the low fuel state has led him. In the next accident, a pilot worked himself into a corner where he no longer had the luxury of making any choices at all.

Bad Bet
by Peter Garrison

A set of Jeppesen charts lay in the trunk of a car in a Pennsylvania parking lot awaiting the return of its owner. Two groups of approach plates were missing: Detroit Metropolitan and Chicago Midway. They, with the pilot and his airplane, were in a patch of muddy ground off the approach end of the runway at Detroit.

An airport car cruised up and down the foggy runways and taxiways for some time without spotting the wreckage of the 402C. When the airplane finally was located, it was found pointing back toward the approach end of the runway, bereft of its wingtips and one aileron. The missing parts turned up later in trees a mile from the runway threshold.

It had begun as a routine Part 135 cargo flight. The pilot, a 4,900-hour ATP, got a weather briefing before leaving his home field of North Philadelphia and flying to Teterboro, New Jersey, where he picked up a load of newspapers bound for Detroit and Chicago. He phoned for a new briefing from Teterboro FSS at about 10:20 p.m. EST. The specialist mentioned Phillipsburg and Cleveland (Phillipsburg was zero-zero, but Cleveland had VFR conditions under an overcast with a pilot report from an airplane on top at 4,500) before reporting Detroit with a 300-foot ceiling and two miles in fog, looking for improvement to 500 and four by two in the morning. Winds aloft at nine and 12,000 feet were out of the west at 20 to 35 knots, with precautions for moderate rime and mixed icing in clouds.

"That will be fine," the pilot said, with slight exaggeration, and asked the specialist to enter his flight plan in the computer. His estimated time en route was two-and-a-half hours, and he had fuel on board for four-and-a-half hours. He did not file an alternate, although one was required.

The distance from Teterboro to Detroit is roughly 450 nm; the pilot's time en route corresponds to a speed of 180 knots, which would be a reasonable figure for a 402C at 10,000 feet (book cruising speed is 213 knots at 72-percent power at 20,000 feet). The trip actually took about three hours, a time that corresponds to a groundspeed of 150 knots. It appears that the forecast headwind was there, and that the pilot, who dictated his flight plan to the specialist before requesting the winds aloft, may not have taken it into account.

Radio communications were normal throughout the trip, and there was no sign of trouble. But the weather at Detroit worsened. When the tower cleared the flight for the ILS approach to Runway 3R at 1:03 a.m., the RVR (runway visual range) was 3,000 feet, and the ceiling was 100 feet. The decision height for the approach was 200 feet, and the minimum RVR 1,800 feet. The airplane never reached the runway, and its pilot, after acknowledging his clearance to land, was never heard from again.

National Transportation Safety Board investigators pieced together what had happened. The airplane had struck trees about a mile short of the runway, shearing off the left and right wingtips and the right aileron. The airplane managed to remain airborne and crashed a little to the right of the runway. The wreckage path indicated that the airplane struck the ground on a course almost exactly opposite to the runway heading.

The pilot was legally permitted to make the approach even though the observed weather was below minimums; if he had the runway environment in sight upon reaching the decision height of 200 feet agl, he could land. If he did not have the runway environment in sight at the decision height, however, he could descend no lower. It is the pilot's weather observation when reaching the decision height, in other words, that determines the legality of the approach.

One of the assumptions governing ILS approaches is that the airplane remain close to the glideslope; unlike a localizer approach, an ILS approach does not permit "stepping" from one minimum altitude to the next as one approaches the runway.

The full vertical scale of the ILS indicator in the cockpit represents a course depth of 1.4 degrees. That corresponds to 130 feet one mile from the transmitter (usually located about 1,000 feet down the runway, to provide a crossing height of about 50 feet at the threshold). In other words, a full up needle deflection a mile from the transmitter indicates that the airplane (or the airplane's glideslope antenna—in big machines the distance from the antenna to the lowest point on the airplane can be significant) is at least 65 feet below the glidepath.

The height of the glidepath above the transmitter is always a little more than twice the full-scale needle deflection, or four times the error indicated by a full up or down needle. But the terrain short of the runway may rise; at Detroit Metro there are charted obstructions in the last mile of the approach that rise more than 100 feet above the runway elevation.

NTSB investigators found evidence that the pilot may have mistakenly selected the ILS Runway 3L approach plate, but this possibility is inconsistent with the location of the initial collision with trees. In any case, however, what made this accident interesting was not that the pilot descended below the glidepath and struck trees. It's not uncommon for airplanes to crash within a mile of the threshold during ILS approaches, despite the rule of thumb that you should never allow any below-glideslope deflection inside the middle marker and, presumably, very little as you approach it. The interesting thing is the pilot's apparently faulty preflight planning and the subsequent course of his decision-making.

The 402C has a usable fuel capacity of 1,236 pounds and burns about 200 pph. With a cargo of newspapers, however, it could not carry its full fuel load. The NTSB estimated that it would have left Teterboro with 920 pounds of fuel—an amount consistent with the endurance stated on the flight plan. In that case, the airplane had enough fuel aboard to remain airborne for more than an hour when it arrived at Detroit. It did not have enough to go on to Chicago Midway, its second destination; but it did have enough to go to Cleveland Hopkins, 80 nm away, where the weather was better than in Detroit. But the approach plates for Cleveland were in the pilot's car at North Philly.

Why the pilot did not bring his Jeppesen kit with him on the flight, rather than only the plates for his two destinations, is unexplained. Possibly he had removed the Detroit and Chicago plates to study them—it was his first flight into Detroit—and then had simply forgotten the Jeppesen kit in his car. It's unlikely that he deliberately left the plates behind to reduce his takeoff weight. He did not even have the Teterboro plates with him. It seems more likely that he discovered on the way to Teterboro that he did not have his charts, decided to make do without them rather than go back, and that his failure to file an alternate at Teterboro was deliberate.

The fact that the forecast weather for his arrival at Detroit was well above minimums may have encouraged him to continue the trip. When he got to Detroit and the weather turned out to be well below minimums, the paucity of his options was brought home to him.

He really had only two. First, he could try to squeeze into Detroit. Second, he could go to Cleveland, confess that he didn't have the approach plates, get a radar approach, and probably get slapped with a violation.

But there was a complication: In nine days he was due to begin training with Republic Airlines as a DC-9 first officer. This was not the time to get in trouble with the FAA. So he did what most pilots in this fix would have done: He attempted the approach at Detroit.

He may have flown the approach badly because of anxiety over his predicament; the fact that the *left* runway approach plate may have been at the top of the stack on his clipboard could indicate distraction or confusion. In any case, we know that he failed to land safely or make the missed approach—*prima facie* evidence either of equipment failure or of bad piloting. Suppose, however, that he had safely flown the approach to decision height without deviating from the glidepath. Suppose further that the runway environment—meaning the approach lights—did not come into sight. Now, 3,000 feet from the runway threshold, he would face for the second time in a few minutes the decision that might set back his prospects of an airline career. And now he would have to make the decision in a split second.

It is pure speculation, of course—we are talking now about a hypothetical situation and a typical pilot, not about what this particular man actually did—but it is hard to imagine that he would not have decided to sniff down a little past minimums. He had already probably made one slightly-too-bold decision: to head for Detroit without an alternate and without approach plates for any of the nearby airports. A posture of boldness, once adopted, is hard to abandon, not only for psychological reasons but because it is likely to have created new circumstances from which escape is increasingly difficult.

By a single act of mere carelessness, followed by a single decision, this pilot had managed to put his career—and his life—in jeopardy.

This accident illustrates the virtue of conservative decision-making. A conservative pilot is one who assumes that things that have a reasonable chance of going badly will; and so he does not make decisions now that may deprive him of his freedom to make reasonable ones later.

A readiness to take risks for the sake of one's job is not the monopoly of young pilots struggling to build time in commuter and cargo operations. Veterans feel it too.

Late for Work
by Peter Garrison

It was a gray dawn at the north end of Tampa Bay, Florida. Tampa International Information Papa told the story: "Indefinite ceiling zero, sky obscured, visibility one-sixteenth of a mile with fog, temperature and dewpoint seven-one . . ."

Arriving aircraft were using the Runway 36L ILS approach—except that no aircraft were arriving. The runway visual range (RVR) was shrinking all the time. At about 6:30 a.m., 15 minutes before sunrise, a DC-9 started an approach with an RVR of 1,400 feet and descended to 100 feet above the runway with the approach lights in sight before losing sight of everything, taking the missed approach, and diverting to nearby Sarasota. A Cessna 172 three minutes behind the DC-9 was given the minimum RVR report for the approach: 1,200 feet. He was in solid fog at 200 feet and went to his alternate, St. Petersburg, just a few miles across the bay, where the weather was 200 and one.

Just after the Cessna started his missed approach an Apache called from seven miles out. The tower gave him an RVR of 600 feet at the touchdown end of the runway and cleared him to continue his approach.

Seven minutes later, after flying a precise ILS approach to minimums, the Apache pilot called a missed approach. "I'd like to go back and try it again," he said. As the Apache circled toward the outer marker, Tampa Approach gave him new RVR readings: 600 feet at the touchdown end, 800 at the roll-out end, and 3,000 in between. The controller thought the improvement in midfield visibility was probably due to the turbulence created by a DC-9 that had just departed, but he didn't say so. "That 3,000 sounds better, I hope," the Apache pilot said.

"Yes, it does," the controller agreed.

Two minutes before seven, when he cleared the Apache for a second approach, the controller reported the midfield RVR as 1,000 feet. Five minutes later, when the Apache was two miles from the touchdown point, the controller gave another update: 600 feet at touchdown, 800 at midfield, and 800 at roll-out. The Apache pilot acknowledged.

At the same time, a Pan Am 727 was rolling cautiously toward Runway 36L. As the captain peered into the fog, a shape materialized and moved rapidly toward him. It was the Apache, flaring, its wheels feeling for the taxiway. It touched down 200 feet from the jetliner. There was time to swerve the Boeing hard to the right before the small twin, which had pitched up and become airborne again, struck the airliner's nose. The Apache's left engine caught beneath the radome and was wrenched from the wing; the rest of the airplane, its ruptured tanks spewing burning fuel, hurtled under the left wing of the 727 and skidded to a stop 100 feet away, where it lay burning on the taxiway.

The Pan Am first officer called in a Mayday to the tower: "Clipper's been hit by a light airplane on the taxiway, I don't think there's any injuries but there may be some damage."

Evidently he wasn't thinking about the pilot of the demolished light airplane, who was dead.

When the news media first reported this accident, it caused many people to say, "Another crazy private pilot. They shouldn't let those guys near airports." But as the details emerged an irony appeared: The pilot of the Apache was a highly experienced Eastern Air Lines captain, a 20,000-hour pilot who had been with Eastern for more than 20 years.

He lived at Pine Shadows Airpark near Fort Myers, 120 miles to the south, and was trying to get to work. He had a Newark-bound flight at 8:05 a.m., and was supposed to report at 7:20 a.m. He had called flight service the night before and gotten a forecast for Tampa; the worst it predicted was a 300-foot ceiling and half-a-mile visibility. He decided to fly to Tampa in the morning rather than drive.

During the night the forecast changed for the worse; when the pilot called flight service after getting airborne a little after six a.m., he heard about the zero ceiling and the one-sixteenth-mile visibility for the first time.

At this point he could no longer drive to Tampa and expect to get to work on time. He could, however, land at St. Petersburg, take a taxi across the bridge, and be only a little late. If he were slightly late, his flight would be held for him. He elected, however, to try the approach.

It was a case of letting one bad decision force another. The first bad choice was not to call flight service the moment he got up, at five a.m. At that point he still had the option of driving if the weather at Tampa had worsened.

By not calling flight service until he was airborne, he put himself in the position of inevitably being late, unless he could land at Tampa. Why did being a few minutes late matter so much?

Eastern had been acquired by Texas Air earlier in the year, and there had been a lot of emphasis on eliminating crew delays. In addition, it was a company policy to "discourage" private flying within 12 hours of a scheduled flight.

The pilot was late once before. Yet more than three years had passed and, under Eastern policies, that previous incident could not be held against him in determining how another instance of tardiness would be dealt with. But he may not have been aware of the three-year limit. The pressure to land at Tampa, concludes the National Transportation Safety Board in its analysis of the accident, "probably was largely self-generated on the part of the Apache pilot."

Exactly what happened during the last moments of the Apache's approach is, of course, unknown. Radar records showed that the pilot flew the approach with exemplary accuracy down to the decision height. There, presumably as he took his attention away from his instruments and searched for visual cues outside, the airplane deviated from the localizer, to the left on the first approach, to the right on the second. There could have been no visual cues to speak of; if you don't see the sequenced flasher on the approach lights you don't see anything, and the radar ground tracks suggest that the pilot could not see the flasher through the fog. Yet he cannot simply have been feeling for the ground. In that case, his eyes would have been on the instruments, and he would not have drifted completely off the ILS localizer.

It was rumored that the pilot of the Apache might have mistaken the 727's taxi light for a runway light or approach light, but according to the NTSB report the airliner had on only its navigation and anti-collision lights.

The accident occasioned debate over the provisions of FAR 91.116, which describes the conditions under which an ILS approach can be continued below decision height.

The decision height is a height above touchdown, usually 200 feet, below which you may not descend unless you have certain things distinctly (albeit not *clearly*) in sight. The FAR lists a number of qualifying items: the threshold, threshold lights or threshold marking; the runway-end identifier lights; the VASI indicator; and so on. A nearby McDonald's is not enough.

The approach-lighting system is in a special category; if the approach lights are "distinctly visible and identifiable"—not just a "general glow"—the pilot may descend to 100 feet agl.

There are other requirements. The airplane must be "continuously" in a position from which a "normal" descent and landing can be made: no wild maneuvering at the last moment. And—this is the most ticklish one—the "flight visibility" must be at least equal to the minimum visibility for the approach.

This last requirement is tricky because the determination of flight visibility is left to the pilot, who has no means of making precise determinations of visibility—he cannot distinguish between 1,000 feet and 1,200 feet in fog. In many cases pilots are pressed by personal or professional concerns to land successfully at their destination, and therefore on occasion they may make overly generous assessments.

The "official" visibility comes in two varieties: RVR and ground visibility. Ground visibility is given in miles or fractions of miles, and is estimated from the degree of obscuration of objects at a known distance. RVR is measured by a transmissometer, a device consisting of a light and a meter located at intervals along a runway and measuring horizontal visual range in hundreds of feet. RVR is based on what pilots *should* see upon landing, looking down the runway.

When an airplane lands while the RVR is below published minimums, FAA personnel may—or may not—take note of the possible infraction and contact the pilot. The astute pilot has a story ready: He could see the threshold (or whatever) from over the middle marker. This is the kind of definite statement that is hard to challenge. The incautious pilot who merely asserts that the flight visibility was such-and-such, but can give no explanation of how he arrived at his estimate, may get into trouble with the FAA's enforcement people.

As a consequence of this accident, the NTSB recommended to the FAA that it eliminate the pilot's "look-and-see" privileges. In recognition of the fact that they operate under greater pressure to make good schedules than do Part 91 (nonrevenue general aviation) pilots, Part 135 (air-taxi and commuter) and Part 121 (scheduled airline) pilots are already forbidden to begin an approach if the forecast weather is below minimums. In variable weather, however, some pilots are careful not to ask for the latest report until they are inside the outer marker, at which point, according to FAR Part 135, "The approach may be continued and a landing made if the pilot finds . . . actual weather conditions are at least equal to the minimums prescribed." Part 121 is similarly worded.

One member of the Board, Joseph Nall, dissented from this recommendation, arguing that the accident in question did not merit a sweeping change to the regulations; it had clearly been the result of a deliberate decision to bust minimums on the part of the Apache pilot. If there was a problem, Nall suggested, perhaps it lay in the FAA's lackadaisical and uneven enforcement of the regulations.

The FAA has not acted on the NTSB recommendation.

Pressure, real or perceived, leads pilots to many errors. In the three preceding cases, it was company or career pressure. In the next, a helicopter pilot takes off in terrible weather under a more complex kind of pressure: the pressure to live up to the high expectations of others.

Angel of Mercy
by Peter Garrison

Certain occupations are inherently more dangerous than others. That is their appeal. One person becomes a policeman, another a file clerk. But both file clerks and policemen become pilots, and National Transportation Safety Board post-mortems treat them all alike.

Safety in flying is an elastic idea; Alaskan bush pilots routinely accept a level of risk, even in for-hire operations, that would not pass in the lower 48. Helicopter pilots doing external-load work don't think about the height-velocity curve; pilots of commuter helicopters who don't think about the height-velocity curve are considered reckless.

Too lively an appreciation of risk makes a bad pilot. Flying requires either a blind (and dumb) belief in the reliability of man-made equipment, or a kind of unconscious abandon, like that of charging troops. Yet there is a point at which troops turn and run, and at which pilots fold up their charts, lock the airplane, and go home. The soldier who does not retreat may become a hero, more often than not posthumously; the pilot is likely to be seen as a mere victim.

The pilot of a Bell 206 was killed when his helicopter hit a mountain in foggy weather. The accident occurred in predawn darkness within a minute or two of takeoff. The visibility was around 125 feet in fog and rain. At first glance, one would say that this was an example of a fantastically reckless operation with a predictable outcome. Examined more closely, the accident seems to fall into the fuzzy zone between recklessness and the honorable pursuit of one's duty in a hazardous occupation.

The pilot, according to the NTSB accident report, had a total of 1,753 hours, with 106 hours in single-engine airplanes and the rest in helicopters. He held an instrument rating for airplanes, but not for helicopters. Nevertheless, his log reflected 255 hours of instrument flying as pilot in command. Mothers tell their children always to wear clean underwear in case they are involved in an accident. Somebody should tell pilots the same thing about their logbooks. In this case, the log—if accurately transcribed in the NTSB report—implies that the pilot had flown more than 149 hours in IFR conditions in helicopters without a helicopter instrument rating.

Helicopter instrument flying is quite different from airplane instrument flying. For one, a helicopter is naturally much less stable than an airplane. Also, the attitude cues provided by the artificial horizon and turn-and-slip and directional indicators have different meanings in a helicopter. The helicopter is easier to fly straight-and-level blind than it is to maneuver, however, and plenty of helicopter pilots have probably made short, illegal forays into the soup without great risk or danger.

In this case, the helipad was located 5,000 feet msl at a hospital on a mountainside. The terrain fell off to the south and west and rose to the north and east. The flight was what is known as a "mercy flight." A medical team from another hospital, about five miles northwest of the first, needed to be transported to the aid of a critically ill child 50 miles to the south. The pilot's mission was to fly from the first hospital to the second, pick up the doctors, and fly them to the child.

Weather was moving in from the northwest; there was already a low overcast over the city, and on the mountain, where the hospitals were located, the weather was much worse than down below. The call came from the dispatcher at about 5:10 a.m. The pilot called flight service for a briefing, but they didn't have weather for the destination. The local weather at the airport was 500 broken, 1,300 overcast, seven miles in light rain. The pilot called his dispatcher back to say, "If they want to try it, there'll be no guarantee." He told the dispatcher he could see the airport in the valley below; at that time the hospital must have been just below the overcast. The pilot asked the dispatcher to call the other hospital and ask if they could see any landmarks below.

The dispatcher made the call, and the answer was no; but the people at the hospital told him it was urgent that the team get to its destination, and said they would put out additional lighting at the helipad.

At 5:30 a.m., the dispatcher later reported, he called the pilot and told him they wanted to try to go. The pilot said he would try it, but if he couldn't get to the second hospital the emergency team would have to drive over to meet him. The pilot then said to a nurse, "I feel really uncomfortable about this flight." She later said that she "really felt he was pressured into leaving."

Another nurse reported, "My attention was caught because the pilot was rotating the engine at what seemed like takeoff speed for about five minutes. It definitely wasn't the usual idling sound. I looked again out the observation window and noticed [him] picking the craft off the pad maybe five or 10 feet and then setting it back down . . . it was unusual to see him do it for such a long time . . . I walked outside and looked over the valley from the ER entrance. It was raining hard, like the sound of sleet, and very foggy. I watched him disappear rapidly into the fog . . . [and] have no trouble gaining altitude . . . I made multiple trips outside, but the fog was so bad I could barely see the heliport from the . . . ER entrance . . ."

A short time later the pilot contacted the airport tower in the valley below requesting radar vectors to a VOR approach. The tower controller got radar contact with the helicopter long enough to advise the pilot that he was below the minimum vectoring altitude and to suggest a heading; the blip then disappeared from radar.

An all-weather jogger saw the lights of the helicopter overhead in the fog and then heard two impacts separated by a long moment. Apparently the main rotor struck the mountain and began to disintegrate before the hull struck the ground about 600 feet farther on. The helicopter had been in a right turn when the jogger saw it. It crashed on an easterly heading, just a little north of the helipad from which it had taken off.

Little could be inferred from the wreckage. There was one possibly significant thing, though: The altimeter was set at 29.80, whereas the actual pressure at the time was 29.70 inches. In other words, the altimeter would have indicated that the helicopter was 100 feet higher than it was.

The flight path of the helicopter was puzzling. Apparently, the pilot at once both gave up hope of locating the other hospital and abandoned his contingency plan of returning to the helipad from which he had taken off in favor of heading for the airport down in the valley. But why did he turn to the right, where the mountain lay, rather than left, toward the valley? And why was he heading straight-and-level eastward when he crashed? Was he trying to locate the helipad he had just left?

Investigators thought fatigue might have played a part in the accident. The pilot, who in addition to his on-demand charter work also flew for the National Guard and was attending school, had averaged five hours of sleep a night for the four days prior to the accident. But the exact role of fatigue is uncertain; it could have led him to set his altimeter incorrectly, or perhaps to become disoriented, or had no influence at all.

What is really at issue here is judgment. The pilot is not the only one who showed bad judgment, but as the pilot, and so the final authority for the flight, he ends up bearing the onus. From the witnesses' descriptions and the transcript of the weather briefing, it's clear enough that the weather at the hospital was terrible, especially when compounded by darkness. The pilot could perhaps have made a safe flight off the mountain and down into the valley, where the visibility was better; but to fly from one point on the mountain to another in dense fog would have been well-nigh impossible.

The two hospitals were only five miles apart; why couldn't the emergency team have driven over to meet the helicopter? Indeed, it would have been faster, because half an hour elapsed from when the first call arrived to when the helicopter actually took off. Perhaps the doctors needed to make preparations while the helicopter was coming to get them.

The pilot could have done a quick calculation and concluded that the medical team would have gotten to its destination almost as quickly by ambulance as by helicopter. Most likely he did the calculation, but could not bring himself to suggest that the low-tech solution be chosen.

The NTSB listed "self-induced pressure" and "pressure induced by others" among the causes of the accident. These are categories recognized by the computer that compiles accident statistics, but what a wealth of human complexities they contain. Countless issues may have impinged upon the choice that was made: the modern love of fancy machinery, the desire of hospitals to justify their helipads, the desire of doctors to make grand entrances, illusions about the speed of aircraft as opposed to cars, the reluctance of a chauffeur to stand up to his boss, the belief of the boss that if the trip is really impractical the chauffeur will stand up and refuse to make it.

But hovering over all these factors is the sick or dying child in whose name everything is being done. Many people (not to mention animals) have given their lives to save a child. Were their decisions improper? Were they victims, or were they heroes?

Nonprofessional pilots succumb to their own kinds of pressure. Often it has to do with the expectations, or what they imagine to be the expectations, of their passengers. Basically, what is involved is the pilot's ego and the not-inconsiderable emotional investment most pilots have in being pilots.

Too Late to Turn Back
by Peter Garrison

On a Thursday evening in February 1989, the pilot-owner of a Piper Lance and four passengers were getting ready to leave the Waterloo-Guelph airport in Ontario. Three of them were bound for North Bay, 170 nm distant, for some ice fishing; the pilot and one of the passengers intended to return that same evening.

The pilot had not talked to a weather briefer; but perhaps he had gotten information from unofficial sources, as many pilots do—newspapers, television, a phone call to a friend at the destination. If he had checked the weather, he knew that a low over New York and Pennsylvania was pulling clouds into the area of his intended flight. Bases were 2,000 to 3,000 feet agl, sometimes lower, with visibilities of three to five miles in light snow and occasional freezing drizzle. The aviation forecast called for some moderate clear icing below 4,000 feet; the freezing level was at the surface, with an inversion and an above-freezing layer between 3,000 and 7,000 feet.

While the pilot was fueling his airplane and getting ready to depart, the weather was stable and looked better than forecast: 2,500 broken, 7,000 overcast, 15 miles. There was a light wind blowing from the east and the temperature was 16°F.

Between Guelph and North Bay the terrain is low; the highest man-made obstacles are below 1,900 feet msl. The Lance was IFR-equipped and carried a loran. The 41-year-old pilot was not instrument rated, nor was his license endorsed for night flying, as Canadian regulations require; but he had had 27 hours of instrument instruction and had logged 20 hours flying solo at night. In any case, it may have seemed reasonable to suppose that he could fly VFR from Guelph to North Bay under those conditions. There would be ample room between the ceiling and the ground, and the loran would make it virtually impossible to get lost. If there were areas of low cloud that precluded getting to North Bay, he could always turn back to Guelph. The pilot was familiar with the route; he had flown it several times previously.

The Lance took off at 5:40 p.m. A few minutes remained before official sunset, but because of the heavy cloud cover it was already nearly dark. A nearby air traffic radar stored the airplane's track as it flew on a beeline for North Bay. Twenty-nine miles from Guelph, the Lance made a 180-degree left turn and angled back toward the track that it had followed outbound. A few minutes later, as it rejoined its outbound track, it disappeared from radar.

Residents in the area had seen the airplane pass by northbound at treetop height and shortly afterwards return. One, who must have heard the sound of an impact, set out on foot and 40 minutes later came upon the wreckage.

The Lance had struck seven feet below the top of a 192-foot tower supporting high-tension cables that run along a ridge at a height of 1,575 feet msl. The cables are marked on charts, but not as an obstruction, only as a fine dashed line. The line would have been very hard to see in a darkened cockpit had the pilot been scrutinizing a chart. But it's unlikely that he was. In the dark 200 feet above the ground is no place to be studying charts.

Accident investigators speculated that the pilot had encountered low ceilings and freezing rain that had probably frosted over his windscreen. A 172 flying in the same area an hour earlier had reported such an encounter, and there was still a thin layer of mixed clear and rime ice on the leading edges of the wings and stabilizer of the Lance when investigators arrived on the crash scene the next morning.

Most likely the pilot had never seen the transmission lines when passing over them northbound; the support towers, being less than 500 feet high, were not required to be lighted. Relying on his loran for position information, he had turned around and attempted to rejoin his outbound track, which was already set up on the loran. He was doing all the right things, and doing them correctly—except a little too low.

Different authorities take different views of night VFR flying. In the United States and Canada, night and day VFR minimums at the time of the accident were the same—in uncontrolled airspace, one mile visibility and clear of clouds. At the other extreme, Mexico does not permit night VFR flying at all. The U.S. recently changed its night VFR minimum visibility in uncontrolled airspace to three miles. In Canada it is periodically urged—the Canadian Aviation Safety Board urged it in connection with this accident—that night minimums should be higher than day. One argument against higher minimums might be that they are meaningless at night anyway, since estimating distance is all but impossible, and, in any case, only self-illuminating objects, which do not include clouds, are visible. So far as this accident is concerned, visibility would not have been an issue anyway; if the pilot's windscreen was iced up, his visibility was about 30 inches, and even if it wasn't, the transmission lines would have been invisible in the darkness.

Setting special minimums for night VFR flying would, on the other hand, have a symbolic effect; it would be as much as to say, "Take care, night flying is more difficult than day." Canada already recognizes the special nature of night flying by requiring an endorsement on the pilot's license. Obtaining the night endorsement requires 10 hours of night-flying experience, of which five must be dual and five may be solo under the supervision of a flight instructor. Ten hours of instrument instruction are required as well. This pilot, although he did not have the endorsement, did have the experience level required by the regulations.

Going and taking a look is a time-honored way of dealing with marginal VFR weather. Done with caution, judgment, and the requisite attention to navigation, it is sufficiently safe. Navigation is the most important thing; the pilot must always know where he is and where he can land.

Loran has made being lost a thing of the past, but it has also paradoxically made pilots less aware of where they are. No longer dependent on pilotage for their position, they can leave their charts neatly folded on the floor. A number of recent accidents have involved a pilot cruising into some obstacle on a perfectly straight line between his point of departure and his destination—the hallmark of loran-guided death.

Loran doesn't help you see clouds or avoid obstacles, and so for night VFR flying it's only as good as the weather is. In this case, the feasibility of the flight really depended on the kind of clouds that the pilot would encounter. If there were a clean overcast with good visibility underneath, a VFR flight would be possible over a populated area where ground lights would show the way; in the absence of ground lights, or in the presence of showers or areas of fog or low stratus, VFR flight would be impossible.

Since the area between Guelph and North Bay is virtually uninhabited, the pilot must have gambled on good visibility under the clouds in making his decision to go. It was a long shot—unless he based his estimate of the weather entirely on the way it happened to look as he drove to the airport.

A pilot may decide to make a flight under certain peripheral circumstances that he would not have made under others. Social pressures, real or imagined, can enter into the decision to go or not to go. Published accident reports rarely delve into the social climate of a flight; this one doesn't. But whatever the reasons for this particular pilot's decision to attempt the flight may have been, the decision and the outcome make one reflect on certain kinds of social dynamics.

What may sometimes happen is this. A pilot arranges to take people somewhere in his airplane. By doing this he gains the gratitude of the beneficiaries, the self-esteem engendered by his own magnanimity, and the prestige of his command of an exotic form of transportation. In other words, he has some ego invested in the trip. As often as not, the flight is supposed to take place at the beginning of a weekend, and part of the value of it to the passengers is that it will spare them a tedious drive and make their weekend longer. Time is therefore of the essence.

Come the proposed departure, the weather is marginal. "Marginal" is important; if there's thunder and lightning with hailstones big as dogs, the passengers won't want to go anyway, and the pilot is off the hook. But if the weather at the airport looks okay, then the pilot, if he has doubts about it, is in the position of having to renege because of purely hypothetical concerns. He may appear to be trying to weasel out of doing the favor, or the passengers, whose disappointment may pass over into irritation, could think him timid or less competent than they originally supposed.

Of course none of these concerns is expressed aloud. The pilot may not even be conscious of them. The passengers rely on the pilot's special knowledge and abilities and certainly don't dream of pressuring him into a fatal misjudgment. But the pilot pressures himself. He leans toward decisions that will permit him to make the trip; he encourages the passengers to feel that they are safe. He may say something like, "Listen, there's a chance we may have to come back, but there's no problem going to have a look." He may even neglect to get a weather briefing because once he has determined that he is just going to "take a look," the briefing becomes superfluous.

Because preflight decision-making can be so important to pilots, they should take care to immunize themselves to social influences by regular mithridatic doses of humiliation. Offers to fly someone somewhere should be accompanied by disclaimers, such as, "I don't have an instrument rating, and I'm a bit chicken, so if the weather's not good we won't be able to do it." That may be hard to say—you may imagine your interlocutor thinking, "Remind me never to get in an airplane with this dork"—but it's probably easier than waiting until the last moment to announce, "I'm sorry. You'll have to take the bus."

The theme of carrying passengers into terrible weather emerges again and again. In the next case, the passenger is the pilot's own son, and the circumstances are again ones in which it might have been better not to rely on an airplane—at least not on one with a faulty flight in-

strument—in the first place. The very fact that the pilot was experienced, instrument-rated, and an instructor probably increased his reluctance to capitulate to the weather.

Hidden Pressure
by Peter Garrison

From extremely sketchy data I have formed the notion that many general aviation accidents in which bad weather and bad judgment are involved take place either at the beginning of a weekend or at the end of one.

I suppose it stands to reason that nonprofessional pilots would do much of their flying on weekends. In that case, however, there would be a lot of Saturday accidents to weaken my impression that Friday and Sunday are the particularly unlucky days. I think there is a factor other than a mere burst of weekend flying: the urgency of making good one's carefully hatched vacation plans or of getting back to work on Monday.

Besides the pressure, real or imagined, of schedules, and therefore of Fridays and Sundays, pilots feel all sorts of other pressures. Some come from passengers, whose expectations and apprehensions play upon the pilot's pride. A pilot whose spouse accepts his flying reluctantly and wishes the money were being spent in some other way may be loath to cancel a planned vacation because of weather or to delay the departure or make a precautionary landing. The pilot does not want to hear, "If we had taken the car we would be there by now."

We can only speculate about what motivated the pilots to press on into conditions that eventually defeated them, since defeat in an airplane is so often fatal. But when we are speculating, it is helpful to think about the day of the week, the purpose of the flight, the relationship between the pilot and his passengers, the expectations of people waiting at the destination. In the interactions of these factors we can sometimes find plausible building blocks from which to construct the state of mind that led to a terrible mistake.

A 48-year-old pilot flew a Piper Cherokee 140 from his home base near the Ohio-West Virginia border to Fort Worth, Texas, to pick up his son (who was a licensed private pilot himself, though inexperienced). They stayed overnight in New Orleans and left together for home early in the morning. The weather along the route was deteriorating; an extensive spring cold front, with icing, thunderstorms, rain, fog, and low ceilings, was moving in from the west toward the mountains over whose western foothills their route lay.

The airplane's directional gyro had failed on the southbound trip. The pilot had had the filter replaced, but to no avail. So, although he was instrument rated (and held flight instructor and multiengine ratings as well), he chose to make the return flight VFR.

They stopped first in Picayune, Mississippi, took 13.5 gallons of fuel, and waited two and a half hours for the weather to improve. A little before noon they took off and headed northeast.

Less than an hour later, the Cherokee landed at Tuscaloosa, Alabama. When FSS personnel pointed out to the pilot that the airport was IFR, he said that he had tried to contact the FSS on 123.6 but had gotten no response.

The pilot obtained a weather briefing for a flight to Chattanooga, Tennessee. The area forecast called for lowering ceilings throughout the afternoon, becoming 1,200 to 2,500 overcast with three to five miles visibility in light rain and fog, and mountains obscured after 1300. The briefer told the pilot, as he was required to do, that VFR flight was not recommended.

The pilot then asked for the weather for Meridian, Mississippi, where the weather was VFR. He said he would be returning to Meridian. By now Tuscaloosa was VFR too; father and son took off, after getting an airport advisory on 123.6, at 1313.

Perhaps when they got into the air the weather to the northeast didn't look so bad, because they headed not for Meridian but for Chattanooga. The distance from Tuscaloosa to Chattanooga is 157 nm. The route runs parallel to the ridges of the Cumberland Plateau, with elevations dropping off to less than 2,000 feet to the west, and rising above 4,000 to the east. Interstate 59 runs up to Chattanooga from Birmingham, and they flew alongside that highway as the ceilings grew lower and visibilities worse.

"We were just trying to stay clear of clouds," the son said later from his hospital bed, "but the ceiling just kept coming down . . . .. It was raining very hard, there was moderate turbulence and sometimes severe."

At one point during the flight they had descended to 1,800 feet or so (msl—the terrain elevation was between 1,000 and 2,000 feet) to stay under the clouds. "I remember showing my father an airport on the left side. It was raining real hard, and the wind was bouncing us around a good bit. I remember talking about that, and then I remember him explaining to me some stuff about the turbulence we were encountering." The airport, the son recalled, was "along a big four-lane highway with a lot of signs that said something about Ruby Falls."

Ruby Falls is a tourist attraction at the southern edge of Chattanooga, but it is heavily promoted on billboards on both sides of the highway both north and south of town. The airport could have been Isbell, some 42 nm south of Chattanooga, or Lovell, in Chattanooga itself.

When you have to fly so low to stay out of clouds that you can read billboards, it's usually considered a sign that you ought to land. But the pilot-in-command continued. After passing Chattanooga he seems to have decided to abandon the four-lane highway and track directly to the Hinch Mountain VOR, about 40 nm past Chattanooga. According to the son's account, they were clear of cloud with the ground in sight up to the moment, some time between four and five in the afternoon, when the airplane snagged trees at the 2,700-foot level on Hinch Mountain and crashed into rising terrain.

The father was killed and the airplane burned. His son escaped with serious injuries and was found the next morning walking down the VOR transmitter access road.

This was a classic example of VFR flight continued beyond its natural limits. One is tempted to pontificate upon the flagrance of the risks taken and upon the obvious faults of the pilot's inflight decision-making. Before one takes the podium, however, it is well to reflect upon the remarkable frequency of this type of accident, despite decades of training, lecturing and "Aftermath" columns. Like other examples of ill-advised human conduct, such as barroom brawling and marrying on impulse, continuing VFR into adverse weather seems to persist in spite of all the moral and didactic artillery arrayed against it.

Many pilots would not have begun this trip at all. Many might have started out from Tuscaloosa and turned back as the weather worsened. Most would have landed at that airport that presented itself, a last wan resort, on the way to Ruby Falls.

But a few would reason that the weather was worse than forecast, and that it might well clear up somewhat in a little while, as it had done a couple of hours earlier at Tuscaloosa. They would keep in the back of their minds that they could, if worse came to worst, go up IFR, using the wet compass in lieu of the DG. It is possible to fly blind without a DG.

Counterbalancing those encouragements would be the fact that they had already been drawn into violations of regulations, first in landing at Tuscaloosa without a clearance when the airport was IFR, then in low flying along a highway; and the fact that since the weather was certain to worsen, the escape route to the southwest was likely to be closing up behind them.

Even for a bold pilot, then, the decision would be an uncertain one. What might push him into taking the risk? Several factors. Sunday. The need to impress, or not admit defeat before, his pilot son. The very fact of already being in violation of one regulation or another—if he arrived at yet another airport under questionable conditions, the feds might get after him.

And then there is something you might call "involvement in the plot." It is always much more difficult to end an activity once one has begun it than to avoid it in the first place.

This last element is probably one of the most important, though it eludes identification in accident analyses. The pilot invests a certain amount of his ego in the struggle with the weather, so that while his reason may recognize at any moment the pointlessness of continuing, his heart is averse to capitulating. (Las Vegas was built upon this dynamic.) And a kind of technical problem arises as well: At what instant, exactly, do you call it quits?

In scud running, your spirits rise to the challenge of a certain level of hazard. But like the sense of smell, which rapidly deadens to a persistent odor, the sense of danger flags. You may feel uneasy, but there is no particular event to precipitate a 180-degree turn. You continue by default, awaiting either the break in the weather that vindicates your dauntlessness, or a fright sufficiently stimulating to make the decision to turn back automatic. At this point, though it appears that you have made a decision, really you have ceased to make decisions; you are waiting for circumstances to make a decision for you. Since the circumstances are neither human nor, most probably, divine, you should not be surprised if the decision they make on your behalf is a heartless one.

Pilots sometimes exercise amazing recklessness on behalf of their passengers. In the previous case, the pilot probably felt right up to the last moment that the weather conditions, however terrible, were still flyable. In the next, it's hard to guess what the pilot could have been thinking.

The Road Warrior
by Peter Garrison

Scud running is like an amusement-park ride: You feel a gratifying sense of risk when there need not, in fact, be much real risk at all. The sense of motion in a three-dimensional world, notably and lamentably absent in most flying, is strong; and the continuing parade of scenery makes the time pass quickly. Many pilots enjoy scud running, look forward to it, and enjoy telling lively hangar stories about their experiences.

Perhaps it was with some such affection about low flying in weather that a 30-year-old, 330-hour Washington pilot noted in his logbook after a January flight of 1.5 hours: "WX VFR SCUD FLYING."

He flew little during the rest of the year, less than nine hours in fact, all in rented Mooneys. But during the December holidays he had another opportunity for scud flying. He and a pilot friend who had flown even less regularly—4.3 hours in the preceding year—rented a Mooney for a sightseeing flight; a woman friend sat in the back. They departed Paine Field in Everett, Washington, just north of Seattle, and flew to Hillsboro, Oregon, near Portland, a distance of less than 200 nm.

At about 4:40 p.m., the pilot visited the Portland Flight Service Station and requested an abbreviated briefing for a flight to Boeing Field in Seattle. He had just come down an hour earlier, he said, and so he knew the weather. The briefer told him that VFR was not recommended for the route, but the pilot said that he was instrument rated and would file en route if he could not continue VFR along the big highway from Portland to Seattle. The briefer then assisted the pilot in filling out an instrument flight plan, which he took with him. The briefer later recalled that the pilot seemed to have considerable trouble filling out the IFR flight-plan form. Obviously, it was something he was not used to doing.

The sun sets early in midwinter, and with the heavy cloud cover lying close to the ground it was dark by the time the flight neared Seattle. The pilot made radio contact with a ground station only once: to request permission to pass through the Olympia, Washington, airport traffic area, which lies athwart the highway.

Getting into Boeing Field with a low overcast would be tricky; the highway the pilot was following passes within a fraction of a mile of Seattle-Tacoma International. From Sea-Tac to Boeing Field is about three miles, and Renton Airport forms an equilateral triangle with the other two. The pilot must have felt that he would be able to pop up nonchalantly on a mile final for Boeing Field without anyone being the wiser.

He almost got to try. He was less than two miles from the threshold of the runway at Sea-Tac when he struck a power line and crashed on the embankment that runs alongside Interstate 5.

It's likely the two pilots aboard the airplane had some second thoughts during the last minutes of the flight. Witnesses on the ground, several of them pilots, reported seeing the Mooney heading up the interstate. Those who heard its engine reported that there was nothing amiss; one thought the airplane was so low, however, that it must be trying to land on the highway. Estimates of its altitude varied from 70 to 200 feet. In fact, it was at a height of 75 feet above the road—about two wingspans—that the Mooney struck the power line. Witnesses' reports on the weather conditions were also variable as, no doubt, were the conditions themselves. One witness reported a mile visibility in light rain and fog, while another, a retired airline captain, at a different location, reported a 200-foot ceiling and a half to three-quarters in fog. A third witness, who lived close to the accident site, said the visibility was "very good."

The idea of flying at night through an urban area at an altitude of 75 feet and in visibilities of a mile or less should give anyone but Luke Skywalker the heebie-jeebies. It probably wasn't what the pilot himself had in mind. It just, as the saying goes, sort of happened.

All the elements were there. The pilot had logged enough time to consider himself experienced, but not enough to *be* experienced. It was a Sunday evening, with the pressure to get back that that can entail. Two pilots were in the airplane—a situation in which the pilot-in-command's decisions may be influenced by the desire to impress the other pilot, by his own beliefs of what the other pilot may expect of him, or by an unexpressed—and utterly groundless—assumption that two pilots are less likely to get into serious trouble than one.

If the flight from Everett to Hillsboro had preceded the return flight by only an hour, as the pilot told the Portland briefer, then the pilot's first and perhaps biggest mistake was to begin the first flight so late. It made a return in darkness inevitable. Given the late start, and assuming that the weather was then no worse than low VFR, it would have made a lot more sense to make a shorter flight and remain within striking distance of Seattle—especially in view of the fact that weather tends to move across the area from the northwest.

Once the pilot was at Hillsboro with his two passengers, he had put himself into a bind. Having gotten them 200 miles from home (actually, the other pilot was from southern California; but maybe he had a plane to catch), was he now to tell them that they were stranded, and would either have to return ignominiously on a bus or buy toothbrushes and wait out the weather, perhaps missing work the next day?

Ever since briefers started having to tell pilots "VFR not recommended"—the phrase is a relatively recent addition to their vocabulary—pilots planning to do a little creative VFR flying have had to play trick-the-briefer. The "specialist" himself, though he has no authority to wrestle the pilot to the ground even if the ceiling be upon it, appears to the pilot in the role of an FAA enforcer, armed at the very least, in the errant pilot's imagination, with a direct line to the FSDO. When our pilot fibs to the briefer that he is instrument rated and will pop up into the system along the way if need be, he is actually doing what few instrument pilots would do: Fly VFR in marginal weather when IFR is possible. He is also putting himself into the position where the ATC system becomes his adversary. He must now not only complete his flight safely, which will be hard enough, but make it appear that he did so legally as well—that is, not call attention to himself when he arrives under the moustache of the Seattle TCA in weather that by general agreement is below the VFR minimums.

Now, he is not entirely without instrument training. He has logged 23 hours in a simulator and 20 in actual conditions, presumably working toward the rating. He actually has some approach plates, including one for Boeing Field. As the ceiling lowers, though, he apparently feels more comfortable staying under it than getting into it. There, his instincts may be good. By the time he is coming down the pike into downtown Seattle at an altitude of 75 feet, however, he must either be completely disoriented or utterly desperate. Of course, he may still think, as the familiar off-ramp signs pass unfamiliarly below rather than above him, that he can pull it off. After all, there are only a few miles to go.

There are some simple rules to remember about scud running. Don't do it at night. Don't fly toward deteriorating weather—by the time you decide to turn around, it may have shut down behind you. Don't follow the bright spots—"sucker holes"—but hold a heading and follow landmarks instead. Don't fly under a ragged, foggy overcast; stick to the nice crisp ones with clear air underneath. If you're down so low that you can read the Surgeon General's warning on the billboards, give up and land.

But all the rules in the world are useless when you fly away and leave good judgment at home.

The most dire weather forecast might not deter a pilot who feels that he has to show his passengers that he can get them home on time. In the next report, a noninstrument-rated pilot presses on into the weather, while an instrument-rated one does the sensible thing.

Uncontrolled Experiment
by Peter Garrison

A 44-year-old Indiana businessman-pilot was homeward-bound from Florida on an Easter Sunday afternoon. With him in his company's

Piper Saratoga SP were six friends and family members, including an infant. They stopped at a small town in Georgia to refuel and get a weather briefing. The 850-hour, noninstrument-rated private pilot apparently had not gotten a briefing in Florida before starting the trip.

The weather briefing was probably the most daunting one he had ever heard. It called for tornadoes and hail up to two inches in diameter in the vicinity of Indianapolis, wind gusts to 70 knots, and multiple lines of thunderstorms building to 45,000 feet.

Layers of cloud between a warm front and a cold front reached above 12,000 feet in Georgia, dropping to 8,000 along the Ohio River; the mountain tops would be obscured. The freezing level roughly coincided with the cloud tops. There would be moderate turbulence, and moderate rime icing in clouds above the freezing level. The cold front responsible for all this extended from Michigan to Louisiana and was slow-moving; the briefer speculated that by the next morning there would still be a wide area of IFR and marginal VFR conditions from Louisiana to Maine.

The pilot, hunting for a ray of hope, asked for the Knoxville weather. "I'd like to go a little further north if I could, then get another briefing—Knoxville or around Louisville."

The briefer continued to emphasize the low ceilings, drizzle, and fog.

"What are the tops of the low-level clouds?" the pilot asked. "All I was thinking about is flying . . . getting on top and then over the mountains and then come down if it's around Knoxville, that broken . . ."

Knoxville actually sounded reasonable: 4,500 broken, 25,000 overcast. But then the briefer found an amendment: 3,500 broken, gusts to 25, occasionally 1,200 overcast with two miles visibility in light rain and a chance of thunderstorms. Having told the pilot twice earlier in the conversation that VFR was not recommended, he now said, "Okay, well, at this point in time based on the Knoxville terminal forecast of the IFR conditions, you know, the overcast conditions, I don't recommend you trying to get on—ah, VFR flight ah, VFR on top."

"Ah, 'cause it's not broken in between there to reach my destination," the pilot said.

"Right," replied the briefer.

The pilot filed no flight plan; nor, as the newspapers occasionally remember to say, was he required to. He had no radio communication with the ground. We know nothing of what happened next, except that the flight never reached Indiana. Relatives notified the authorities two days later, and after another three days searchers combing a four-state area found the wreckage at the 2,900-foot level on a ridge about 50 miles north of Knoxville. All the occupants had died on impact. The accident site lay almost exactly on a straight line from the point of departure to the intended destination. Such are the advantages of loran navigation.

It appears likely that the pilot took to heart the dreadful weather around his destination and the briefer's cautions about not trying to go on top. Despite having a good IFR panel with autopilot, HSI, and a recently installed Northstar loran, he did not succumb to the temptation to get on top and then fake it when he had to come back down. Instead, he seems to have decided to try to slip underneath the weather.

Staying under the weather is often the better choice for a VFR-only pilot. The cards are on the table. If the weather is shutting down ahead, he can see it and make a decision. If he has a little common sense, he can land before getting clamped between clouds and earth.

But flying below the weather requires pilotage. The pilot needs to watch his map, study the terrain, follow roads, know at every moment where he is, have escape routes and nearby airports at his fingertips. VORs are a help, but it doesn't do to rely on them except as a backup to visual navigation.

Flying under the weather also requires a sense of the interactions of weather and terrain. The pilot's route would take him over 7,000-foot mountains southeast of Knoxville; with the low situated well to the north and the circulation flowing counterclockwise around it, he could expect a westerly flow and the worst of the cloud buildups on the northwest slopes. He made it successfully across the highest mountains. Did he find a way over the ridges, or did he fly through the fortuitously situated pass at Asheville, where the terrain drops below 2,000 feet? We don't know. Oddly, the ridge he hit was the last one of any significance that lay between him and the low, rolling hills of eastern Kentucky. It, too, had a pass, at Middlesboro, just five miles or so west of the crash site. And less than 20 miles to the west the ridge broke up, and a major highway, an excellent navigational aid, led north from Knoxville.

That he hit the ridge rather than fly through the pass suggests that he was not using pilotage, but was instead relying on radio navigation to make good his track. He could have been inbound to the London VOR, or he could have been using his loran. The autopilot was not engaged—a fact which suggests that he was not simply boring along through cloud waiting to pop out. More likely he was trying to slip between the ridge and the clouds and either suffered a momentary visual disorientation that caused him to misjudge the angle to the treetops, or else was pulled down at the last moment by a lee-side downdraft. The airplane struck the ridgetop trees at a shallow angle, traveling 2,000 feet before it came to rest on the north slope of the ridge.

There are so many variables involved in weather flying that it is difficult to say that this pilot made any single big mistake. That he took off at all is surprising, given the dire face put on the weather by the briefer; he took off, too, more than 300 pounds over gross weight, and was still over gross when the accident occurred. All of this suggests a certain nonchalance or perhaps just the all-too-familiar homeward urgency of Sunday afternoon.

A case can be made that flying in such weather is an experimental procedure and that pilots contemplating it should consider whether their unwitting friends and relatives ought to be made guinea pigs. Most likely the other people in the airplane had no idea how bad the weather ahead was, nor had they any way to estimate the competence of their pilot to deal with it. They resorted to the blind faith of the utterly powerless.

A letter solicited by National Transportation Safety Board investigators from another pilot who flew that day in that area is included in the accident docket. He, too, was bound from Florida to Indiana with passengers. The letter implies an alternative attitude to weather, passengers, and time.

"My family and I were returning from vacation and had left Leesburg [Florida] at approximately 9:45 a.m. Weather was obtained from the local FSS. Weather was forecast VFR for the route from Leesburg to Athens [Georgia]; about 2,000 to 3,000 scattered, visibility greater than six. We were advised of a front from Cleveland through eastern Tennessee. One of our passengers was a nervous flyer [sic], so we opted to go VFR to Athens. Forty-two miles south of Athens we were down to about 800 feet agl with visibility about three or four miles. Weather to this point had been 3,000 scattered-broken visibility unrestricted. We decided to land at Milledgeville to wait on weather to improve. We stayed overnight there and departed Monday, April 4, 1988, morning on an instrument flight plan and were never in a cloud."

Weather isn't the only trap. In the next scenario, an overconfident pilot takes a deliberate gamble.

Pride Before the Fall
by Peter Garrison

The excitement of flight and the professional pride of pilots spring in part from the general perception of flying as dangerous. This is a reasonable enough perception at the visceral level, if not at the cerebral; any aborigine would hesitate to confide his body to a rickety contraption miles above the ground, and we are all born aborigines. Statistics—always surprisingly favorable to aviation—come later.

Pilots, by their skills, make the dangerous environment safe for themselves and others. Because they have the power to do this, they regard themselves as entitled to higher esteem (and pay) than other transportation workers. Pilots are the apotheoses of busmen, chauffeurs, rickshaw-wallahs, and drivers of big rigs; they are the noblest flowers to sprout from the age-old enterprise of hauling goods and persons.

If we anatomize the pilot's pride a little further we find that it embraces not only coolness in conditions and situations that uninitiated people might find unnerving, but also "ship-handling"—skill in the execution of mechanical tasks of running an airplane. Pilots pique themselves on being able to hold exact altitude and heading for a long time, to place the wheels delicately on the runway, to estimate their time over checkpoints with surprising accuracy, to freeze the ILS cross hairs on their target.

When pilots fly with other pilots watching them, their pride often gets the better of them. They may do things that they would not ordinarily do. On one hand, they may try to redouble their precision, holding altitude within 25 feet rather than the required 50 and speed to within a knot or two. On the other hand, they may occasionally take a risk or omit a precautionary ritual, as if to say, "Rules for ordinary pilots do not apply to me." The marriage of recklessness and skill is one that people find easy to admire; but it sometimes produces ugly offspring.

A single accident a few years ago took the lives of four pilots (possibly five; the status of the fifth victim is unclear from the NTSB report). All of them were in the last stages of preparation for Part 135 check rides, which were to take place during the next few days. The pilot was taking up the Cessna 411 that he would be using for the check ride; it had just come out of the shop and had been troubled lately with nagging, minor problems.

It was late on a Monday afternoon in spring; the weather was clear, and in an excess of airport camaraderie the pilot collected an airplaneful of passengers to accompany him on the flight. Three were charter pilots like himself; the fourth man had just come down from a ride with a friend in a Skylane, but apparently his appetite for flying was unsatisfied.

What they did on the flight is unknown; there's a suggestion that they may have buzzed someone's house, but the witness is careful to say that he can't be sure the airplane he saw was the same one that had the accident. At a little before six o'clock the Cessna droned back into view in the traffic pattern of the airport. Witnesses saw the left engine stop; although they later described the airplane as "losing" an engine, post-crash examination of the engine revealed no evidence of a failure, nor did the right-seat pilot, who was handling the radio communications and announced the downwind entry in a calm, nothing-special tone of voice, give any indication of trouble. Investigators assume that the pilot deliberately caged the engine and feathered the prop in order to make a single-engine landing.

One witness near the airport emphasized that the twin seemed to fly the downwind unusually close to the runway, and unusually low; he watched "wondering how the pilot was going to be able to turn on final." Many witnesses commented on how low the airplane was.

The 411 flew a left-hand pattern with an extended downwind. It banked steeply onto final—or perhaps witnesses mistook the stall departure for a steep bank; in any case, it stalled into the dead engine on the turn to final. It was too low for any hope of recovery; the twin crashed and exploded into flames.

The accident raises two obvious questions. First, why did the airplane crash? That is, why did a 6,000-hour professional charter pilot, his skills presumably honed for an impending check ride, fail to fly a single-engine approach under controlled conditions? Second, why did the pilot attempt an actual single-engine landing (as opposed to a zero-thrust simulation) at all?

The first question has several answers. First, the 411, with big engines and a small vertical fin, is notorious for its heavy handling in single-engine flight. One test pilot, evaluating the airplane for the plaintiffs in a liability suit against Cessna, described its rudder pedal forces as "intolerable." Obviously, that pilot may not have been impartial; Cessna has always maintained, to the contrary, that the airplane meets certification requirements and has no unsafe flight characteristics. But in any case, no one dreams of spending his vacation flying a 411 on one engine; the airplane is at the very least no better than other medium twins in single-engine handling, and all of them present the same potential difficulties. Those difficulties are well known. In recognition of them, most single-engine work is done at altitude, and low-level practice is conducted with an engine at zero thrust, not stopped. The airplane is light; one does not carry a planeload of passengers for single-engine practice.

When one makes a single-engine approach, one takes every precaution. One flies a stabilized approach, straight in, with enough excess altitude to make it unnecessary to carry a lot of power (but not so much as to force a go-around). Above all, one does not fly a tight downwind at low altitude, with steep turns into the dead engine on base and final.

In this case, the pilot violated every one of these precepts.

Why? That brings us to the second question: Why in the world did he cage the engine just before landing in the first place?

It would be absurd to pretend to know, from the sketchy information in an NTSB report, what motivated the *dramatis personae* to act as they did. We can only generalize, from knowledge of self and others, about how some people might act in certain circumstances, and to construct from that kind of general knowledge a hypothesis about what by definition always remains hidden: the workings of another's mind. Such an analysis is general, not particular; its interest for us is not in what it may suggest about the victim of this particular accident—to whom such illumination as it may provide has no further use—but in what it may reveal about us, the living, who may gain useful knowledge from it.

To me it appears that in this accident one hears the faint echo of the wedding music of Recklessness and Skill. Even if the pilot did not cage the engine purely to show off to his large audience—to give them a little *frisson* of anxiety and then deliver them safely from it—he may still have been caused to show a little more bravado than usual by the fact that while his companions were pilots, he was *the* pilot. It's the old roll-the-LearJet phenomenon, where you'd finish an hour and a half of hauling the jet through simulated emergencies, holding patterns and ILS approaches, and on the way home the instructor would say, "Here, I've got it," and do a roll or two just to show that he's really a good guy and knows that the rulebook isn't everything.

It's a rare pilot who can look back at his flying career without finding a few instances—perhaps many—where he went closer to the edge than he needed to. And in many such instances there was an audience, on the ground or in the airplane, that made the risk seem worthwhile. Recklessness and Skill don't elope; they invite their friends, and their friends' friends, to their wedding.

Not all bad inflight decisions are caused by personal pressures, of course; there can be a host of different causes. One is confusion over the proper role of ground-based air traffic controllers. Although pilots

*generally find themselves following controllers' instructions, the final
authority for the safety of the flight is vested not in the controller but in
the pilot. Sometimes, however, pilots forget, or don't want to use, that
final authority.*

Dropping the Reins
by Peter Garrison

It was a September morning, clear but hazy. A V35 Bonanza was en
route from Worcester, Massachusetts, to Chatham, on Cape Cod, for a
Bonanza fly-in. The pilot's wife was the only passenger. The visibility
was four miles, but the pilot had filed an IFR flight plan. He had just
leveled out at his assigned cruising altitude of 5,000 feet and been
handed off from Bradley (Connecticut) Approach Control to Quonset
(Rhode Island) Tracon when he experienced an engine problem.

The following transcript covers the period from the pilot's first report of his engine problem to Quonset Tracon to his attempted landing on Interstate 95, the main New York-Boston highway, less than
five minutes later. (V35 = Bonanza N5NG; QUO = Quonset Tracon;
HEL = a Guard helicopter.)

TIME: 1020:13

V35: [Unintelligible] problem.

QUO: Okay, aircraft calling Quonset, N53167 are you calling me?

V35: [Unintelligible] like to land at Providence. Is that my nearest
airport?

QUO: Okay, who was that calling with the problem, please?

V35: N5NG, my rpm is falling off.

QUO: 5NG roger, understand, sir, descend and maintain 2,100, turn
left heading 140, that's vectors to the localizer at Providence.

V35: 5NG.

QUO: 5NG, disregard the heading, just continue on your present
heading now, vector to Providence, report the airport in sight.

V35: 5NG.

QUO: Providence weather is VFR, visibility three in haze, wind 260 at
eight, altimeter 30.10.

V35: 010, 5NG.

QUO: Beechcraft 5NG, Providence airport is at 12 o'clock now and
eight miles.

V35: 5NG.

QUO: And 5NG, turn 10 degrees right now, that's a better vector to
the airport.

V35: 5NG, I don't know if I have engine power or not, I'd like to maintain altitude until I'm in close.

QUO: Roger, sir, maintain any altitude you'd like.

   TIME: 1022:36

QUO: And 5NG, the wind is 260 at eight, any runway you'd like is yours.

QUO: 5NG, how many people do you have?

V35: Two people on board. How far am I from the airport?

QUO: You're now five miles, five and a half miles north of the airport.

V35: 5NG may not be able to, ah, [unintelligible] five miles.

QUO: Say it again, please.

V35: [Unintelligible] engine power.

QUO: Okay, understand you're losing engine power, the airport is now at 12 o'clock and five miles, sir.

QUO: Beechcraft 5NG, the airport's at 12 o'clock now, five miles.

V35: 5NG, 12 o'clock and five miles, I don't know if I'll make it.

QUO: Roger, I understand, sir.

HEL: Quonset Approach, Guard 60860, would you like assistance on that aircraft?

QUO: Guard 860, yes sir, if you can . . . 5NG, are you in VFR conditions?

V35: Affirmative.

QUO: Okay. Guard 860, Quonset, maintain, can you maintain VFR conditions?

HEL: That's affirmative, sir.

QUO: Sir, you can turn right heading 170 and I'll vector you toward that aircraft. Maintain VFR and I'll keep you advised.

HEL: Okay, right turn heading 16 . . .

   TIME: 1024:32

V35: 5NG will not make the field, I'm going to have to find an emergency field.

QUO: 5NG roger, you are over 95 at this time.

QUO: 5NG, that's Interstate 95 you're over at this time.

V35: 5NG.

QUO: 5NG, I have a helicopter coming toward your position and I'll keep you advised. Radar contact lost at this time.

HEL: Quonset, Guard 860, what's his apparent, approximate location?

QUO: 5N, ah, Guard 60, he is two and a half miles north of Providence Airport. I just lost radar contact with him over Interstate 95.

The Bonanza struck a highway barrier while attempting a gear-up landing on the interstate. The airplane disintegrated and both occupants were killed.

The cause of the power loss was found to be a broken crankshaft. Curiously, broken cranks sometimes announce themselves by a gradual loss of power rather than, as you might suppose, the abrupt and noisy deconstruction of the whole engine. An engine with a broken crankshaft can produce quite a bit of power; it all depends where the cleavage occurs. So the pilot of the Bonanza may not have had any way of knowing at first how complete his engine failure was or how imminent was his landing. A 1,600-hour pilot with 1,300 in the Bonanza, he may have known quite well that without power and with a windmilling prop, his airplane would descend at about 1,000 feet a minute in a glide; the pilot's operating handbook figure is two statute miles per 1,000 feet agl at 105 knots indicated with gear and flaps up, cowl flaps closed, and prop in coarse pitch (low rpm).

Nevertheless, engine trouble is engine trouble, and one has to be prepared for the worst at the first sign of it. If it occurs, as it did in this case, at relatively low altitude, the pilot's first order of business is to conserve his altitude while slowing to the best glide speed and setting the propeller in coarse pitch (low rpm), which produces the least drag while windmilling.

The pilot of the Bonanza appears not to have reacted in a very systematic manner. The reconstructed radar track shows him at 4,900 feet, doing 176 knots true, a few seconds before he first called Quonset to report a problem. Two minutes later his speed was undiminished, and he was at 3,000 feet. Only then did he gradually begin to reduce speed, but he never maintained the Bonanza's best glide speed of 105 knots.

Nevertheless, this engine failure did not have to be fatal. That it was was due to a multitude of factors, including the dynamics of the Bonanza's arrival on the interstate. But the fact that the Bonanza landed in desperation on the interstate rather than at an airport or on some other road or field was due to the actions of the pilot and controllers, and those are the aspects of the accident from which other pilots (and controllers) may learn something.

The crux of this accident was misunderstanding, due in part to radio traffic and garble, and in part to misinterpretation of the words that were correctly heard.

As far as we know, the pilot at no time declared an emergency. This may seem like a technicality, but the use of the word "emergency" or "Mayday" would have made clear to the controller what he otherwise only gradually came to understand: that the pilot was in dire straits.

The pilot began by announcing that he had a problem. Most of his first transmission was unintelligible, but from the fact that it ended with the word "problem" it appears likely that it contained little other information. Probably he said something like, "Quonset, Bonanza 5NG, I believe we have an engine problem."

The controller at first thought a different aircraft had called. Before he got that confusion cleared up, the pilot made an absolutely critical transmission: He said he would like to land at Providence. He then added, "Is that my nearest airport?" but the controller, who still didn't know to whom he was talking, apparently didn't pick that up. Sadly, there were in fact two airports closer to N5NG's position than Providence; one, with a 5,000-foot runway, was five miles away, off his left wing.

Once the controller understood that 5NG had an engine problem, he issued a puzzling clearance: Turn left, descend to 2,100, vectors to the localizer. This was a standard clearance for a localizer approach to Providence; it made no sense in terms of emergency action after an engine failure.

Why did the controller issue it? Probably because the pilot had merely reported dropping rpm, and the controller had no way of knowing whether the drop was large or small or what it signified.

By now the pilot had probably interpreted the controller's clearing him to Providence as implying that there was no other airport nearby. But there was most likely also another, subtler misunderstanding: The pilot felt that he had placed himself in the hands of the controller and that the controller (who is, in a sense, an omniscient, godlike figure compared with a pilot enmurked in industrial haze) had made some kind of informed judgment about the feasibility of his limping to Providence. At the same time, the controller, who knew that the final responsibility for the safety of the flight rests with the pilot, probably interpreted the pilot's acceptance of his clearance as implying that the pilot felt he could get to the airport; in any case, the controller had no reason at the time to second-guess what appeared to be the pilot's own decision.

If the pilot could have seen Providence—that is, if the visibility had been 20 miles rather than four—he would perhaps have judged that he could not get there; and, incidentally, he might have spotted the other airport off his left wing, or have selected a promising-looking off-airport landing place. Instead, he proceeded through the haze, away from relatively open country, and toward an unseen urban destination.

At this point the dice were cast. The pilot had turned over his decision-making responsibility to the controller, and the controller, who was not in the airplane and didn't even know whether conditions outside were VFR or IFR, could do nothing but alert the crash trucks and hope the pilot made it to Providence.

This accident clearly illustrates the reason why pilots, not controllers, have final authority over their airplanes. They know, or at least are supposed to know, exactly what the situation is in the airplane at all times. Controllers know only the airplane's position, and nothing else unless the pilot elects to tell them. And even if he tells them, there is always a chance of misunderstanding.

In an ideal world, the pilot would have been following his progress on a VFR chart and would have known that there was an airport in easy gliding distance when he first had his problem. In an alternative ideal world, he would have had one of the new smart lorans that can drag two or three nearby airports out of their databases in fractions of a second. But not everybody has one of those fancy lorans, and few pilots traveling on IFR flight plans, even in VFR weather, keep constant track of their position.

Nevertheless, the pilot could have made an informed judgment about reaching Providence if he had applied that basic rule about his airplane's gliding range—two *statute* miles per 1,000 feet agl. But to do that he would have had to make it his business to ask the controller the distance to Providence.

That the pilot didn't try for another airport is understandable; he *thought* the controller had understood his query about alternative airports and had implied by his answer that there were none. But that the pilot tried to reach Providence without establishing that he could really get there was entirely his own fault. After all, the basic rule about engine failure is to make a controlled landing *here*—not to stretch your glide to get *there*.

Not until one-and-a-half minutes after the pilot first announced his problem did the controller tell him the distance—then eight nm—to Providence. His altitude was then probably around 3,500 to 3,800 feet, and so he could expect to glide only seven or seven-and-a-half *statute* miles. By that time he must have known that he couldn't count on his engine for much help. The pilot could still have abandoned the attempt to reach Providence and begun looking for an appropriate emergency landing site instead; but, without realizing it he had given up the initiative to the controller and was not likely to make such a decision now.

Only when Providence was five miles away did the pilot begin to suggest that he couldn't get there. By now he was down to 2,000 feet msl. But what was the controller supposed to do? It was too late for any corrective action, and all the time the pilot had been flying away from the suburbs and toward the densely populated city.

We may say to ourselves that in this pilot's shoes we would have acted differently, but it behooves us to recognize that his actions were probably not different from what many other pilots would have done. To begin with, nothing is more difficult to cope with than a partial or progressive engine failure, because it's so difficult to decide to make an off-airport emergency landing when the engine is still responding, even reluctantly, to the throttle.

Pilots, furthermore, are not as attached to command responsibility as they're supposed to be. For one thing, being on an IFR flight plan predisposes us to accept direction from controllers and to accept their version of what we should be doing; after all, they know all the time where we are, and we, frankly, don't, except in rough numerical terms. For another, it must be very comforting, when the only engine aboard is failing, to turn to someone else and say, "You've got it."

Trying to reach a particular airport, rather than the nearest one, is out of the question when a single-engine plane has engine trouble. With a twin, the pilot may feel he can pick and choose. In the next accident, a pilot tries to nurse his ailing twin a few extra miles.

Deferred Maintenance
by Peter Garrison

In October 1987, a Cessna 421A was cruising at altitude near Page, Arizona, when a cylinder head on its left engine separated. The pilot feathered the engine and flew 188 nm west to Las Vegas, Nevada, where prompt service was available. The incident demonstrated unarguably the superiority of multiengine airplanes to singles in certain sorts of situations.

It also demonstrated a high level of confidence in his skills and equipment on the part of the pilot, a 55-year-old businessman with more than 7,000 hours of flying time. It was a confidence bordering upon overconfidence: When, in the course of replacing the broken cylinder, the Las Vegas maintenance shop found cracks between the spark plug and injector bosses in all the other cylinders on the engine, the owner was unmoved. "No cracks allowed per telephone conversation with TCM [Teledyne Continental Motors] West Coast rep," the supervisor wrote on the work order, continuing, "No action taken per customer request." The section of the work order regarding the cylinder cracks was stamped "THIS ITEM NOT APPROVED FOR RETURN TO SERVICE."

Thirteen months later, the pilot was bound from Torrance, California, near Los Angeles, to Tucson, Arizona, on a business trip in the same 421. Near March Air Force Base, just west of the parenthesis of mountains that brackets the Los Angeles basin, an engine again failed. But the pilot's belief that the cracking discovered in Las Vegas would not do him any harm was borne out by the event: The cylinder whose head blew off this time was on the right engine.

A partial transcript of radio communications follows. (85Q = the 421A; ONT = Ontario Tracon; 14K = an itinerant aircraft.)

TIME: 1601:04 PDT

85Q: Ontario, twin Cessna 3385Q, 121.5.

ONT: Twin Cessna calling Ontario Approach on the frequency, go ahead.

85Q: Roger, we're a Cessna 421/R, we've had an engine go out, we're about over March Air Force Base heading for Palm Springs, we're 5,500 feet, I think we can hold this and get into Palm Springs okay. Could you get me the frequency? I should be talking to a controller in this area.

ONT: 134.0 . . . Squawk 0253 . . . you're radar contact seven miles east of the March Air Base, your altitude indicates 5,100 . . . I won't be able to give you flight following through the pass, sir, at that altitude. You are only eight miles from March Air Base and only five miles north of the Hemet-Ryan airport.

85Q: Okay, I think I'd like to try and get into Palm Springs if I can, I know I can get service there.

ONT: 85Q roger, I'll continue advisories as long as I can and I'll forward the information to Palm Springs . . . altitude indicates 4,800 now, are you able to maintain altitude 5,000 or above?

85Q: Yes sir, I think we can get it back up to 5,000.

ONT: Okay, keep me advised and how many persons on board, sir?

85Q: One person on board.

ONT: Okay, and say your fuel remaining and time.

85Q: We're full of fuel, we've got five hours.

ONT: Okay, thank you . . . and 85Q, are you familiar with the Banning airport in the event that you encounter any more difficulty en route to Palm Springs?

85Q: Yes sir, I am. I can just barely see the ground here. I think I could find it if I'm not able to sustain, I'm not getting a full feather on my right engine so I'm not going to be able to hold altitude, I'm down to 4,000 feet now.

ONT: 85Q, roger, I'll maintain radio and radar communications with you as long as possible. The Banning airport is about 12 to one o'clock and 9.6 miles and they do have a fit runway and the frequency there is 122.8 in the event you are unable to make it through the pass.

85Q: Okay sir, thank you, 122.8.

TIME: 1605:29

ONT: Twin Cessna 85Q, radar contact lost seven miles southwest of the Banning airport.

85Q: Okay sir, thank you, we'll head straight for the Banning airport and then head on into Palm Springs.

ONT: November 85Q, roger, abeam the Banning airport, if you're going to continue, Palm Springs will be 126.7, they do have the information.

85Q: Okay sir, thank you.

ONT: And 85Q, I'd ask you one other thing, if you'd forward back to us when you are on the ground just for our own edification that all went well.

85Q: Okay, really appreciate the help, thanks a lot.

TIME: 1612:07

14K: Ontario, Cherokee 6714K, did you get the emergency call from 85Q?

ONT: I'm sorry, say again.

14K: This is 14K, did you receive an emergency call from 85Q saying he had an emergency and was landing on the freeway?

ONT: No sir, I did not hear that.

14K: Okay, we just picked it up about 30 seconds ago.

ONT: And where are you, sir?

14K: I'm currently 37.8 miles out of Seal Beach on V-64.

ONT: Did he cite any location, which freeway he may have tried landing on?

14K: Negative, he just said, "This is 85Q, we have an emergency, we're going to land on the freeway," and about 10 seconds after that he said, "This is 85Q," and then there's no more transmission.

The pilot's final transmissions were on Banning's unicom frequency. According to the airport manager, the pilot first said he had the Banning runway in sight but wasn't sure he could make it. After flying past the runway on a low left downwind leg, the pilot reported that he didn't think he could turn back to the runway and would try to land on the nearby interstate. He then keyed the microphone for six to 10 seconds, and the airport manager saw "a fireball in the direction of Cabazon."

A man returning home from work on his motorcycle, traveling east on the interstate through the pass that connects the Los Angeles basin with the desert and Palm Springs, was near the Cabazon overpass when he saw the 421 overhead at low altitude. He heard no engine sound and saw the right propeller rotating slowly. The left propeller was hidden from his view. The airplane suddenly veered to the right when 50 or 75 feet from the ground and, continuing to turn, it struck the ground with one wing, cartwheeled, and exploded.

The pilot had used up all his altitude and speed trying to reach Banning; and in doing so he had used up his options as well. Why he was unable to land on the interstate isn't clear; perhaps there was traffic at the moment he reached the road, or perhaps he felt he had gotten too slow even to risk the 45-degree turn into the dead engine that would have been necessary to align him with the pavement. The terrain in the area is open but uneven; he may have been making a bid for a smooth spot, but the airplane struck an electrical transmission line and crashed into a house.

Inspection of the engines recovered from the wreckage revealed that all the cylinders had been chromed, some repeatedly, despite a 1976 TCM service bulletin strongly recommending that this not be done on GTSIO-520-series engines. The left engine was about 100 hours past the published TBO of 1,200 hours, the right engine about 100 hours shy of it. The number-three cylinder of the right engine had failed from a fatigue fracture at the beginning of the threads that connect the aluminum head to the steel barrel. The reason for the failure of the propeller to feather properly could not be determined.

Experience is not always the best teacher. The pilot's previous success in reaching a major service facility on a single engine undoubtedly contributed to his decision to try to do the same thing again. Having once decided to reach Palm Springs, he seems to have developed the well-documented fixity of mind that besets people in emergencies; there is so much solace in having made a decision that they balk at abandoning it.

In retrospect, it is obvious that the moment the pilot saw that he could not maintain altitude, he should have hedged his bets and headed for the nearest airport—according to the controller, Hemet-Ryan. After all, there is always a possibility of something going wrong to delay a landing, and so in an emergency one ought to husband altitude, not squander it.

The pilot was in VFR conditions on top when the engine failed; below him was a thick haze, limiting visibility to little more than a mile. The afternoon sun lit the haze obliquely, making it more difficult to discern the ground, and a broken stratus layer at 1,000 agl further hampered visibility. The pilot may have been concerned about locating Hemet-Ryan or, for that matter, Riverside, a major general aviation airport with complete repair facilities that lay behind him; at least Palm Springs was in the clear. But the pilot was instrument-rated, and tracon could have provided him with vectors. Palm Springs is about 35 nm from the point where the pilot first reported his problem, Banning 15 nm, Riverside 14.

Even though twin-engine airplanes can usually drag themselves along well enough on one engine if they have to, the best policy after losing an engine is to land as soon as practicable. What is meant by "practicable" is left up to the pilot. Most would interpret it to mean that you should land at the nearest airport with adequate runway length, approach facilities if the weather is IFR, and so on. In this case the pilot seems to have made a more liberal interpretation of practicability, introducing a concern about the quality of repair facilities. Is this practicability, or is it convenience?

There's an adage, usually applied to midfield takeoffs, that notes that there's nothing more useless than the runway behind you. With an engine out and nowhere to go but down, the same adage applies.

In the next report, a pilot tries to land at the nearest airport after an engine fails. Hindsight permits us to weigh the odds better than he could at the time. Like the crash of Avianca 052, this one reminds us that no matter how carefully we fly an approach, landing is never absolutely assured.

Point of Know Return
by Peter Garrison

A former writer for *FLYING* once proposed, I believe in all seriousness, that among the good reasons for encouraging all pilots to acquire some training in aerobatics is that if they should happen to find themselves flying up a blind canyon, they could escape from their predicament by performing a simple half-loop with a roll off the top. Most authorities take a different view, and urge pilots not to fly up blind canyons in the first place.

The two opinions represent polar perspectives upon the potential hazards of flying. The first accepts the hazards and prepares to confront them with skill; the second, doubting the adequacy of skill in the abstract (to say nothing of the skills of individual pilots), turns back at the first glimpse of danger. The apothegm about old and bold pilots is too familiar to need repeating; as a passenger, at any rate, I always prefer to fly with cowards.

In the fall of 1987 a de Havilland Caribou, operating on a cargo flight in the Yukon Territory, crashed during an attempted go-around from a single-engine approach. The accident took place in near-darkness, in mountainous, rising terrain, at the bottom of a river valley. The situation was as close to the hypothetical blind canyon as you'd care to get, and there was no hope of escaping by aerobatics. Judgment was everything; and the pilot's judgments turned out badly.

The Caribou is a big, homely twin-engine STOL airplane whose aft fuselage resembles a dislocated finger. It first flew in 1958 and was used for a long time as a transport by the U.S. Army. Powered by two Pratt & Whitney R2000 radials of 1,450 hp, it has a gross weight of 28,500 pounds, can carry 30 passengers or three tons of cargo, and, with its full-span double-slotted flaps, can take off and land in less than 600 feet. It cruises at around 150 knots and can climb at 1,500 fpm. Its single-engine climb rate at gross weight is 270 fpm.

Like most piston twins, the Caribou is sensitive to speed and flap setting in single-engine operations. The best single-engine rate of climb may be obtained either with 14 degrees of flap (the takeoff setting) at 77 knots, or with flaps retracted at 94 knots. Presumably it can be maintained along some line of increasing speed and diminishing flap setting between these two points, but doing so would be as delicate as walking a tightrope; a surer technique for cleaning up the airplane is to maintain level flight while bleeding off the flaps and gradually increasing the airspeed, and then beginning to climb after reaching 94 knots. To accelerate to 94 from 77 knots in level flight while retracting the flaps takes about 30 seconds.

The chain of events leading to this accident—there is almost always a chain in an aircraft accident, not just an isolated catastrophe—began 10 days earlier, when a mechanic changing the propeller governor on the right engine inadvertently damaged a gasket. No replacement was in stock; to permit rigging the governor control cable, he fabricated and installed a temporary rubber gasket. To be sure that no one would operate the engine with the temporary gasket, he left the governor mounting nuts loose and attached a yellow tag to the governor explaining the situation. But he did not advise anyone of the makeshift, nor did he make an entry in the maintenance log.

A few days later other mechanics, having completed the rest of the work on the airplane, performed a ground run-up. There was an oil leak on the right engine; they traced it to the loose governor base nuts. At this point the yellow tag had mysteriously disappeared. They tightened the governor base nuts and sent the airplane up for a test flight. After it returned they noticed a small puddle of oil beneath the right engine but did not consider it worth investigating.

The flight that ended in the accident began at the maintenance base at Calgary, Alberta. After a stop at Fort Nelson, British Columbia, the airplane was to continue to Ross River, Yukon, where it was to be used for hauling silver ore concentrate. It was carrying 5,500 pounds of spare aircraft parts and support equipment and took off from Fort Nelson about 1,000 pounds over gross weight. By the time of the accident it had burned off about 2,000 pounds of fuel.

The last leg of the flight was conducted on an IFR flight plan; the arrival at Ross River, which has no instrument approach, involved going 30 miles past Ross River to Faro, making an NDB approach to get below the clouds, and then returning down the river valley to Ross River.

The minimum circling altitude at Faro is 2,709 feet agl. The cloud bases were at 400 to 600 feet agl, with a mile visibility in light snow, when the Caribou attempted the approach. After failing to get sight of the ground at Faro the pilot advised the airport radio operator that he was going to his alternate, 180 miles distant, but might, weather permitting, attempt a landing at Ross River, which lay along the route.

When the flight had again leveled out at cruising altitude the right engine low-oil-quantity light lit up, followed shortly by the low-oil-pressure light. The crew kept the engine running until the oil pressure dropped out of the permissible operating range, and then shut it down and feathered the propeller.

The sun had been setting as the flight began its abortive approach to Faro. Now, as the dusk deepened, the lumbering Caribou, making perhaps 100 or 110 knots over the ground, faced a long flight in darkness on a single engine. The only alternative was to try to get into Ross River.

Witnesses later reported that the airplane could be heard circling above Ross River; then the sound trailed off to the southeast as the Caribou positioned itself for the approach.

The 5,500-foot gravel runway at Ross River was unlit, but it was equipped with a visual approach slope indicator system and was clearly visible from the airplane despite the darkness. It was necessary to begin the approach slightly high because of terrain three miles from the threshold. The pilot had set flaps, and he called for landing gear about a mile and a half out. No green light showed for the nose gear. The crew cycled the gear. This time the green light appeared, but too late; the airplane was no longer in a position to land.

Witnesses described the denouement: The airplane overshot, turning to the right to hug the valley side and seeming at first to climb. It then began to lose altitude as it disappeared in the darkness.

The Caribou sank into the trees two miles from the runway. Parts of the right wing were sheared off first, and then the airplane cartwheeled onto the river shore and began to burn. Two passengers survived; both pilots were killed.

The accident was investigated by the Canadian Aviation Safety Board, which devoted a good portion of the "conclusions" section of its report to suggesting that enforcement of safety regulations by the Department of Transport was not all that it might be. The emphasis upon this theme seemed to suggest that the accident had raised questions about the propriety either of the approach at Ross River or of the maintenance practices that had led to the failure of the right engine; but these issues are only implicated in the report.

From an operational standpoint—and from our standpoint as pilots studious of avoiding the repetition of history—what is interesting in this accident is the decision to land at Ross River. The CASB correctly observes that neither of the alternatives offered to the pilot— the long flight over mountains and in darkness on a single engine, nor the approach in bad weather and near-darkness at Ross River— was attractive. But I doubt the choice was made altogether dispassionately; in fact, I think it was half-made even before the right engine quit, when the pilot told the radio operator at Faro that he might attempt the approach at Ross River. It had been a long day— both pilots had already been on duty for 10 hours—and it's easy to imagine the crew wanting to get the trip over with. After all, the prospect of an hour or so's flight on a single engine isn't all that alarming; many pilots fly single-engine airplanes over mountains and other inhospitable terrain at night without thinking much of it. But perhaps single-engine flight appears much more dangerous to people who have just lost one engine than to those who had only one to begin with.

Most likely, the captain thought the approach at Ross River would almost surely be successful; and indeed it would have been, but for the utterly unforeseeable problem with the landing gear. Once the airplane was no longer in a position to land, however, what should the pilot have done? The only possible answer is crash under control.

Now, this is the sort of general principle that is of little use when you are in the grip of circumstances. Disaster impends; bent on avoiding it, does one easily embrace a lesser disaster? The pilot didn't; he tried to get a little altitude and turn in the valley; maybe he could get back to the runway and land the other way. Perhaps if he had had more than 90 hours in type and if his checkout had included a few single-engine go-arounds in an airplane *loaded to gross weight* he would have made a very different decision.

But backtrack to the point where the stricken Caribou was cruising over Ross River. The pilot could have applied a general principle: Don't attempt an approach if a go-around is impossible, unless there is no alternative. There was no reason to think a go-around would be necessary, but who knows? Moose on the runway, a sudden snow flurry obscuring visibility, even—it could happen—a landing gear malfunction . . . .

Now, the pilot obviously felt that the chance of something going wrong on the approach was about as remote as the chance of the good engine giving up on the way to the alternate, and so the *land as soon as possible* rule outweighed the *don't make an approach if you can't go around* rule. Did he discuss the matter with the copilot? The accident report doesn't say, even though one of the two surviving passengers was seated on a jump seat located between the two pilots.

In nursery schools these days, children too prone to rely on their fists or feet to clarify their opinions are urged, "Use your words!" Pilots should take this advice to heart; words give us a chance to simulate action before embarking upon it—and may lead us to salutary second thoughts.

In retrospect, it's clear that before descending from cruising altitude the crew should have discussed the decision to make the approach at Ross River. In the enfolding darkness, and with only one engine, they weren't likely to make it out of the narrow valley if they didn't make the runway. The implication needed to be made explicit: "If we don't make the runway, we'll have to put it down straight ahead in the best spot we can find."

Saying things like that out loud has three important effects: First, it gets the decision-making taken care of in advance, when there is still time to think calmly; second, it removes ambiguities and clarifies what is happening; third, it ensures that both crewmembers are thinking the same thing. Perhaps if someone had said straight out, "If anything goes wrong, we crash—no false hopes," the crew would have seen the 130-mile trip to the alternate in a different light.

2

Attitude

Certain personality types don't make good pilots, but the FAA has no way of screening them out. It's remarkable how many accident reports concern pilots who seem to have considered themselves exempt from the rules that apply to the rest of us. A manic nonchalance about rules and procedures is often accompanied by indifference to maintenance; the pilot behaves as though he or she thinks himself or herself invulnerable. Often the danger such people present is recognized in advance by others, but it's rarely possible to stop them.

Patterns of Destruction
by Peter Garrison

In what follows, the names have been changed to protect the innocent, the guilty, the inept, the careless, and the deceased.

Two men who lived in the South—call them Joe and Fred—perhaps influenced by such slogans as "Discover Flying" and "Anyone Can Fly," decided to acquire an airplane and learn to fly it.

Accordingly, they purchased a Cessna 150 and a large book of instructions. At a small but busy suburban airport they began their studies by firing up their new chariot—which, had they been classicists, they would no doubt have dubbed *Argo*—and taxiing it around between the rows of parked airplanes. This they did without incident, Joe presumably holding the book in his lap as Fred pounded on the rudder pedals, or vice versa.

Next, they approached a freelance instructor, Wally, who worked at the airport. They told him that they had just purchased the Cessna and had already taught themselves to taxi and were now interested in flight instruction. Wally agreed to instruct them at a rate of $16 per hour and forthwith gave each of them an hour of dual, after which he, being duly cautious, taxied the airplane back to the tie-down area himself.

This took place on a Sunday. The next Sunday, Wally flew an hour and a half with each of his new students, learning in the process that Joe had never flown before and that Fred had ridden as a passenger with a cousin in California. At the end of the lessons, some difficulty arose over the payment. Joe finally made out a check for less than the $48 that was due, explaining that he was short on money that week. Furthermore, he remarked, he had a friend who was a pilot and would teach them to fly and wouldn't cost so much.

His 90 minutes in the air with Joe had persuaded Wally that Joe was not likely to make a good pilot. He only wanted to learn to make the airplane go up and down and head in the required direction; he had no interest in learning to be a pilot in any larger sense. Fred, on the other hand, had the necessary basic skills and coordination. But by this time Wally had already decided not to give any more instruction to either man, because he had concluded that their oft-proclaimed intentions of vacationing in the Bahamas had something to do with drugs and had heard rumors that one of the men involved with the Cessna had a record of drug use.

Now Joe and Fred approached their friend Hank, who held a private pilot certificate. Hank was not exactly a seasoned ace; he had a total of 181 hours, 158 of them in a Cessna 150. His third-class medical certificate had expired three and a half years earlier, and it had been almost five years since his last biennial flight review. Nevertheless, Hank consented to fly with Joe and Fred, and the following Sunday found the trio back at the airport. Joe went up first. When they came down Hank remarked that the one functioning radio in the Cessna seemed to receive but not to transmit. He then took Fred up for half an hour, landed, and took Joe up again.

Hank and Joe left the pattern and returned after a 45-minute flight. They entered a straight-in approach from two or three miles out. A low-wing trainer was flying a left-hand pattern; as the Cessna was on short final, the other airplane overtook it and struck it from behind and above. The low-wing airplane lost half of its horizontal tail in the collision and plunged toward the ground; it struck a steep embankment, killing its occupants, an instructor and a 10-hour student.

The Cessna, meanwhile, recovered from the collision, made a normal landing, and taxied to parking.

Fred saw it all happen. He anticipated the collision and ran toward the runway waving his arms frantically, but in vain. He ran to the wreckage of the trainer, saw the student pilot breathe his last, and, realizing that both men were probably dead, ran back to the parking ramp to meet Joe and Hank. He told Joe to go to the office and call an ambulance. He then returned to the wrecked airplane, this time taking his camera with him. Several minutes passed before anyone else arrived.

Midair collisions can be completely random events, like the collisions of celestial bodies, or they can, on rare occasion and generally in wartime, be deliberate, kamikaze rammings. Usually they fall somewhere in between, closer to the random, but with a tincture of human causes. Those causes run the gamut from the purely physical and physiological—parts of his own airplane may obstruct a pilot's view or traffic may be virtually indiscernible against a certain background or in a certain light—to missteps of varying degrees of gravity: laziness, recklessness, indifference to safety, disregard of regulations or of proper operating procedures.

Investigators arriving on the scene of this accident found the usual material evidence: wreckage, bodies living and dead, severed airframe parts, smears of one airplane's paint on the skin of the other. And of course there were witnesses. First of all, there were the occupants of the Cessna and their friend on the ground, and, fortuitously, there was Wally, who happened to be in the pattern with a student at the time. By the end of the next day, the survivors and the witnesses had told their stories to the National Transportation Safety Board investigator.

Joe and Hank agreed that Joe had been in the right seat and Hank in the left. Fred didn't differ with them. Hank said he had been showing Joe a few things about flying. Hank also said that he had first seen the other trainer on a left base as he was on final, and had then lost sight of it. Fred, too, described the airplane as having been on a left base. Hank said that he had heard no radio transmissions from the other airplane.

Later, after consulting a lawyer, Hank remembered that when he had first seen the other airplane it had actually been leaving the downwind leg on a 45-degree angle, low, apparently headed elsewhere; he also down-played the vaguely instructional cast of the flight, saying instead that it had been a "sightseeing trip" intended to show Joe "some real estate he was interested in purchasing and essentially to give him a ride in his own aircraft, which he could not fly because he is not a licensed pilot."

Wally, who had also been in the pattern, had heard the trainer report its position on the downwind leg and the base leg, but not on the turn to final. He had heard nothing from the Cessna—not surprisingly, since its transmitters were both inoperative. Wally insisted, though he would not say how he knew, that, contrary to their assertions, Joe had been in the left seat of the Cessna, and Hank in the right. He also said that the Cessna had been in the pattern prior to the accident, "making hazardous approaches and [with] no radio."

The news media arrived in due course to report on the accident and recorded a heated exchange between Hank and the owner of the flight school whose trainer, student, and instructor had crashed. The exchange reflected an "intense animosity" that turned out to exist between the flight school and the Cessna operators.

Animosity also seemed to exist between other users of the airport and the flight school. Several pilots reported incidents of being cut off in the traffic pattern both by the Cessna and by trainers similar to the one involved in the accident. The difficulties, one pilot wrote to the NTSB investigator, arose from "a long-standing 'attitude' problem on the airport"—a reference, obviously, to the flight school, not to the Cessna.

The pilot described a couple of cases in which he had been cut off in the pattern; in one, a trainer resembling the accident airplane had turned ahead of him onto a quarter-mile final from a 200-foot base leg. "Thank you for cutting off my final," he had transmitted, and the trainer had returned, "Anytime, guy," and then broke off his approach. He went on to say that such incidents could have been avoided "by better communication on the common frequency and a realization by all pilots that there are other people with equal needs who use the airport . . ."

The operators of the Cessna seem to have disregarded a fair number of regulations, to say nothing of common sense. Their interest in aviation seems to have had less to do with the romance of flight, or whatever got the rest of us into this business, than with some kind of nefarious, half-baked ideas about cashing in on the drug wars. But if they emerge as less-than-admirable characters in this tale, that really has no clear bearing on the accident.

There are, however, two aspects of the Cessna's operation that are pertinent. One is the question of who was in what seat. Instructors are prepared by their training to handle the airplane and monitor traffic from the right seat. The combination of a low-time private pilot with no recent experience in the right seat and a no-time nonpilot in the left seat is not a good one.

The other aspect is the inadvisability of making a straight-in approach to an uncontrolled airport when several other airplanes are in the pattern and your radio transmitter isn't working. In fact, there is some indication that the Cessna's receiver, which was working, wasn't even tuned to the correct frequency; Hank and Joe may have had no radio contact whatever with other people in the pattern.

Hank said he had seen the trainer, then lost it. By his first account, the trainer was on a base leg, 60 degrees off his nose when he first saw it. Later, when he decided the trainer had really been elsewhere, he added that it must have been traveling at a *much higher speed* (emphasis his) to have overtaken him.

If we assume that Hank's first account, unpolished by consultation with a lawyer, is reliable, then it sounds as though the Cessna cut off the trainer, and as though the trainer, in the classic situation of a low-wing airplane descending on another airplane from above and behind, never saw the Cessna at all.

On the other hand, the reputation of the school's trainers for cutting other airplanes off suggests a cavalier view of traffic, and is consistent with the occupants of the trainer, while still on the base leg, failing to notice the Cessna approaching from the right on a straight-in.

If this incident is to be read as a cautionary tale, its lesson, apart from the obvious one of always looking around and taking nothing for granted in the traffic pattern, has to do with that "attitude" of ownership of the traffic pattern to which one pilot alluded in his letter to the NTSB.

Many of us have probably experienced that attitude; we fly into and out of an airport regularly, we consider ourselves "old hands," we fly a certain kind of pattern and feel irritation and contempt when strangers appear and fly too wide, or too high, or too long to please us. If they go out far enough we may even turn inside them, not regarding such a move as something reckless or egotistical, but rather as a natural remedy for the inadequacies of the other guys' flying.

It is, as often as the ineptitude of the novice, the nonchalance of the experienced pilot that brings trouble. We need to remind ourselves to be cautious, to fly defensively, to distrust flair and boldness. A little fear is a good thing in the air. Old hands need occasionally to refresh the innocent awe with which they first viewed the traffic pattern and the other pilots in it.

An indifference to training is one of the hallmarks of the scofflaw pilot. Once he gets the hang of handling the airplane, he sees no reason to waste time on more instruction. Unreasonable self-confidence can go unpunished for a while—even a long while—but seldom forever. The pilot in the next report flew for years before the simple facts of blind flying caught up with him.

End of a Rule-Breaker
by Peter Garrison

In 1985, a 27-year-old man bought a K35 Bonanza, a four-seat, 260-hp V-tail model manufactured in 1959. Three years later the Bonanza rained down in a million pieces out of a 1,000-foot ceiling into a farmer's field 50 miles from the pilot's home. The man, his wife, and their two daughters died—an ignominious end, wreathed in illegalities.

There was no record of the pilot's ever registering the airplane or, for that matter, maintaining it. Neither airplane nor pilot logbooks could be found; an associate of the pilot reported that no aircraft logs existed, and relatives said that annual inspections had not been performed. The ELT battery had expired in 1985. (On the other hand, the 1987 mandatory service bulletin for the V-tail beef-up had been complied with.)

The pilot, furthermore, was unlicensed. He had obtained a student certificate four months before the accident, reporting on his application that he had flown 20 hours in the previous six months. The holder of a student certificate is specifically forbidden to carry passengers or to leave the local area except with the particular authorization of an instructor.

When the crash occurred, the airplane had been airborne for two hours and 20 minutes, homeward bound from an airport several hundred miles distant. There was no record of the pilot's having obtained a weather briefing. In a final irregularity, the pilot had neglected to pay for the fuel and oil put into the airplane before taking off on the final flight—whether deliberately or inadvertently could not be known.

Now, it is one thing to flout the law and another to have an accident. The FAA likes to pretend that flight is impossible without the aid of certain official documents and is prone to make a direct connection between a pilot's coming to grief and his not having his papers in order. Yet it's easy to imagine an unlicensed pilot—a libertarian, perhaps—carefully maintaining and operating an unregistered airplane for a lifetime without hazard to himself or others. In fact, it's easy to imagine a movie being made about such a person in which we come to like and admire him. It all depends on his attitude.

This pilot owned and operated an airplane for three years without benefit of clergy; that his flying career ended with a fatal crash was due, however, not to his outlawry but to his carelessness.

We know the details of the final flight because the pilot was using VFR flight following. Evidently the weather must have looked good at the beginning of the flight, but then it got cloudy, with rainshowers, occasionally heavy, and scattered to solid layers at 1,000 feet and above. The visibility below the clouds was good, but the Bonanza wasn't below the clouds. Perhaps if the pilot had obtained a weather briefing he could have anticipated the destination weather and descended in time to get below it; instead, he was at 8,500 feet when the clouds started to get in his way. Evidently there was a layer below him; half an hour before the accident he had already reported to center that he was "VFR on top." The following transcript covers the final minutes of the flight. (25R = the Bonanza; JAX = Jacksonville, Florida, Center; 43E = a Cessna; 954, 105 = commuter aircraft; TIME = Eastern Daylight Time.)

TIME: 1543:00
25R: Jacksonville Center, Bonanza 25R.
JAX: Bonanza 25R, go ahead.
25R: Going to have to descend . . . well, maybe not . . . okay, I'm going to have to descend to maintain VFR.
JAX: N25R, roger.
25R: [Unintelligible] 6,500.
TIME: 1543:16
JAX: Roger, report reaching 6,500.
25R: 65R [sic], roger.
TIME: 1544:40
25R: 25R's through 8,000.
JAX: N25R, roger.
TIME: 1546:16
25R: 25R leaving 7,500.
JAX: 25R, roger.
TIME: 1551.46
25R: Jacksonville Center 25R, ah, we're level at 6,500, sorry it took so long.
JAX: N25R roger, contact Jacksonville Center 135.75, 135.75, and advise them of your new altitude.
25R: 5R, roger . . . Jacksonville Center, N9525R, 6,500, VFR.
JAX: N9525R roger, maintain VFR, Gainesville altimeter 29.88.
25R: 29.88, 5R, roger.
TIME: 1559:17
25R: Jacksonville Center, Bonanza 25R.
JAX: Bonanza 25R, Jax
25R: Roger, we're going to descend a little more [to] remain VFR.
JAX: Okay, if you could hold off for a minute there, you got traffic 12 o'clock and three miles northbound, northeast, northwest-bound IFR at 6,000.

25R: 25R, I've got to do something here, well, okay, I'm gonna be in the clouds.

JAX: Okay, what's your altitude now?

25R: 6,250 feet.

JAX: Roger. 8243E Jax, traffic off your right side there at two o'clock position three miles southbound, a VFR at 6,200 feet.

43E: Ah, roger, I'm solid at this time.

    TIME: 1559:59

JAX: Roger. 25R, I suggest about a 30-degree turn to the left.

25R: 30 degrees left, roger.

JAX: 43E Jax, fly heading of 290, vectors around traffic.

43E: [Unintelligible]

    TIME: 1600:52

25R: Oh yeah, we're, we're in a spin; I'm not sure which way we go here. I lost it. I'm sorry.

JAX: Calling Jax, say again please.

JAX: N8243E Jax, clear of traffic, now fly heading of 340, receiving Greenville proceed direct.

43E: 43E, roger.

JAX: N9525R, clear of traffic. 25R, Jax. N9525R Jax, how do you hear?

    TIME: 1603:08

JAX: November 8243E Jax, that VFR that was descending on top of you there I seem to have lost . . . see if you can raise it for me, his call sign is N9525R.

    TIME: 1604:15

954: Jacksonville, Bar Harbour 954.

JAX: Bar Harbour 954, Jax.

954: Yeah, that call about three minutes ago that you asked who it was, sounded like somebody that was a little disoriented there for just a moment.

JAX: I thought that might have been him, but, ah, I wasn't sure, he never called me back. I think he was in the clouds there, he was trying to maintain VFR, but he was descending down upon some IFR traffic.

954: It sounded like he said something about not being sure which way he was going or something like that.

JAX: Okay, thank you . . . 25R, if you hear the center ident.

105: 105, what was that guy's position? It sounded like he was getting into a spin.

It seems that everyone in the vicinity heard the Bonanza's distress call and drew the obvious conclusion from it, except the controller. Or did the controller understand what was going on all along? The transcript is worth careful study, particularly the exchange between the controller and 954 in which the controller appears to know that the distress call came from 25R without the other speaker's ever having suggested it.

In any case, however, our concern is with the pilot, not the controller. Few pilots have as casual an attitude toward rules and regulations as this one apparently did, but it's not unusual for a VFR pilot to find himself heading into worsening weather.

The first and foremost rule about this type of situation is to avoid it by getting a weather briefing and interpreting it conservatively. Sometimes, however, you need to go take a look; in that case, you should not get suckered by the bright sunlight above the clouds into staying on top. Unless you have a reliable, up-to-date report of scattered to broken at the destination—just "broken" isn't good enough— you shouldn't risk getting caught on top without enough fuel to reach a point where you can safely descend.

You also need to understand the nature of VFR flight following. The controller's first responsibility is to IFR traffic. In this case, had the pilot not been using flight following, he would probably have begun his descent earlier—being known to controllers discourages pilots from maneuvering at will—and, if he had stayed sufficiently far from clouds, he would not have risked a conflict with IFR traffic. He might have ended up below the clouds and made his way home safely.

Once he had involved himself with controllers, however, the pilot had compromised his freedom of movement. Controllers, after all, are called *controllers*—not advisors, counselors, or facilitators. And though experienced pilots know the limits of controllers' powers, many naive pilots do not. This pilot seems to have thought that because he was talking to a controller, he was entitled to fly into a cloud because the responsibility had somehow been shifted to the controller.

Actually, the controller was entitled to assume—in fact, *had* to assume—that the pilot was maintaining legal VFR cloud clearance, and so when he told the pilot to "hold off for a minute there" he thought that in the worst case the pilot would have to circle until the IFR traffic below him had passed.

The pilot, on the other hand, does not seem to have considered circling. He just barged on ahead.

When the pilot said, "I'm going to be in the clouds," the controller, who could not know the pilot was not instrument rated, said, "Okay," and asked for the Bonanza's altitude. To the pilot, the controller must have seemed to be approving the pilot's actions.

The airplane was equipped with an autopilot, but it was not turned on; probably it was inoperable from lack of service. The pilot, once in cloud, evidently got into the familiar and inevitable "graveyard spiral"; a true spin out of cruising flight is unlikely and inconsistent with the airplane's breaking up in the air. It all took less than a minute.

The relations between controllers and pilots are complex. They are carefully defined by regulations and by the mass of procedural guidelines contained in the controller's handbook, but the infinite variety of real situations defies complete specification. Controllers are like taxi dancers—pilots latch onto them for a few intimate moments and then say good-bye. During those moments of closeness, however, it's important, just as in some kinds of dancing, to know who has the lead.

In the next accident, careless maintenance combines with a pilot who barely knows his airplane. The presence of friends and impatience to get a delayed vacation trip underway probably played roles in the ill-advised launch into bad weather.

Flying Squirrel
by Peter Garrison

The Navajo was giving its new owner trouble. His departure with two friends for the Bahamas had been delayed most of Wednesday by a bad magneto harness on the left engine; the whole thing had to be replaced. They finally left Long Island, New York, after midnight and got to Jacksonville, Florida, in the wee hours of Thursday morning, only to find a tropical storm blocking their way. They landed, fueled, and serviced the airplane—the left engine took seven or eight quarts of oil, the right took three quarts—and laid over a day in Jacksonville. The men were back in the airplane at the crack of dawn on Friday.

The engines were hard to start. The pilot got them both going after some time—he told one of his passengers that he knew how to *fly* the airplane, he just didn't know how to *start it*—and then sat on the ramp for half an hour or so with the engines idling.

He finally called for his IFR and taxi clearance and, on beginning to taxi, promptly left the taxiway and rolled into the grass. After recovering from this indignity he found his way to the active and, after holding short for some time, he was finally cleared for takeoff.

The following edited transcript is taken from Jacksonville Tower tapes. (982 = the Navajo pilot; TWR = tower local controller; DEP =

departure control; APP = approach control; CTR = Jacksonville Center. Times are Eastern Standard Time. Land-line communications are in italics.)

TIME: 0740:08
TWR: Navajo 982, turn right heading 100, cleared for takeoff, wind 070 at 17.
982: Roger . . . what was that heading for 982?
TWR: Heading 100, one-zero-zero.
982: Roger, thank you.
TIME: 0741:43
TWR: Navajo 982, fly heading 100 and contact departure control on 118.0.
982: Roger 982.
982: Departure control, Navajo 74982 with you at 1,000, going to 11,000.
DEP: *Go ahead, green.*
TWR: *Watch that guy, he's a squirrel.*
DEP: *982 Jacksonville.*
DEP: *Green light.*
TWR: *That Navajo don't have a transponder.*
DEP: *I ain't seen him yet, where is he?*
TWR: *That's him just to the east, heading, uh, he looks like he's turning 070, I'm gonna turn Eastern.*
DEP: *Yeah, turn Eastern northbound, that's easier.*
DEP: Navajo 74982 JAX, you with me?
982: 74982 roger, at 2.3 going to 11,000.
DEP: Okay, Navajo 982 squawk 0752 please.
982: Roger, 982.
TWR: *South, local.*
DEP: *Go ahead.*
TWR: *That 982 get everything squared away out there?*
DEP: *I don't know, what's his problem?*
TWR: *He, I gave him a turn to 100 and he turned 100 and then when everything was cleared I let Eastern roll behind him, he turned back to 70 on me, that's why I had to give Eastern a 50 heading and point him out to the north, I just wanted to make sure. That 982, Chuck, he's a squirrel. Watch him.*
DEP: *All right, thank you.*
TWR: *It took us 30 minutes to get him on the runway.*
TIME: 0746:03
DEP: November, 982, turn right heading 170.

982: Right to 170, roger 982.

TIME: 0746:45

DEP: 982, JAX, say your heading please.

DEP: November 982, JAX.

982: Heading 070.

DEP: Okay, you were turned right 170, one-hundred-and-seventy degrees.

982: Roger, 170, thank you.

TWR: *Local.*

DEP: *You're right about that, I turn him 170 so he decided to fly 50.*

TWR: *Yeah, that's what I'm telling you. The guy is, the guy is a squirrel.*

DEP: *I don't think he's any more instrument-rated than I am.*

TWR: *Uh, uh.*

DEP: November 74982, when receiving Ormond resume own navigation direct.

982: Roger, 982.

DEP: *Daytona, JAX 32.*

CTR: *Go.*

DEP: *Yeah, you gonna work 982?*

CTR: *Yeah.*

DEP: *I really hate to do this to you this early in the morning, but watch that guy, I don't think he's any more instrument-rated than I am. He's, uh, I've given him about 12 turns in the last 12 miles.*

CTR: *All right, thank you.*

TIME: 0755:49

982: Jacksonville Control, Jacksonville Control, uh, Navajo 74982, we got an emergency.

DEP: Navajo 74982 JAX, all right sir, say intentions.

982: Right engine just went out on us . . . can we get radar vectors back to the airport?

DEP: Roger, sir, turn left heading 360, a left turn heading 360.

DEP: *Daytona, JAX 62 line, disregard 982, he just lost an engine, coming back to me.*

DEP: 74982, you can descend and maintain 4,000 at pilot's discretion.

982: Roger, thank you.

DEP: 74982, Craig is available at, Runway 4, they're presently VFR, estimated ceiling 1,100 broken, 2,500 overcast, visibility three miles light rain and fog, wind 060 at 12, altimeter 29.77. Can take you down right there for a VOR Runway 31, circle-to-land Runway 4 approach at Craig if you'd rather go there.

982: Uh, what's the length of that runway, do you know offhand?

(Unidentified voice): Craig Airport Runway 4 is 4,000 feet.

DEP: Four thousand feet long for 982.

982: Four thousand feet long. What's the length of Craig's runway?

DEP: Craig's runway, Runway 4 is 4,000 feet long.

982: I'd rather go into the 8,000-foot runway at Jacksonville, if possible.

DEP: 74982 roger, turn right heading 310.

TIME: 0758:30

DEP: November 74982, say souls on board and fuel remaining in time, please.

982: Three souls. I have about six-and-a-half hours of fuel, uh, I seem to have gotten part of the engine back. I'm working on the fuel thing now, so I'm heading back anyway for the moment.

DEP: 74982, fly heading 310.

TWR: *Local.*

DEP: *Local, look down there six miles south of Craig if you can see that far, 74982.*

TWR: *Yeah.*

DEP: *He's coming back. He lost an engine.*

TWR: *Oh, thanks, Chuck. I appreciate it.*

DEP: *Hey, how do you think I felt?*

TWR: *Okay.*

982: Jacksonville, this is 74982, uh, it seems as if our prop governor or something went [unintelligible]. I got a partial . . . a partial power back on the right engine but I'm gonna have to return, something's wrong with the airplane.

DEP: 74982, roger, turn left heading 290 now, 290 is the assigned heading, descend and maintain 5,000.

982: 982, we'll be making an instrument landing to Runway 7, is that affirmative?

DEP: 74982, roger, expect vectors ILS Runway 7 approach, International's presently estimated ceiling 700 broken, 1,600 broken and visibility's four miles in fog, wind 070 at 17, altimeter 29.78.

DEP: November 74982, turn right heading 340, 340.

982: Roger, right to 340.

DEP: November 74982, contact Jacksonville Approach on 119.0, so long.

982: 119.0, roger.

TIME: 0803:22

982: Jacksonville Approach, Navajo 74982, we have one engine that's intermittent and the other engine is okay.

APP: Navajo 982 roger, understand partial power on the engine.

982: Roger, that's affirmative, partial power one engine.

APP: *Sequence.*

TWR: *Yeah, if you'll find out what 982, what the sequence of him is.*

APP: *He's gonna be [unintelligible] after Osprey . . . following Osprey 152.*

TWR: *Okay, what I'm trying to find out, find out the condition of that engine. I'm gonna call Alert Two.*

982: Jacksonville Tower, about how far is 982 from landing?

APP: 982, you're presently about nine miles south-southwest of the field. You're on a right base of the ILS to Runway 7, sir.

982: Roger, that's affirmative, thank you.

APP: Navajo 982, turn left heading 300.

982: 300, right.

APP: Navajo 982, you copy?

982: Roger, 300 right.

APP: No sir, that's a left turn heading 300.

APP: Navajo 982, continue descent and maintain 2,000, and make that heading 290, two-ninety, sir.

982: Having a little trouble keeping the heading but going to 290, roger.

APP: All right sir, I'll keep you advised. Try to fly the best 290 you can. We're gonna try to give you a turn right about three miles outside the marker. The weather is IFR, we're 700 broken, sir.

982: Roger, I appreciate any help I can get.

APP: Roger sir.

APP: *Sequence.*

TWR: *Visibility one-and-one-quarter and falling.*

APP: Okay.

TIME: 0808:48

APP: Navajo 982, turn right heading 340.

982: Roger, 982, having a lot of trouble with this engine, it [unintelligible] goes in and out on us, uh, I don't know.

APP: All right sir, let me know if you have any more problems sir, right turn heading 340.

APP: *Mike?*

TWR: *Yeah.*

APP: *You have to watch this guy on final 'cause he's having problems with the headings because the engine picks up and up and down, okay?*

TWR: *Okay, we'll keep an eye on him and I've already called, we called Alert One but I'll upgrade it to a Two if it gets any worse.*

APP: *All right.*

APP: [unintelligible] 982 is four miles from DINNS, turn right heading 050, maintain 2,000 until established on the localizer, cleared for ILS Runway 7 Approach.
982: [unintelligible] got problems, oh my God [unintelligible] Mayday! Mayday! . . . lost control . . . God . . . in a spin . . . oh my God . . .

The Navajo crashed with its wings level and in a 15- to 30-degree nose down attitude. It hit 60-foot trees in a swampy area, struck several more trees and traveled 400 feet before coming to rest. The nose and cockpit were demolished by impact, but there was no fire. Both engines and propellers separated from the airplane and were found 25 feet behind and to the left of the main wreckage.

The pilot died in the crash; the two passengers survived, seriously injured. One described the last moments of the flight:

"I was just so scared I put my head down and I was holding on for dear life and they were screaming and saying we got big trouble, big problems, big problems, and Larry was screaming something and Steve said oh my God I can't believe, oh my God . . .

"All of a sudden we hit some really heavy turbulence or something and our altitude dropped and we were going down and all of a sudden the plane just went crazy. We just lost control and started diving. First we went straight up and then we started going down. I was looking out the window and I saw that we were going down straight at the trees and then we leveled off right before the trees. And that's it, that's all I remember."

The first sign of mechanical trouble had been a heavy stream of oil coming from under the oil access door on the right nacelle. It was later determined that the dipstick was missing. The number-five piston had a hole burned in it by detonation, there was burn damage on number-five and number-six connecting rods, and the number-six rod bolts had failed.

To the credit of the engine, it continued to run—smoothly, the passenger thought—despite major component failures; and the engine's refusal to stop dead seems to have persuaded the pilot not to shut it down and feather the prop, but instead to continue to coax power out of it.

The pilot, a 46-year-old man, had an estimated 800 hours' total time, with 75 hours in multiengine aircraft. His instructor and occasional safety pilot, who had checked him out in the Navajo, reported that the pilot had practiced "to an acceptable level, normal and emergency procedures including multiple precision and nonprecision approaches . . ."

Most likely, in a training situation the pilot could have controlled the airplane and gone through the proper engine-out drill, and could even have flown the ILS approach on one engine. The training situation is like that; the instructor reaches over and chops a throttle, the robot pilot runs through his catechism. There may be nervousness, but there is no real anxiety. The "dead" engine will come back to life on request, and the instructor, who presumably has everything under control, provides an additional measure of security. There is no threat of imminent capital punishment for error.

Real engine failures are different. Shutting down the engine and flying the airplane isn't difficult; those steps are no more difficult than in the training situation. The greater problem is making the decision to cage the engine that isn't quite dead and to commit to single-engine operation.

Some pilots, like the victim of the next accident, seem to consider being legal or illegal a matter of taste, like the choice of a tie. They also use lack of time as an excuse for not facing their own shortcomings as pilots.

Flying Above the Law
by J. Mac McClellan

No sane pilot believes that following the rules is an ironclad guarantee of safety. Conservative and usually logical, our FARs are only guidelines to safe flight. But what about the other extreme? Can an FAR scofflaw fly safely? For a time—maybe even a long time—but not forever.

The basic facts of the accident that killed an FAR scofflaw are sadly routine. The Cessna T303 Crusader, flying on an IFR flight plan, disappeared from radar in an area of heavy snow southeast of Denver. The T303 had departed Centennial Airport and had been flying about 10 minutes when the pilot apparently lost control of the airplane. He had been handed off from Denver Departure Control to Denver Center and was given a routine clearance. He responded normally, and that was the last anyone heard from him.

Witnesses near the crash site reported near-blizzard conditions on the ground, with strong winds blowing heavy snow. It was a dark night, and blowing snow cut visibility to an estimated quarter-mile. The owner of the ranch where the airplane crashed said he heard an airplane fly over and thought it odd because the weather was so bad.

When the controller lost voice and radar contact with the T303 he immediately asked other pilots in the vicinity for reports on flight conditions. Nobody reported any icing or significant turbulence, but several pilots said there were localized areas of heavy snow. One pilot volunteered to deviate from course and fly over the area of last radar contact. He found very heavy snow in a small band directly over the crash site.

The right wing of the Cessna twin hit first, and the engines bored deep holes into the frozen ground. No evidence of any pre-impact failure of the airplane or any of its systems could be found. The circumstances all pointed to a depressingly familiar accident pattern: Pilot loses control while flying in terrible weather.

But a check of the records quickly uncovered that this was no routine IFR accident. First and foremost, the pilot had no instrument rating. He was flying on an IFR clearance, had filed a flight plan, and had behaved in every way as though he knew what he was doing, but he had no instrument ticket.

He had a valid third-class medical certificate but with a restriction that prohibited night flying. The restriction resulted from problems the pilot had had with the color-vision test over the years.

Having an instrument rating does not guarantee that you are a good instrument pilot. It would be possible to learn to fly IFR without taking the steps necessary to earn the rating. A valid medical does not make a safe pilot, either. The night-flying restriction was based on color-vision problems related to differentiating colored light signals used by control towers when radio communications are lost. Reading tower light signals correctly has absolutely nothing to do with one's ability to control an airplane on instruments in a snowstorm. But doesn't an attitude of total disregard for the rules indicate an unreasonable attitude toward all aspects of safe flight?

Investigation of the dead pilot's background revealed a years-long pattern of disregard for rules and normal operating procedures. A computer search of the enforcement records found that he had been charged with careless operation for landing gear-up in a Mooney. This was not a basic "oops" event. The pilot had electrical problems before takeoff, got the Mooney running with a power-cart start, and then lost all electrical power in flight. He had departed with a known deficiency in the airplane, encountered subsequent problems in flight, and had so little knowledge of the airplane's systems that he was unable to lower the gear using the manual extension system. While investigating the gear-up incident, the FAA learned of an even more bizarre event. A few years earlier the pilot had landed his

Baron on a deserted Texas highway at night after running out of fuel. He had refueled the Baron with autogas and had managed to take off from the road without incident and without telling authorities.

Investigators interviewed an instructor who said the pilot had come to him for instrument training. The pilot said he was "tired of being illegal" and wanted to get his instrument rating as soon as possible. He reported that he had already logged between 300 and 400 hours of instrument flying. The instructor began with the basics of weather briefings, clearances, reporting-point requirements, and so on. After about four hours of ground training the pilot lost interest and quit. He did, however, tell his instructor about running out of fuel in the Baron and several other "blatant" incidents. The instructor never flew with the pilot.

Investigators did find an instrument instructor who had flown with him. Again, it was a rushed affair. After about 23 hours of instruction in a six-day period the pilot "was nowhere near" being ready for the instrument check ride. The pilot would "forget little things, like missing an altitude or forgetting to time an approach," the instructor recalled.

When the pilot purchased the T303 the dealer included 20 hours of instrument flight instruction. The pilot received 12 hours of training over a six-day period a few months before the accident, and the instructor described his flying performance as "squirrelly." The pilot was unhappy with the instruction and never returned to finish the 20 hours included in the airplane deal.

A large segment of the accident report deals with the pilot's medical history, particularly his difficulties with color vision. When the pilot first applied for a third-class medical, 14 years before the accident, he failed the color-vision test and was prohibited from night flying. Five years later he asked to take the light-signal test from the tower so he could get a demonstrated-ability waiver and have the night-flying restriction removed from his medical. Only three signal colors are used: red, white and green. The pilot misread seven out of 10 light signals from the control tower.

He then asked for a waiver from the night-flying restriction based on his wearing "X-chrome" contact lenses, which can correct color vision. The FAA refused to grant a waiver based solely on the wearing of the special lenses but did offer the pilot another opportunity to take the signal test from the tower. The pilot said the first test was taken in daylight and was invalid, so this time the FAA agreed to a night test. The authorization for the night signal test was good for 90 days, and this period passed. The pilot asked for a 30-day extension, which was granted, and that also passed without the pilot showing up for the test.

If you think it's trite to say that safety is an attitude, this accident report will likely change your views. If not, at least you'll know that there is most certainly such a thing as an unsafe attitude.

Even though the point of flying is to get places quickly, pilots are sometimes called upon to exercise a great deal of patience. Impatience can be deadly. In the next case, a pilot worked himself into such a frenzy over delays that when an emergency struck, he was utterly unprepared for it.

Hot Head
by Peter Garrison

"Jess" (not his real name) was just an impatient kind of guy. He ran an exterminating company, but he wanted to be a professional pilot. He applied to a couple of local carriers even though he only had about 600 hours, but they turned him down because of his weight. Jess was five-foot-ten and about 275 pounds. He was very disturbed about being turned down.

He had built up his hours pretty quickly. He got his multiengine rating late in 1987, his commercial ticket the following day, and bought an old Cessna 310 less than two months later. Apparently he put hours on the 310 at a pretty good clip, averaging more than 25 a month. Actually I think there might have been some P-51 time in there, because the airplane logs reflected only 56 hours since the last annual, which took place a month before Jess bought the airplane, whereas he had recorded 156 hours in the 310 in his own logbook. Jess added a single-engine CFI to his roster of certificates early in April 1988—which was also the month he got killed.

That 310 was a pretty tired airplane. It was a 1962, a G model, and it had about 3,200 hours on the airframe. It had had various engines and overhauls, but there were big gaps in its service history. For instance, there were no entries at all in the airplane logbooks between March 1974 and December 1983. Then the next annual—a big one, you can imagine—was in October 1987. That was the one that was done just before Jess bought the airplane.

But Jess wasn't a guy to let a little spotty maintenance bother him. He liked to do maintenance himself. He always thought he was being ripped off by mechanics, and he kept a supply of old parts at home that he had got off old airplanes and engines, and he would put them on his airplane as replacements. He had just replaced the oil cooler on the right engine of the 310 a couple of weeks before the accident, and then got an A&P to sign it off. Jess didn't have any training or certification as a mechanic himself, though. He just didn't like paying someone else to do what he thought he could do just as well himself.

There was a lot of self-deception or maybe just crazy optimism in his attitude toward maintenance. For instance, he had tried to sell the 310 about three weeks before the accident. The prospective buyer's mechanic had done an inspection on the airplane and had come up with a five-page list of squawks. There were 32 discrepancies, including inoperative nav lights, cut and torn air ducting, worn and stiff engine controls, control system play, loose magnetos, oil and fuel leaks, ADs not complied with, improper log entries and a missing airworthiness certificate. Jess just shined it on. Apparently he had quite an argument with the mechanic, said that the squawks didn't require immediate attention, and left.

Ironically, though, what ended up doing him in, or at least helping to do him in, wasn't some piece of neglected maintenance or one of his garage-cupboard replacement parts. It was a piece of genuine, approved maintenance. A real, officially rebuilt fuel pump had been installed in the right engine the day before the accident, and it seized up on him just after he took off. Of course, maybe the reason the fuel pump seized up was that it ate some piece of junk from the fuel system. You never know.

But you aren't supposed to crash a twin just because of a fuel-pump failure. There is an electric fuel pump, after all, and it's supposed to be turned on for takeoff; and at least according to the pilot's operating handbook the 310G can climb 350 feet a minute on one engine at maximum takeoff weight. Jess was already cleaned up when the engine failed, and he was well below maximum weight. So he should have been in pretty good shape. But evidently he wasn't, because he didn't feather the prop, and witnesses said he never lowered the nose but just held it up until the airplane stalled, snapped over and went in straight down.

So the thing you have to wonder about is why the fuel-pump failure ended up causing a crash. If he'd had the electric boost pump on, the engine-driven pump shouldn't have made any difference, so evidently he didn't have the electric pump on or else it wasn't working, which I guess wouldn't have been too surprising.

The fact that he didn't feather the right engine when it lost power isn't too surprising either, in light of the fact that he stalled the airplane. After all, if a guy is so far behind things that he stalls at 100 feet, it isn't too likely that he'd be right on top of feathering the engine.

The first thing you have to understand is that Jess actually didn't have a whole lot of flying experience. He had a few hundred hours, or at least his logbooks said he did, but most of that is spent just sitting there watching air go by. There was no evidence that anyone had put him through engine-out procedures in the 310 or that he had done any engine-out work at all since getting his multi rating.

Now, doing the drill with an instructor in the right seat is quite a different thing from doing it yourself, all alone, in a different airplane, with an actual engine failure. For one thing, with the instructor there you really don't have to worry too much about getting killed; the worst thing that's likely to happen to you is a little temporary humiliation—and not too much of that, since instructors need all the business they can get. And of course you know in the back of your mind that whatever happens, you can always cob that "dead" engine and haul out of there. But when the engine is really dead, and that's the first time it's happened to you, it's a different story.

Then there's another aspect, namely Jess's state of mind at the time.

It was a Saturday morning. He was supposed to be flying to meet a bunch of people to go on a group trip. His wife was already with the group, and he came down to the airport to get his airplane and found that the right engine was running as though the plug wires were crossed. This was at 6:30. Mechanics were already on it at seven—he couldn't complain on that account—but it took a long time to get the engine straightened out. First they had to change the points in the left mag, then they had to clean and gap a couple of plugs, then they had to track down and clean a fouled injector. In the meantime he was on and off the phone to his wife, and she was yelling at him about why didn't he get his airplane serviced before this.

Finally they got the engine running well, but by then it was almost 11, and Jess was as mad as Rumpelstiltskin. The mechanics cowled it up and went in to fill out the logbook, and when they came out Jess had already taxied away. A couple of minutes later Jess took off and everybody stood and watched him go up and come right back down.

Now, Jess must have had a sneaking suspicion that his airplane wasn't in such great shape, because he had said to a friend on the phone just the night before that he was going to fly his airplane on that trip "whether it worked or not." The mechanic who was working on the 310 could see that Jess was under a lot of pressure and tried to persuade him to put off his departure and join the group later, but he said he couldn't do that.

As the morning wore on, Jess fumed. At one point he said that if he had someone to punch, he would. Later, he said he was "going to get drunk on the way down and tonight," and at one point even said, "I don't care if this plane goes in." I doubt he meant that last statement literally, but it gives you some idea of his state of mind. He was in a tizzy of frustration and impatience, probably the more so because he had no one but himself to blame for his problems. It was he, after all, who felt that maintenance could wait; and now he was having to wait for maintenance.

You can imagine his emotional state as he taxied away from the hangar. He had kept a bunch of people waiting for four hours. His wife was furious with him. Everybody has felt that way at one time or another. Usually you take it out on your tires for a few blocks and then calm down. But he was in an airplane instead of a car, so he probably taxied too fast, skipped the run-up—after all, what had they been doing for the last four hours but run-up after run-up?—and roared into the air, grumbling and mumbling to himself the whole way. He wasn't exactly mentally prepared for what happened next. Ideally, you're supposed to collect your thoughts before takeoff, review what you'll do in an emergency, and think engine-out procedures all the way down the runway. I don't know what Jess was thinking about, but I guarantee you it wasn't "dead foot—dead engine." He was probably stewing about what incompetent s.o.b.'s mechanics were. And so when the right engine suddenly revved down just as though somebody had turned off the switch, Jess had to come back from a long way away.

I think he just froze up. He was in a steep climb, and he just stayed there, yoke back, hand frozen on the throttles, completely at a loss. It took only a few seconds. There wasn't time for him to sort things out.

The fuel-pump failure, the failure to feather—those are the things that go down in the official list of causes of Jess's death. But the real cause was his impatient, choleric character. Everything else just set the stage for the final meeting between Jess and his own worst enemy.

Overconfidence about equipment usually takes the form of delaying maintenance on engines or radios or taking off despite known mechanical deficiencies. The next accident presents an interesting variation on this theme: a pilot who kept flying despite known mechanical deficiencies in his own body. He was abetted by an opportunistic and corrupt medical certification system.

Heart Trouble
by Peter Garrison

The medical examinations regularly taken by pilots don't seem very rigorous; but perhaps the reason is that the doctor is quietly sizing us up and will subject particularly wobbly-looking candidates to a more scrupulous examination than those who appear healthy and fit.

A few pilots do get more than the usual cursory going-over; and a few are disqualified because their eyes, ears, hearts, brains, or souls are suspect. Those who rely on flying for their livelihood may then begin an uphill battle with the FAA to regain their medical certification.

Many of those who have petitioned the FAA have succeeded. One of these was a 49-year-old helicopter pilot, an ATP with 16,500 hours in his logbook, who found out at the age of 44 that he had heart trouble.

The pilot was a big man, six-foot-three, 220 pounds, "personable and robust," who obviously did not take the popular literature on cardiac health too seriously. He had smoked since he was 15 and still smoked half a pack a day; he drank alcohol five or six days a week and consumed four or five cups of caffeinated beverages each day.

His sole concession to mortality was to walk or jog one or two miles a day—at least when he was ashore, for his work involved flying from fishing boats, spotting tuna.

In December 1980, the pilot got a second-class medical certificate. At some time in the following year, he was diagnosed with atrial fibrillation—an irregularity of heart rhythm.

In October he consulted a cardiologist, who prescribed medication for him and advised him to give up smoking and drinking. A few days later he saw the cardiologist again and told him that he had not stopped smoking and drinking but had made an attempt to taper off.

The medicine had been ineffective in controlling his fibrillation, however, and so the doctor then recommended a treatment called "electrical cardioversion" to attempt to stabilize his heart rhythm. The pilot declined.

He returned to the cardiologist in May 1982. He had stopped taking his medication. He was still working as a helicopter pilot on a fishing boat, and when he was in port, he said, he drank heavily. Not surprisingly, his heart irregularity persisted. The doctor again recommended electrical cardioversion, which the pilot again declined; so the doctor again prescribed medication.

Finally, in October, the pilot underwent electrical cardioversion, but it was unsuccessful. In the meantime, he continued to drink and smoke.

His comparative indifference to his condition is perhaps understandable in light of the fact that he suffered absolutely no symptoms. According to his cardiologist, "he had no particular awareness of the abnormal heart rhythm."

The pilot's second-class medical lapsed at the end of 1981 but, although he continued to fly professionally, he did not apply for a new medical until early in 1984, when he engaged an FAA examiner at a heart-disease rehabilitation clinic to evaluate his condition. The examiner was experienced in sponsoring pilots with disqualifying histories of coronary disease and alcoholism in petitions for medical exemptions from the FARs.

A coronary angiography was performed and the pilot was found to have mild to moderate occlusion of several coronary arteries, but his heart function was within "normal limits." The examiner wrote to the FAA Aeromedical Standards in Washington to recommend that the pilot be granted a second-class medical certificate.

Five months later an FAA medical consulting panel of seven physicians, three of them board-certified cardiologists, recommended that the petition be denied, and three months after this—the pace of these Washingtonian operations suggests a hope that the petitioner will resolve the matter by expiring of his own accord—the Federal Air Surgeon (FAS) turned down the pilot's application for medical certification.

One month after the FAS turned down his application—October 1984—the FAA Administrator appointed a new FAS. The pilot lost no time in scheduling a personal meeting with the new FAS, in the course of which the FAS assured the pilot that his petition would be reviewed.

Late in January 1985 a new medical certificate was issued, unrestricted in third class, with a "not valid for pilot-in-command duties" restriction in second class.

In August the FAA's Civil Aeromedical Institute (CAMI) in Oklahoma City wrote to the pilot to remind him that his medical would expire in January, and to request that he undergo a cardiac examination by a cardiologist or internist. Shortly after this, the pilot sent a grateful letter to the FAS asking that the "not valid for PIC duties" restriction be lifted from his medical, and the FAS obligingly telexed CAMI ordering that this restriction be lifted if the medical reports were favorable.

The pilot now went back to his former sponsor, the examiner, who was neither an internist nor a cardiologist, but who administered a modified coronary protocol (which he had developed for patients too feeble to survive the standard one) and subsequently recommended to CAMI that the pilot be given an unrestricted second-class certificate.

CAMI forwarded the recommendation to the FAS, who then instructed CAMI to issue the second-class certificate, citing the support of a consultant who was, it turned out, none other than the ubiquitous examiner/sponsor himself.

The certificate was issued in May, together with a letter requiring the pilot to report any adverse change in his medical condition and to cease all flying activities immediately, should such a change occur.

It probably reached him while he was in the hospital recovering from a heart attack.

In May 1986 the pilot had chest pains and went to an emergency room for treatment. It was there that he suffered the heart attack, from which he was resuscitated by the attending doctor.

An angiogram disclosed partial blockages in several coronary arteries. He remained in the hospital a week. Two weeks later he returned for a stress test and an electrocardiogram. He could not complete the stress test because of "general fatigue," but the EKG indicated that there was an adequate blood supply to the heart muscles.

The doctor instructed the pilot to "increase his activity" and scheduled a follow-up visit, but the pilot never came back. There is no evidence that the pilot ever advised either the FAA or his medical examiner of his heart attack.

In August the pilot, who had a documented predilection for buzz jobs, was taking his boss on one such buzz job when their Bell 206B, after circling a residence twice, suddenly keeled over and plunged a short distance into trees. Both men aboard were killed.

Although the pathologist who performed the autopsy attributed the pilot's death to multiple traumatic injuries, he found severe coronary atherosclerosis as well as at least three separate heart problems that could have caused sudden death, which suggested that the pilot "may have suffered a myocardial ischemia and/or dysrhythmia at the time of the accident."

The National Transportation Safety Board divided the blame for the crash between the pilot and the Federal Air Surgeon. The Board felt that the FAS had too cavalierly rejected the recommendation of his own medical panel and consulting cardiologist, preferring to rely on the pilot's advocate, the FAA medical examiner, who the FAS assumed was a board-certified cardiologist because the word "heart" appeared in his letterhead, but whose specially was, in fact, public health.

The pilot, on the other hand, had not merely been cavalier—he had been dishonest.

He had a history of ignoring FARs and had paid civil penalties for two previous infractions, one of which involved low flying. It seems likely that he didn't try to renew his 1980 medical certificate because he knew that he might be rejected on account of his heart trouble. At the time of the accident he was in defiance of CAMI's instruction that he cease flying if his condition changed for the worse, as it had, in fact, done.

This "personable and robust" man would not accept the fact that his flying days were over. One can sympathize with him—at age 49, ill and without the self-discipline to do anything about it, he was in a poor position to start a new life.

Up against the wall, he simply turned his back on it.

Pilots need to take their responsibility for the lives of others more seriously than this pilot did. Your health is, no less than your skill and your good judgment, part of the pact that you make with your passengers. Perhaps you can fool the FAA's system for a while, but you cannot fool your own.

3

Ice

Weather was a factor in many of the accidents we've seen so far, but they were grouped under the rubrics of decision-making or attitude because those factors, more than the weather itself, seemed to point to the useful insights the accidents provide. In the next two chapters, weather itself is the culprit. Not that attitude or decision-making are absent. On the contrary, both ice and thunderstorms, two of the deadliest aspects of flying weather, are usually forecast, and pilots who encounter them have usually chosen to do so, or at least to risk doing so. But ice and thunderstorms are in a special class among the causes of accidents, because they represent special technical problems—aerodynamic degradation and structural overload—that pilots may misunderstand or underestimate.

In the first of this selection of icing-related accidents, an unrealistic optimism impels a pilot into a situation from which only Lady Luck could extricate him—but she stays home.

Too Long in the Ice
by J. Mac McClellan

While icing is dreaded for its slow, accumulated destruction of lift, a Mooney 201 pilot discovered that it can also strike with fatal swiftness.

The pilot was awake long before dawn on a December morning talking to Phoenix Flight Service as he planned an IFR flight from Mesa, Arizona, to Cedar City, Utah. The route was over the intermountain West, with its high-altitude mesas that are peppered with substantial peaks. In VFR conditions it would be an easy trip below 10,000 feet in the nonturbocharged Mooney. Under IFR conditions, some of the MEAs were at 13,000 feet.

The weather was not VFR. The Phoenix briefer described a slow-moving cold front that was approaching from the northwest, causing some low clouds, fog, precipitation, and surface winds gusting to 30 knots or more. There are few weather-reporting points between Phoenix and Cedar City, particularly at three a.m., so the briefer could provide little current weather information.

Cedar City was forecasting lower scattered clouds with a ceiling at 5,000 feet. There was, however, a chance that the ceiling would be down to 2,500 feet with visibility three miles in light snow or blowing snow. The winds at Cedar City were forecast to gust to 35 knots. Weather over the northern part of the route was forecast to be about the same, or perhaps even lower in moderate snow showers.

The few observations available hinted that the weather might be better than forecast and that the cold front might not be moving as fast as predicted. But, the briefer warned, "You've got warm air over-riding cold air and that translates to an unstable condition, which translates to maybe, well, you know, obviously cumuliform clouds. And they don't always play by the rules."

Flight precautions in the area forecasts called for "moderate icing, rime and mixed, in clouds or in precipitation" plus "frequent moderate turbulence below 18,000 feet." That forecast precaution placed the conditions beyond the capabilities of the non-deiced, normally aspirated Mooney 201. But the few sequence reports available, especially for the first part of the flight, sounded better than forecast, with only thin layers of clouds.

The pilot apparently didn't believe the forecast conditions would occur because, by definition, they made a safe trip impossible. According to the *Airman's Information Manual*, moderate icing means that "rate of accumulation is such that even short encounters become potentially hazardous and use of deicing/anti-icing equipment or flight diversion is necessary." The 201 had no deicing equipment and, flying at an MEA of 13,000 feet with four people on board, would have little ability to divert. The terrain would block a descent and lack of turbocharging would restrict climb capability. If the forecast was right, the 201 had no chance.

The NTSB could not determine the exact level of the pilot's experience. He was instrument-rated, held a commercial certificate and had reported a total flight time of 460 hours, with 250 hours flown in the previous six months, when he applied for a first-class medical just 14 months before the accident. When he applied for insurance on the Mooney just five months before the accident he reported a total flight time of 1,200 hours, with 650 of those hours flown in the 201. If those times were both accurate the pilot would have flown 760 hours in eight months. No confirming logbook was found, and the NTSB lists pilot experience as unknown.

The pilot departed Mesa, a suburban Phoenix airport, at 5:05 a.m. For the first hour the trip proceeded smoothly, with the 201 cruising at 13,000 feet. In that first hour it had covered about 120 nm, not bad when you include the climb to 13,000 feet with the airplane at maximum allowable weight. The airplane was also about to enter the area where the forecasts called for thicker and lower clouds—and the probability that icing was in those clouds.

The ice struck suddenly. At 6:18 the pilot called Los Angeles Center: "I'm picking up a little bit of ice—call you back in about five minutes. I might be turning around." The pilot's first thought of turning around was an excellent idea. He had just flown for more than an hour in ice-free air and that safety zone was still there, waiting for him. The five-minute plan was stretching his luck but still offered hope. He didn't know that by not turning around at the first sign of ice, he sealed his fate and that of his three passengers.

The controller volunteered a pilot report from a nearby Merlin showing only light rime ice on a descent through 13,000 feet. He also told the pilot that he was showing precipitation on his radar but that it was to the west. The controller reminded him that only moderate or greater precipitation would show on his radar.

The pilot's next response was to ask for a lower altitude, and the controller cleared him to 11,300 feet, the MEA. Less than four minutes after the initial report of "a little bit of ice" the pilot called to say, "I'm turning around. I'm going to stay at 13,000." The controller asked: "Mooney 12 Hotel, would you call that severe rime ice?" The response was, "I think so."

Ten minutes after the initial report of ice, and six minutes after the Mooney started to reverse course, the controller asked: "Are you out of that ice yet?" The NTSB transcribers determined the reply to be: "No, I got problems but I think I can handle it . . . we're going down . . . are we . . ." The controller told the pilot he could descend to a minimum safe altitude of 9,600 feet and that Grand Canyon Airport was at 12 o'clock and 23 miles. "I got prop ice and I'm at 10,000 and descending. I'm at 10,000 feet just going up and down. I got prop ice, trying to fling it off—what do you show me, right over the Canyon?"

That was the final transmission from the Mooney. The wreckage was located by a military C-130 later that day on a 9,000-foot plateau on the north rim of the Grand Canyon. The heavily wooded area was covered by five to six feet of snow and was considered to be inaccessible. Winter storms continued to keep investigators away until the following April, more than four months after the crash. Even then an impending storm limited investigators' time at the crash site. There was no evidence of any preimpact aircraft or system failure. The airplane had initially struck a 70-foot tree, and was badly crushed. There wasn't much else to investigate. The engine had been turning at impact. The important evidence—ice—was all around. The wreckage was buried under snow.

The NTSB found the probable cause of the crash to be "icing conditions" and "flight into known adverse weather—initiated—pilot in command."

The Mooney pilot demonstrated reasonable judgment by announcing his plan to turn around when icing was encountered. But, like many of us, he apparently didn't realize that a little bit of ice can become a fatal amount of ice so quickly. When you encounter ice your escape plan cannot be delayed, particularly when there is only one available option.

Icing and high terrain make a particularly deadly combination. But even over the low, flat Midwest, ice can overpower an airplane given enough time. In the next occurrence, two highly qualified pilots, evidently suffering from "get-home-itis," carry a commando raid into icing country a little too far. They're right to fly VFR rather than in cloud, but they seem fatally unwilling to take the weather's "no" for an answer. Up to the end they retained the option of making an off-field landing—in the last minutes it was their only chance—but they didn't want to admit defeat.

Ice Box
by J. Mac McClellan

"A Cessna 182 can carry a ton of ice," I've said to myself several times as I watched the wings of the sturdy Cessna single frost over. I've said the same thing to other pilots, and have often heard it from others. Perhaps a pilot trying to escape a soggy early spring weather system in Montana had heard—or even said—the same thing. But any of us who have said or believed such a thing were merely whistling past the cemetery.

A Cessna 182 pilot and his friend planned to leave Miles City, Montana, early on a cold April morning. Both were experienced, IFR-qualified pilots. The passenger was a former naval aviator. The owner had more than 3,500 hours' total time. The weather was messed up by an upper-level trough that was moving slowly eastward. Few pilots understand weather troughs—I don't—but you don't need to fly for long before you figure out that a trough is a forecaster's all-purpose explanation for low clouds, rain, and poor visibility that are slow to move and have no other apparent meteorological reason to exist. The forecasters said this trough would douse eastern Montana with marginal VFR conditions including the chance of light rain, light snow, and fog. Icing, of course, was prominently mentioned as a flight hazard. Temperatures and dew points were both in the low 30s.

After many years of flying, the 182 pilot knew the only way to make progress in a light airplane in poor weather is to start, if you can, and go as far as you can before the weather halts progress. He initially telephoned for a VFR weather briefing from Miles City to Rapid City, South Dakota. His home was in Manhattan, Kansas, and that was probably his actual destination, but Rapid City would have cleared most of the forecast low weather and left the rough terrain behind, making a continuation to Manhattan easy.

The FSS briefer painted a bleak picture, mentioned the icing forecast, and recommended against VFR flight. About an hour later two men walked into the FSS station, gave the same N number as the pilot who had phoned earlier, and this time asked for a VFR briefing from Miles City to Scotts Bluff, Nebraska. Apparently the pilot had examined the charts and decided a more southerly route would clear the bad weather more quickly. But the FSS briefer again recommended against VFR flight because of the low weather and icing forecast for Miles City and east. The pilot filed a VFR flight plan and departed.

Flying VFR is one of the few options available to the light airplane pilot when icing is forecast in the clouds. The terrain around Miles City and to the east is not particularly high compared with the mountains west of there, but an IFR flight would require a minimum altitude of 7,000 to 10,000 feet, placing the 182 squarely in the icing forecast area. Staying below the clouds must have looked like a better option.

The 182 pilot was next heard from when he called Rapid City FSS from Broadus, Montana, asking that his VFR flight plan be closed and requesting weather conditions at Rapid City. He also mentioned that he had landed "to get rid of the ice" on the 182. The briefer reported that conditions at Rapid City were 900 broken, 2,000 overcast with visibility of 25 miles. He repeated the flight precautions for icing conditions and the pilot said he knew there was "icing up in it . . . we're not going up in it." If the pilot had encountered enough icing to force a precautionary landing without actually entering the clouds during the 60-mile flight to Broadus, conditions were unusually hazardous. If he had been flying VFR in the clouds when he encountered the icing, his attitude was extremely hazardous.

Despite the grim forecasts and reminders that VFR was not recommended, the pilot filed another VFR flight plan, this time to North Platte, Nebraska. He told the briefer he "had to get across these hills . . . over to Belle Fourche . . . and then around out on the flats. Then I can make it." The terrain flattened out east of Belle Fourche, Montana, so the pilot's plans were clear—he intended to scud-run under the clouds and ice.

The next contact with the Skylane pilot was about 70 minutes after take-off from Broadus when he called Ellsworth AFB Approach Control, asking for an IFR clearance into nearby Rapid City Regional Airport. He told the controller he was maintaining VFR, but was about to go IFR, and had a big load of ice. The pilot reported he was climbing to 3,500 feet. Ellsworth elevation is 3,278 feet and Rapid City is 3,202 feet. The controller cleared the 182 to Rapid City at 5,000 feet for the VOR/DME 14 approach. The pilot said he could not climb that high because of the ice on the Skylane. The controller offered an approach to the closer Ellsworth Air Base, but the pilot said he could make Rapid City. The 182 never did reach the assigned 5,000 feet and gradually sank below radar coverage. Minimum descent altitude on final approach was 3,740 feet.

Ellsworth approach and Rapid City tower controllers exchanged worried comments about the progress of the 182. The tower controllers reported rapidly deteriorating weather to the northwest, the direction from which the Skylane was approaching. A single-engine Cessna landed and reported significant icing. A Piper Aztec reported accumulation of more than 1.5 inches of ice at 5,000 feet. The official weather observer on the airport reported 500 feet broken, 1,000 overcast with four miles visibility in drizzle, temperature 33°. Snow covered much of the ground.

Several witnesses northwest of the Rapid City airport saw the 182 flying low below the clouds at an altitude not more than 300 feet above the ground. There was heavy drizzle and visibility of less than a mile. The 182 was reported to be flying slowly with the nose at an unusually high attitude. Two witnesses observed the wings rocking in an unstable manner and all agreed a wing dropped sharply, followed by an abrupt nose-down pitch just before the crash. The airplane struck a gentle upslope in a steep nose-down attitude with the left wing low. The impact killed the pilot and his passenger.

Investigators found rough ice fragments three-quarters of an inch to one-and-a-quarter inches thick, matching the contour of the wing and tail leading edges. Some of the ice clung to the airframe and antennas through the crash. There was no mystery to solve. The National Transportation Safety Board ruled that ice accumulation caused the airplane to stall and crash.

Perhaps this pilot had survived icing encounters in his 182 before. Or maybe he thought weather conditions would improve in the next few miles. But whatever the reasons, he elected to take off in marginal conditions with even worse weather forecast. After collecting enough ice to force a precautionary landing during the 60-mile trip from Miles City to Broadus, he still elected to press on. The icing didn't sneak up on this pilot, it took hours. The weather conditions worsened very slowly. Only the end came suddenly.

There's known icing, and then there's possible icing. Neither makes good company in a light plane, but the second type attracts gamblers. In the next report, a pilot gambles on an Appalachian cold front—and almost wins.

Ice Is Where You Find It
by Peter Garrison

People never tire of saying the same things over and over. One of the things they say is, "Ice is where you find it." By this they mean that forecasts are unreliable; the only way to know for sure where ice is, is to go and see.

People also never tire of having the same accidents over and over. In one tried-and-true scenario, the pilot receives a weather briefing warning of possible icing. He then flies off to investigate the possibility, gets iced up and crashes, taking his heightened understanding of ice to heaven with him.

Why does this keep happening? Probably because for every pilot who goes up into "possible icing," ices up and crashes, there are a hundred or even a thousand who either encounter no icing at all, encounter only light rime, or pick up some ice, change altitude, and have the ice melt off. Thus, the odds that ice will kill you on a given trip are fairly slight, and few experienced instrument pilots ground themselves at the mere mention of icing. Most feel that they can study a weather report and make a rational assessment of icing danger; and if they can stay either below the freezing level or well above it, and if their airplane has a good rate of climb (so that if they have to go above the freezing level, they can get far above it quickly), they will venture out even if some icing is forecast.

The 51-year-old owner-pilot of an A36 Bonanza probably felt that way. He had a private instrument ticket and 1,100 hours total time. He needed to fly from his home airport on Long Island to Nashville. The weather wasn't very promising; he called twice for briefings, first at 11:30 a.m. and then at four p.m. The first briefing said to expect low ceilings and low visibility along most of the route of flight—at the pilot's home field it was 300 overcast and three-quarters with fog—but the weather at Nashville, where he expected to arrive at around eight at night, sounded almost pleasant: a postfrontal 2,000 overcast with unrestricted visibility. The second briefing was more extensive: "occasional moderate turbulence below 8,000 . . . moderate rime icing in clouds and precip from the freezing level up through 15,000 . . . freezing level 4,000 feet around here . . . 8,000 down by Nashville . . . low clouds the whole route of flight . . . precip; you'll be flying right behind the cold front . . . low-level wind shear . . . light to moderate rime icing . . . from 4,000 all the way through 21,000 . . . over West Virginia, 10,000 feet, moderate clear icing; that was a Cessna 172 . . .."

The winds aloft at 6,000 and 9,000 feet were 240 at 30 to 40 knots in the New York area, going to 270 at 30 knots or so in Kentucky and Tennessee. When a pilot hears a briefing like this he listens for certain key words like "moderate" or "heavy," "clear icing," "chance of" followed by some dire condition, and the names of the aircraft types that have given pilot reports. This report was bad, but it was not the worst; after all, a pirep came from a 172. If a 172 could be up there, certainly an A36 could.

The minimum en route altitude (MEA) for most of the route is 4,000 feet, with a couple of stretches at 6,000. So he probably figured that he could take his chances above the freezing level at the start of the flight, and then if necessary drop down below it toward the end. He filed for 6,000 via Charleston, West Virginia, and took off with his wife at 4:40 p.m.

Center took him through the New York area at 7,000 feet. About 30 minutes after departure, he requested and got 6,000 to stay out of icing conditions. The trip then apparently remained uneventful for almost three hours. He checked in with Atlanta Center at 6:55 Central Standard Time. It was probably around 7:10 or 7:15 that the trouble started. (CTR = Atlanta Center; 29R = the Bonanza; 90K = another aircraft. Times are Central Standard Time. Irrelevant transmissions are omitted.)

TIME: 1918:57
29R: Atlanta Center, 29R.
CTR: Bonanza 29R, Atlanta Center, go ahead.

29R: We're trying [sic] to pick up a trace of rime. I'd like to descend down to 4,000 if possible.

CTR: Bonanza 29R, descend and maintain 4,000.

TIME: 1954:16

29R: I'm gonna pick up some more [unintelligible], request 3,000.

CTR: All right, 2929R, you were broken, say again.

29R: [Unintelligible]

CTR: Beech 29R, say again, please, you were broken.

90K: 2929R wants to go down to 3,000.

CTR: All right, 290K, would you relay to N2929R he has clearance to descend to 3,000?

90K: Okay . . . 2929R, are you on the frequency still?

29R: Yes, I am, I hear Atlanta Center loud and clear. Maybe he hears this radio better.

CTR: Well, I hear this radio loud and clear now.

90K: Got the message, he's going to 3,000, he can hear you okay.

29R: 29R, we're out of 4,000 for three.

TIME: 1958:21

CTR: Beech 2929R, if you are going to stay at 3,000 feet inbound to Nashville fly outbound on the Livingston 290 radial expecting radar vectors to Nashville. If you do not wish to do that, you need to climb back to 3,800 feet.

29R: Uh, we can see down here and—uh—290 radial outbound.

TIME: 2004:39

29R: We're picking up a load of ice; we're unable to maintain altitude.

CTR: Roger, do you need to land? There's an airport back at your eight o'clock position about three miles.

29R: All right, I got roughness on the engine, we may have to descend.

CTR: Okay, you can descend, there's an airport at your eight o'clock and three miles. It's the Spring Creek airport.

29R: [Unintelligible]

29R: [Unintelligible] 29R.

29R: Do you have the Nashville weather?

CTR: Yes, sir, hold on just a minute . . . the Nashville weather is measured ceiling 1,300 overcast, visibility four miles with fog, the wind 340 at 11, the temperature is 37°, the dew point 33.

29R: All right, we just shed a bunch of ice down here, we're at 2,200 feet and holding okay. Can I maintain 2,200 feet out here?

CTR: Uh, no, sir, you cannot, that is 800 feet below my minimum en route altitude.

The Bonanza was not heard from again. The wreckage was found the next day in a wooded area at an elevation of 950 feet msl, only a short distance beyond the point at which the pilot had made his last transmission. It had struck trees 20 feet above the ground, apparently in controlled flight.

How the airplane got from 2,200 feet to 970 feet so quickly isn't clear. If there had been an altimeter error, it should have turned up earlier in the flight, since the airplane was presumably equipped with an altitude-encoding transponder. An ice-induced static-system error is a possibility; if ice blocked the static vents, the altimeter would have failed to register altitude changes. The pilot may also have made a 1,000-foot error in reading the altimeter. The pilot's final transmissions give no indication that he knew he might be critically close to the ground.

In any case, the irony of the accident was that it occurred where it did—at the "easy" end of the flight, with the freezing level well above the airplane and the conditions at Nashville, 60 miles distant, VMC. The Bonanza encountered no significant icing until it was flying 6,000 feet below the freezing level, in 37° air. It must then have hit a cell of freezing rain. The ice buildup must have been fast if in fact the A36, low on fuel and with only two people aboard, could not maintain altitude at 3,000 feet. (The engine roughness was probably due to ice on the propeller.) Under those conditions, the windshield would be iced up, and the pilot would not be able to see forward; this may account for his lack of enthusiasm for the Spring Creek airport.

He would know in the darkness that he had shed ice from the clattering sound it makes when breaking away; but he would not know if his altimeter were wrong, because he was flying over dark, unpopulated terrain. He might have supposed that all he needed to do was wait a few more minutes and the ice remaining on the airplane would be gone, leaving him an easy visual approach into Nashville.

Was the pilot wrong to have made the flight, given the forecast he had received? The National Transportation Safety Board thought so, and many would agree, but not because he hit freezing cell in Kentucky. The problem with the weather was that the freezing level sloped up through the entire band of altitudes normally used for unturbocharged flight. The MEAs were generally just below the freezing level, and the terrain, while not high, was irregular. This, with strong westerly winds, was likely to generate local instabilities. And the flight would be conducted in darkness, which would make everything even more stressful.

It seems that, until the pilot's luck ran out, it had been rather good: He managed to run the gauntlet of the Alleghenies and the Appalachians right behind a winter cold front without meeting any serious trouble. What got him in the end was a freak: a pocket of ice that nobody knew was there. It was a freak—but a *likely* freak, considering how near the edge the whole flight had been.

Statistical norms aren't reliable with icing; it can strike too hard, too suddenly, and many airplanes—and pilots—aren't equipped to cope with it. The veteran's trick is to distinguish between stable and unstable conditions, and to recognize when and where freakish events are likely to occur. After all, even though there are *on the average* only 10 cockroaches per square meter in New York City, people there know not to look under the sink.

In recent years small accumulations of ice on the wings of jet airliners have been implicated in a number of takeoff accidents. Once obscure, this hazard is now well-known, and more stringent pre-takeoff deicing requirements have been enacted to combat it. The next two occurrences took place before the leading-edge icing hazard was fully appreciated by flight crews.

Frost Bite
by Peter Garrison

It has been said many times, and so there is probably no harm in saying once again that accidents often occur not because of a single glaring act of negligence or ineptitude, but because of a chain of casual omissions or errors, commonplace or inconsequential in themselves, but fateful in the particular manner of their concatenation. It's proverbial: For want of a nail . . .

The crash of a Continental DC-9 at Denver Stapleton late in 1987 was an accident whose causes consisted of just such a chain of minor missteps. There was no single major factor; no engine failure, no flaps left up, no microburst. There were only little things, banefully arranged.

The accident sequence, in rough outline, was as follows. It was snowing. The airplane, with 88 aboard, taxied from the terminal to the deice pad, where it was sprayed with a heated glycol solution to wash off snow and ice. From there it taxied to the runway, where it was held for 27 minutes awaiting takeoff clearance. Finally it rolled into position and began its takeoff. After rotation, it began to rock from side to side, stalled and crashed. Fortunately there was no fire; nevertheless, 28 died and 28 sustained serious injuries.

The best-publicized aspect of the National Transportation Safety Board's analysis of the accident was the finding that two "inexperienced" pilots had been assigned to the flight, and the Board's recommendation to the FAA that steps be taken to assure that when one pilot on a flight is inexperienced, the other isn't.

To a flying public uninitiated into the arcana of type ratings, recurrent training, simulators, proficiency checks and the rigors of ATP certification, the notion of two rank beginners noodling together in the cockpit of a DC-9 must have been disquieting. (Did they at least have the instructions with them?) To pilots, who understood that "inexperience" in the cockpit of a major airline is a relative thing, the cause of the accident was still mysterious. How could a line pilot, even an "inexperienced" one, not know how to take off?

In the NTSB's view, the stall on takeoff was due to overrotation by the first officer. The overrotation in itself would not normally have caused a stall, however; it had to be combined with another factor: the presumed presence of a thin layer of snow, ice, or frost on the upper surface of the DC-9's wing. This was an early DC-9, without leading-edge slats; according to its manufacturer, its wing may lose a substantial fraction of its lifting ability if even ½₂ of an inch of roughness builds up on it.

The frost is assumed to have been there because the airplane stalled; nobody saw it. That no one saw it, or even looked, was another small link in the chain. According to company procedures, the crew is to inspect the flying surfaces if the airplane sits in freezing precipitation for more than 20 minutes after deicing. Presumably someone is to walk back into the cabin and look out the windows. The airplane sat for 27 minutes, and no one mentioned inspecting the wings, though the captain did increase engine power momentarily to improve engine anti-icing. The captain may have forgotten about ice on the wings, or he may have thought of it and decided to stretch the rule since takeoff clearance was expected at any moment. Perhaps he could see other waiting aircraft and judged from their appearance that his own wings, invisible from the cockpit, were satisfactorily clean. And why exactly 20 minutes, after all? Should he have delayed the takeoff to walk back into the cabin if clearance had come 20.5 minutes after the airplane left the deice pad?

The lengthy wait occurred in spite of flow-control procedures that held Stapleton to about 30 arrivals an hour. It was the result of a series of minor blunders on the part of airplane crews and ground control, and which began when the flight taxied from the gate to the deice pad without contacting ground control. At about the same time, another Continental flight called ground for clearance to taxi from its gate to the deice pad. It got clearance, but was blocked by other traffic. Several minutes later, when it was able to proceed, it called ground again. This time ground cleared it to the run-up area. The crew ignored this discrepancy and taxied to the deice pad instead.

Now the tower was confused about the identities of the airplanes at the run-up area, believing that Flight 1713, the accident airplane, was at the deice pad, when it was really holding for takeoff; and that Flight 594, which was being deiced and had its radios and engines turned off, was at the run-up area. Neither crew paid much attention to the garbled taxi instructions and puzzling traffic warnings it received; and when tower attempted to clear Flight 594 onto the runway and received no response, it directed the next airplane in line to taxi around it and take off. Continental 875 hence taxied around the waiting Flight 1713, which was physically in the number-one position but was believed by the tower to be Flight 594, and took position on the runway.

Flight 1713, hearing the local controller talking to Flight 875, tried to call the tower and point out that it was in number-one position; but it got no response. About a minute later the farce began to unravel; tower finally understood that the DC-9 holding short was not Flight 594 at all, but Flight 1713. Flight 875 held on the runway for several minutes before taking off, however, and it was not until 14 minutes after arriving in the number-one slot that Flight 1713 actually got its clearance to roll.

Those 14 minutes, lost in a comedy of errors that a television writer would have been hard-pressed to improve upon, proved critical; if there was an excessive buildup of frost on the wings, much of it was due to those minutes of mistaken identity.

The captain, a 12,000-hour pilot, had logged more than 3,000 hours as first officer in 727s for Continental, having hired on with the company in 1969. He had comparatively little experience in the DC-9: 133 hours as first officer and only 33 hours as captain, but he was a pilot of better-than-average skills.

The first officer, on the other hand, had only 36 hours of turbojet experience, all of it in the DC-9; he had completed his initial DC-9 training with a proficiency check only two months before the accident.

His previous flying history was spotty. He had been fired by the charter operator for which he was working in 1985 because he failed an IFR multiengine Part 135 check ride three times after 30 hours of training. His former employer described him as tense and unable to cope with deviations from the routine, prone to make the same mistakes again and again, and easily disoriented.

Nevertheless, immediately after losing that job he found another as a first officer on a commuter line flying Beech 1900s. Fourteen months later he failed an ATP check ride, sailing through a holding fix at cruising speed, and going out of tolerances on an ILS approach.

A private subcontractor performed a background check on the first officer when he applied for a job with the airline. Its report was inaccurate, omitting his most recent employment entirely, and stating that he had left his previous job of his own accord and that his performance had been "very good." Continental hired him.

At first he had a lot of trouble in simulator training; but with remedial work his performance improved, and by the time he was recommended for his proficiency check he was getting comments ranging from "average" to "nice job!" He began line flying with an instructor-captain six weeks before the accident, but after two and a half weeks went into reserve status. The accident flight was his first after 24 days of inactivity.

This was also the first flight the captain and first officer had made together; the captain knew nothing of the first officer's experience or skills, though he knew he was new to Continental. The captain himself, having fewer than 100 hours in the left seat, was a "high minimums" captain, temporarily restricted to landing minimums of 300 feet and one mile.

The flight was a round robin to Boise, Idaho; the captain probably gave the first officer the first takeoff so that, trading legs with his subordinate in the traditional manner, he himself would end up doing the landing at Stapleton on the return flight.

At the moment the DC-9 began its takeoff roll, the stage was set for a disaster, and yet no one would have supposed that anything was amiss. The contamination on the wings was so slight that the captain of the airplane that taxied around Flight 1713 on the run-up ramp later testified that he concluded his own airplane must be satisfactorily clean from looking at 1713. The triggering factor was the first officer's rotation technique. His skills—acquired it seems with difficulty and unseasoned by experience—were rusty after three-and-a-half weeks away from flying. The flight-data recorder showed that the first officer rotated at about double the normal pitch rate, and overshot the target pitch attitude by two degrees. If the captain tried to take corrective action, it was too late; the wings had already stalled.

The effect of overly rapid rotation is to exaggerate any excursion to a high angle of attack. With normal rotation—about three degrees per second—the airplane lifts off before reaching the target deck angle of 12 degrees; it begins to ascend, and the angle of its flight path is subtracted from the fuselage pitch angle to get the angle of attack, which does not exceed about nine degrees on a normal takeoff.

If rotation is rapid enough, however, the airplane does not have time to begin to climb; the target deck angle—or in this case an angle exceeding it—and the angle of attack are the same, and are uncomfortably close to the stalling angle of the clean airplane.

One casts about with difficulty to find the linchpin in the fateful series of events that led to the crash.

The confusion and delay in taxiing and taking off were certainly contributory, but, even in the absence of confusion, delay is endemic to foul-weather operations at busy airports.

Were the deicing procedures faulty? The airplane was deiced with a 35-percent glycol solution; the hot glycol removes snow and ice from the airframe, but does not itself freeze. The NTSB recommended that the FAA take a leaf out of the Europeans' book; in Europe, a "thixotropic" deice solution is used—one that clings to the airplane and then blows off, along with any snow or ice that collects on top of it, during the takeoff roll.

Was it a flaw in the design of the DC-9's wing that it could be made to stall at a significantly lower lift coefficient by accumulations of frost so slight that a pilot taxiing past could not see them? Later models of the DC-9 had leading-edge slats, which greatly reduce the wing's sensitivity to contamination; but it is not clear from the NTSB's report how aware pilots of the no-slats version of the airplane were of its inordinate susceptibility to contamination.

Perhaps the captain was at fault in not taking the takeoff himself, and letting the first officer have the landing and takeoff at Boise. But this is hindsight; until the crash, no one would have supposed that a mere takeoff would be any more difficult or risky in bad weather than in good—no one, that is, who was unaware of how adversely a tiny bit of frost could affect the wing.

Was there a logical bind in a situation in which an airplane could conceivably be deiced, taxi to the run-up area, wait 20 minutes, and then have to return to the deice pad to start all over again a cycle that might never end until the airplane ran out of fuel or the storm ended? If such a bind existed, did its lurking presence disincline crews to follow deice procedures to the letter?

Continental's screening of the first officer's previous employment left a lot to be desired; but his training once he was hired was thorough and conscientious, and his performance in the end was satisfactory. Perhaps if instructors had been aware of the first officer's history of rough flying technique, they would have guessed that the improvement seen at the end of his initial training might prove temporary; but at the time, that would have been an unfair speculation. In any case, he had no history of overrotation; in fact, one of the last comments recorded during his training was that he rotated too slowly. If anything, the first officer seems simply to have been a worse-than-average ship handler; but whereas the airline had a category for "high minimums" captains, there was no pigeonhole for "low-skills" pilots.

For want of a nail . . .

Jets without leading edge slats, such as early DC-9s and Fokker F28s, have more trouble with ice contamination than slat-equipped planes do. The next accident brought out just how slight ice contamination can be and still interfere with flight.

Just a Little Ice
by Peter Garrison

A Ryan International Airlines DC-9, carrying night mail between Buffalo and Indianapolis with a stop at Cleveland, landed at Cleveland Hopkins Airport a little before midnight in February 1991. The stopover was brief; some mail from Buffalo was offloaded, some mail for Indianapolis taken aboard. The temperature was 23°F, and a dry, blowing snow was falling.

The crew remained in the cockpit during the stopover. Twenty minutes after arriving, the flight called for departure clearance. The jet left the gate at 10 minutes after midnight, and began its takeoff eight minutes later.

Eyewitnesses differed about exactly what happened next, but generally agreed that the airplane climbed normally to 50 or 100 feet. Then, in rapid sequence, it first rolled slightly in one direction, then back in the other, continuing to roll past the vertical. Several witnesses reported flames or a fireball emerging from one or both engines before the plane struck the ground. The DC-9 came to rest inverted 6,500 feet from the approach threshold. Both crewmembers, the only persons aboard the airplane, were killed.

National Transportation Safety Board investigators concluded that the crash had been due to the airplane's wing's having stalled a few seconds after rotation. The puff of flame emerging from the engines was consistent with compressor stall caused by the sudden detachment of airflow from the wing roots.

The flight data and cockpit voice recorder tapes showed that the takeoff had been normal up to the moment of the stall; but whereas the DC-9 usually experiences a brief vertical acceleration of 1.2 to 1.3 Gs during initial climb, this time the airplane reached 1.17 Gs and then lost vertical acceleration. The first officer was flying; the captain exclaimed "Watch out!" three times in rapid succession *after* the loss of acceleration began. The stick shaker was not triggered before the stall, which occurred at a much lower angle of attack than normal.

Dry blowing snow is not normally thought to present a ground icing hazard. The NTSB hypothesized, however, that the wing leading edge was hot; the crew had most likely used bleed air deice during the approach, since pireps had indicated a possibility of moderate rime ice. Normally, moisture vaporizes on contact with the leading edge, which is heated in flight by 350°F bleed air. But as the wing cooled, snow falling on it may have melted and then refrozen, roughening the surface. (This explanation, while technically plausible, leaves one wondering: Why doesn't this happen all the time?)

Leading-edge deice is disabled on the ground to avoid overheating the structure; the deicing system would not have begun to heat the leading edge until after the landing gear was unloaded—too late to be of any value.

You might suppose that the crew was negligent, under the circumstances, in not requesting ground deicing, which consists of bathing the wings and empennage with glycol—the slimy stuff in automotive antifreeze. But no other aircraft requested or received deicing service that night at Cleveland.

Prior to this accident there had been four other crashes of this same type of series-10 DC-9 under similar circumstances. (Only 93 series-10 DC-9s are in service in the United States.) After the fourth one, the NTSB had recommended that the FAA make ground deicing of series-10 DC-9s mandatory when icing conditions exist. In a letter written 13 months before the Cleveland accident, the FAA rejected the NTSB's suggestion, arguing that the hazards of ice were well known and that the DC-9-10 is affected no differently from other airplanes. Now that more than five percent of the fleet has crashed for the same single reason, the FAA might reconsider its earlier judgment.

A few weeks after the Cleveland crash, Douglas Aircraft Company, the manufacturer, sent out a letter to DC-9 operators to remind them of the hazards of taking off with ice on the wings. At one point the letter said, "Dangerous reductions in handling qualities and stall margins can occur because of icing roughness equivalent to that of MEDIUM GRIT SANDPAPER" [emphasis theirs]. Later the writer, T.M. Ryan, Jr., vice president for flight operations, labs, safety, and training, observed that "Ice accumulation on the wing surface is very difficult to detect. It cannot be seen from ahead of the wing during walk-around, is very difficult to see from behind the wing, and may not be detectable from the cabin because it is often clear and wing surface details may show through."

This suggested that, short of getting a ladder and climbing up to palpate the wing, there isn't much chance of a crewmember's detecting potentially hazardous levels of contamination during walk-around. "Even suspicious conditions justify inspection or precautionary deicing," Ryan wrote. "Crews should be encouraged to taxi back for a second deicing if a delayed takeoff in freezing precipitation raises any question of wing condition."

Ryan was at pains to emphasize that all aircraft, not just the DC-9, were at risk. In a related paper written for presentation to a symposium on the adverse effects of weather on aerodynamics, another Douglas spokesperson, R.E. Brumby (MD-80/DC-9 deputy chief design engineer), presented a list of takeoff accidents between 1968 and 1989 in which ice played a part. While one purpose of the list was probably to buttress Douglas's contention that the DC-9-10 is only one of many kinds of airplanes that have had takeoff accidents related to ice, one couldn't help noticing that of 13 cases listed that involved airliners, nine involved DC-9-10, DC-8-62, or Fokker F28 aircraft. (Of two incidents involving Boeing 737s, at least one, the 1982 Air Florida crash, was probably precipitated more by the flight crew's failure to deice an engine inlet pressure sensor, and then to apply full power when the airplane failed to climb, than by loss of control due to wing surface icing.)

What the DC-9-10, DC-8-62, and Fokker F28 have in common is a "hard" wing—that is, one without leading-edge slats. Given that more than 90 percent of airline jet aircraft are equipped with leading-edge slats, the rate at which slatless airplanes appear in Brumby's list is disproportionately high.

Graphs accompanying Brumby's paper indicate that when roughness is spread over the entire upper surface of a wing, slatted and unslatted wings are equivalent if the roughness height is .00035 times the wing chord, or about 1/16 inch (coarser than any sandpaper you or I have seen) for a wing of 15-foot chord. With finer roughness, the slatted wing is markedly superior, retaining its maximum lift coefficient when that of an unslatted wing has dropped by 15 percent.

With that ¹⁄₁₆-inch roughness on a 15-foot chord, both slatted and unslatted wings experience an increase of about 20 percent in their stalling speed. That number is significant, because rotation speed in jet aircraft is usually less than 1.2 times the stalling speed. In other words, given a certain amount of frost on the wing, a crew may rotate at the stalling speed, rather than 20 percent above it. Slight variations in rotation speed and roughness distribution could cause a stall immediately after rotation, or a stall of one wing and not the other.

Lighter aircraft are at less risk because it is easier for them than it is for a jet to add a comfortable cushion to their speed before rotation. In general, furthermore, the airfoils used on personal aircraft, including most turboprops, are not so sensitive to very small accumulations of frost as the sections used on high-subsonic aircraft are. Nevertheless, the FARs (91.209 and 121.629) prohibit taking off *any* airplane with *any* snow or ice adhering to its flying surfaces.

With increasing recognition of the hazards of ice on flying surfaces, several remedies are possible. One is to raise the rotation speed whenever freezing moisture is present in order to restore stall margins; but that means increasing accelerate-stop distances and field length requirements. Another is to provide pre-takeoff deicing for all aircraft; large mobile deicing rigs that can even accommodate a 747 are now available. In view of the fact that thousands of successful takeoffs are made in freezing conditions for every one that fails, however, the most cost-effective remedy may simply be better crew education, and *extreme* caution with slatless wings.

In the conclusion to its report on the accident, the NTSB noted that "both the FAA and Douglas Aircraft have been aware for several years of the propensity of the DC-9 series 10 to the loss of control caused by wing contamination, but neither of them took positive action to include related information in the approved Airplane Flight Manual." The Board faulted the crew for not inspecting the wings during the stopover, but attributed their complacency to a lack of information from various organizations.

Two NTSB members, Chairman James Kolstad and Vice Chairman Susan Coughlin, filed additional statements. Kolstad, dissenting, felt that the ultimate responsibility was the crew's. "It is vitally important," he wrote, "not to dilute or mask this message by scattering the responsibility among impersonalized organizational structures . . ."

Coughlin took an exactly opposite tack. Believing that the crew was unaware of "information that was apparently readily available and known throughout much of the aviation community," she blamed the FAA and the NTSB itself for leaving this aircrew (and others who had been victims of similar accidents) "hopelessly ignorant of the situations they faced."

Everyone agrees that better crew education is needed. There's nothing like a catchy slogan to foster the spread of an idea, and a suitable candidate appears in the NTSB report: "There's no such thing as 'a little ice'."

In the next report, a professional crew operating in an area known for its icing risk picks up the expected load—but then fails to foresee the combined effects of the ice and a high approach. They can hardly be blamed—probably only an aerodynamicist would have anticipated what happened.

Ice Stalled the Tail
by Peter Garrison

On the night after Christmas in 1989, a British Aerospace Jetstream, United Express Flight 2415, crashed short of the runway threshold at Pasco, Washington, after a 60-nm flight from Yakima. The accident took place at about 10:30 p.m. local time, in visual meteorological conditions, under a 1,000-foot overcast. The cloud tops were at 4,000 feet, and there was no moon. The aircraft struck the ground in a 50- to 60-degree nose-down attitude; all six aboard were killed instantly.

Although the cloud layer was only 3,000 feet thick, it contained a lot of moisture, and conditions were conducive to icing. A Fairchild Swearingen SA227 approaching the Pasco airport three and a half hours before the accident reported accumulating half an inch of rime ice between entering cloud and arriving at the outer marker. Crossing altitude at the marker is 2,400.

Another Jetstream that landed at Pasco three hours before the accident had accumulated half an inch of rough clear ice by the time it descended to 3,000 feet, and required additional power to maintain level flight. The captain reported a strong temperature inversion aloft, with the temperature dropping rapidly from 15°C to 0°C above the cloud tops.

Yet another Jetstream landed at Pasco less than an hour before the accident. The pilot reported a rapid ice buildup after entering clouds, with airspeed loss and an increased rate of descent. According to the NTSB report, "He stated that he had not seen such a high rate of ice accumulation at such a low altitude."

Flight 2415 had already encountered icing on its approach to Yakima. While the airplane was on the ground, the airline station agent watched the crew walking along the leading edges of the wings, knocking ice off. Ice was also sliding off the wings. She offered several times to have the airplane deiced by new glycol-dispensing equipment that was available and ready to use. The captain declined. The station agent also suggested using the equipment to deice the tail, which could not be reached from the ground, but the captain again declined, saying that it would be no problem.

Flight 2415 took off from Yakima at about 10:04 p.m., and was cleared to an en route altitude of 11,000 feet (the MEA between the two airports is 6,000). The airplane presumably accumulated some ice during the climb-out from Yakima. It was only in cloud for two minutes, however, and spent 10 minutes or more at above-freezing temperatures before reentering cloud on the approach; so ice accumulated during climb-out was not a likely factor in the accident.

The Jetstream probably reached its cruising altitude at around 10:13; two minutes later center cleared it to descend to 6,000, and the crew acknowledged and reported out of 11,000. A clearance to 3,000 followed two and a half minutes later. By about 10:26 the flight was back down at 3,000 feet, and in cloud. At this point center transmitted the approach clearance: "Sundance 415's five north of Dunez, right heading 180, maintain 3,000 until established on the localizer, you're cleared straight-in ILS approach."

The flight was, at that point, about four miles from the outer marker, and the bearing to the marker was about 160 degrees. Normally, one would expect to intercept the localizer at least two miles outside the marker, and 105 degrees would have been a more appropriate vector. The glideslope intercepts the 3,000-foot level two miles outside the marker; the 180-degree vector, on the other hand, brought the flight onto the localizer about two miles *inside* the marker. At that point the glideslope is 1,200 feet below the 3,000-foot altitude restriction.

The controller selected the 180-degree heading because it represented the maximum permissible angle for intercepting the localizer for Runway 21. It was less apparent to him than it should have been that the heading was inconsistent with the relative positions of the flight and the outer marker, because he had his radarscope set to its maximum (150-nm) range.

Controllers often switch their scope range back and forth between higher and lower settings to provide approach guidance; alternatively, they sometimes set an adjacent scope for a smaller range. The controller working Flight 2415 did neither. Furthermore, he had displayed on his scope an overlay map that did not include the ILS approach "gate" for Runway 21. At the 150-mile setting, the transponder return from an airplane is two to two-and-a-half miles wide; and so even had the approach gate been displayed, the controller could not have provided precise guidance to it.

The clearance thus forced the flight into a position far above the glideslope. If the ADF was tuned to the LOM frequency (or for that matter if the DME was tuned, which is likely, to the Pasco VOR), the crew knew that it was joining the ILS high and inside. By the time the localizer needle came to life, the glideslope was showing a full-down reading.

The crew had several options at this point. One was to miss the approach, go around, and try again. Another was to treat the approach as a localizer approach and descend immediately to localizer minimums, which were well below the overcast. Once having broken out, they could complete the approach visually.

Evidently the crew initially decided to continue the approach. Then, just as they intercepted the localizer and began to descend, they got a warning flag on the glideslope and declared a missed approach. They began to climb, then got the glideslope back and decided to resume the approach.

The warning flag, it turned out, was due to the location of the glideslope antenna above the radar in the airplane's nose; it was not due to a fault in the onboard receiver or in the airport equipment. But the crew could not know that at the time.

At the point the crew elected to resume the approach, the Jetstream was four miles from the runway threshold, and 2,300 feet above it. Center gave the airplane's position as four north; the crew acknowledged. That was their last transmission.

A witness in the control tower saw the airplane descending, high and fast, toward the runway; suddenly it nosed over and crashed.

What happened is uncertain. The NTSB weighed several possibilities, including inflight use of prop beta (reverse thrust) to hasten the descent. That possibility was judged remote. More likely, the NTSB thought, the crew dropped max flaps (50 degrees) and pushed the nose over. As they subsequently attempted to pull the nose up to arrest the descent, the horizontal stabilizer stalled because of ice accretion on its leading edge, and the airplane pitched into an uncontrollable dive.

The mechanism of stabilizer stall is less familiar than that of wing stall. Conventionally configured airplanes generally operate with a downward load on the horizontal tail. This download is required because at least one, and often two, forces usually act to push the nose of the airplane down. One of them is the moment produced if the CG is ahead of the wing's center of lift, as it often is. The other is the so-called "pitching moment" of the wing, which in most airplanes is negative, or nose-down. Deflecting the flaps greatly increases the wing pitching moment. The worst case for nose-down force therefore occurs when the maximum moment due to CG position and airplane weight is combined with the pitching moment from the maximum flap extension. Just like a wing, a stabilizer can stall at a higher-than-normal airspeed if its leading edge is deformed by ice and it is called upon to produce too-high a lift coefficient. The Board's belief is that this is what happened to Flight 2415.

The NTSB named the controller's error in positioning the airplane as a contributing cause, and the crew's decision to continue the approach after it had gotten off to a bad start as the probable (i.e., principal) cause. Icing is mentioned as a second contributing cause.

As usual, it is possible to disagree with the NTSB. On one hand, the Board argues that the Jetstream may have accumulated as much as an inch of ice in the few minutes it spent in cloud during the approach; in fact, the stabilizer-stall scenario *requires* an accumulation of ice well beyond the half-inch buildup tested during certification of the Jetstream for icing conditions. Yet the Board faults the crew for not wanting to spend another 10 minutes in cloud flying the missed approach. In fact, if the stabilizer stalled with an inch of ice on the airplane, it would have stalled even sooner with two inches. (The Board does not explain at all why the tail deice boots failed to protect the stabilizer.) Furthermore, the Board's implication that even temporarily losing the glideslope would have obliged a conscientious crew to terminate the approach is incorrect; the localizer was still perfectly good, and the weather was not low enough to require using the glideslope.

A strong case could be made that a major accumulation of airframe ice is a greater hazard than an unstabilized approach, and that the crew in fact acted wisely in electing to continue the approach rather than miss, especially given the high ceiling and good visibility that existed below the clouds. In this interpretation, blame for the accident would fall not upon any individual person, but upon the virtually unforeseeable conjunction of a controller's actions and an insufficiently stringent set of certification standards.

4

Thunderstorms

Thunderstorms contain extremely violent weather and pilots are trained from the outset to give them a wide berth. Inevitably, however, pilots who fly in the parts of the country where thunderstorms are common find themselves forced to keep company with them.

When convective storms form a solid line along a front, pilots can still use radar, which detects heavy rain, or an alternative device, the Stormscope, which detects lightning, to find the gaps and punch through. The pilots of airplanes not equipped with radar or Stormscope rely on the ground-based radar of traffic controllers for storm information.

If a pilot is cautious, a partnership with a controller needn't entail an undue risk. But the uncertain division of responsibility between a pilot and a controller can lead to trouble when the pilot doesn't realize that the bulk of the decision-making burden is always his.

The first of this group of thunderstorm-related accidents involves a pilot who put his fate too completely into a controller's hands.

By Jove
by Peter Garrison

When the ancient Romans were arming the chiefest of their gods, Jupiter (also known as Jove), they selected thunderbolts for his weapons, and identified him with a convective storm. *Jupiter Pluvius* they called him—Rainy Jove. He was the mightiest of the gods—mightier even than Neptune of the sea and Vulcan of the earthquakes and volcanoes—perhaps because it seemed to the Roman collective consciousness that thunderstorms were the mightiest and most intimidating things to be found anywhere.

Today many people are not so impressed by thunderstorms as the Romans were. They see in them not the legendary ill temper of Jove but only some churning air mixed with rainshowers and decorative flashes of light. This view does not fully prepare them for what thunderstorms have to offer. True, it is possible to fly through a thunderstorm, enjoying the darkness, the grand scale of the turbulence, the lurid blasts of the lightning and the engine-obliterating tattoo of the rain. It is also possible to come in the side and go out the bottom.

One who came out the bottom was a 370-hour instrument-rated commercial pilot who flew a Bonanza into a level-three cell in Kentucky in the spring of 1989. He had left Florida at 9:20 p.m. for St. Louis to visit his girlfriend. Ironically, she had sent him an airline ticket for the trip, but when his boss offered him the use of his Bonanza, he had cashed it in. The canceled ticket was found in the wreckage of the Bonanza.

The conditions that night were classic. Several convective sigmets had been issued on a string of thunderstorms that lay on an east-west line near the Kentucky-Indiana border, moving eastward. The line was narrow and less than 200 miles long, but it was violent. Aircraft of all types were deviating around the line; but the relatively inexperienced pilot of Bonanza N6863Q decided to plunge straight through it.

The following transcript, which has been edited for conciseness, covers a period of a little more than an hour. It provides a useful insight into the relations between pilots and controllers, and, in particular, into the potential misunderstandings that arise when a pilot wants more guidance from a controller than the controller feels authorized to give.

(ATL = Atlanta Center; 63Q = the Bonanza; MEM = Memphis Center; BLG = Bowling Green FSS. Times are Eastern Standard Time. Communications between controllers are in italics. Asterisk [*] indicates unintelligible portions of the tape.)

TIME: 2230:46

ATL: Attention all aircraft, Kansas City convective Sigmet 8C valid until 0455Z for Indiana, Illinois, and Kentucky from 30 miles south-southwest of Cincinnati to 30 miles west-southwest of Bowling Green to 70 miles south-southwest of Evansville to 30 miles northwest of Evansville to 30 miles south-southwest of Cincinnati, an area of severe thunderstorms moving from 270 at 15 knots, tops above FL 450, a tornado reported about 50 east-southeast of Evansville at 0230Z. Tornadoes, hail to two inches, wind gusts to 65 knots possible.

TIME: 2330:09

ATL: N63Q, I'm painting some light precip about 60 miles in front of you, it's in Memphis Center's airspace, sitting around Nashville. I'll be switching you to Memphis so you can get some weather advisories from them. I don't have much information on it—just what I'm painting on my radar, which isn't much.

63Q: Okay, that's great, thank you.

    TIME: 2334:13

63Q: Atlanta Center, 63Q.

ATL: 63Q go ahead.

63Q: Okay, sir, I'm seeing quite a bit of lightning activity out about 20 to 25 miles ahead of me. Do you have anything reported on that?

ATL: Yes sir, stand by one . . . Bonanza 6863Q, Memphis Center should have some information on that weather activity for you, contact Memphis Center 132.1.

    TIME: 2336:17

63Q: Memphis Center, Bonanza 6863Q with you IFR at 8,000.

MEM: Bonanza 6863Q Memphis. Center, roger.

63Q: Okay sir, [*] the weather about 25 miles ahead of me, do you have anything reported on that?

MEM: N6863Q, yes sir, I've got precipitation in and around the Nashville area, uh, you see anything you want to deviate around just let me know, that'll be approved.

63Q: 63Q roger, uh, know of anything severe out there?

MEM: No real complaints of anything that bad but they are deviating around it, sir.

63Q: 63Q roger, thanks a lot.

(For the next 45 minutes 63Q is silent. On the center frequency that 63Q is monitoring, several aircraft, including airliners and a C-5, request and get deviations around the weather.)

    TIME: 0022:43

63Q: Memphis Center, this is 6863Q, we're just starting to get into the stuff here northeast of Nashville, can you tell me how wide it is?

MEM: Yes sir, it goes for . . . let me see, about 65 north of Nashville, northwest of Nashville you should come out of it.

63Q: Okay, and, ah, what intensity is, is the, uh, cells at?

MEM: Okay, it's not going to be, it looks like it's going to be not too bad until you get about uh 50 . . . 45 or 50 miles northwest of Nashville, and there's about a 10- or 15-mile band of it that's pretty thick.

63Q: Okay, and what's it topping out at?

MEM: I'm not sure, sir.

63Q: Thank you.

(Several other aircraft discuss the weather and deviations with center.)

    TIME: 0033:00

MEM: N6863Q, what are your weather, uh, flight conditions?

63Q: 6863Q, it's getting pretty nasty here, heavy lightning, uh, light rainshowers, uh, turbulence isn't too bad yet, it's moderate, but, uh, this lightning's starting to, uh, be pretty intense here.

MEM: N6863Q roger, you got about 15 more miles, sir, and you'll break out.

63Q: 63Q, thank you.

MEM: *I've been saying that for the last 80 miles or so.*

TIME: 0034:15

63Q: Memphis Center, 63Q, can I get a vector?

MEM: 63Q, say again, sir.

63Q: 63Q, can I get a vector around this stuff? It's getting pretty bad.

MEM: Okay sir, the shortest route out of it would be straight ahead, it's about uh, uh, five or six miles straight ahead should be the shortest route out of it sir . . . And 6863Q, if you're gonna turn around it a right turn would probably be better than a left turn.

63Q: Okay, I'll turn right about 090.

MEM: Roger.

MEM: *I didn't tell the mofo to fly through that shit, I just told him where it was . . . What . . . what . . . he's* [expletive] *flying around out there* [*]

MEM: N6863Q, if you were to go northbound, sir, it's, uh, you'll come out of it in about eight miles . . . N6863Q Memphis.

63Q: 63Q, sir, I'm in a serious downdraft here.

MEM: N6863Q say again, sir . . . *Sounds like we have a problem here, he is* [*]

63Q: 3Q, we're going down.

MEM: N6863Q say again . . . *Sounds like he said "we're going down"* [*] *off . . . Goddamn it* [*] . . . N6863Q Memphis . . . *Told the mother where he was at* [*] . . . N6863Q Memphis . . . N6863Q Memphis . . . *I told him about it* . . . (sound of dialing).

BLG: *Bowling Green.*

MEM: *Yes, have you heard anything from a 6863Q?*

BLG: *6863Q, not that I know of, what's he doing?*

MEM: *Well, it was a BE35 en route to St. Louis and trying to get around some weather approximately 15 miles southwest of your position now of Bowling Green, and last I heard was she* [sic] *said she was going down so I think she's out there somewhere, uh, probably took it in . . .*

BLG: *Yeah, you know there are some, I'm just looking at the radar weather here, and it's just bad.*

MEM: *I know it is, I told her, I told her it was pretty thick out there.*

BLG: *A solid line of level fours and a lot of five in there too.*

MEM: *Yeah.*

BLG: *There's no way anybody in a light plane could make it, there's no way any kind of plane could make it there.*

Subsequent analysis of the transponder returns from the Bonanza showed that it had remained more or less level at 8,000 feet until it began abruptly to descend. The rate of descent was from 3,000 to 5,000 fpm. The NTSB states that the pilot "lost control" of the aircraft; it struck trees at an elevation of 850 feet msl in a steep, nose-down left bank.

Obviously, the pilot took a chance in penetrating a line of thunderstorms clearly marked by intense lightning. Why? One reason may have been the length of the flight, the lateness of the hour, the distance remaining to the destination and the fuel remaining in the airplane. The pilot had somewhat optimistically flight-planned a five-hour-55-minute duration for the 74-gallon fuel capacity of the Bonanza. In fact the airplane is good for about five hours at normal cruise at 8,000 feet. At the time of the accident he had been airborne for three hours, 15 minutes, averaging 167 knots, and was still about one hour, 20 minutes away from St. Louis. He would arrive, therefore, with only a 30-minute reserve. If he made a significant deviation, he might be obliged to land before reaching St. Louis, and then might have difficulty finding fuel at one in the morning. If he didn't get to St. Louis until the next morning, a significant part of his weekend would be lost.

The transcript makes it apparent that the pilot overestimated the ability of controllers to guide an airplane through weather. It also makes it apparent that what a controller says is not always what he thinks, and what you understand him to mean is not always what he really means.

After the airplane went down the controller repeatedly exclaimed that he had warned the pilot that the weather would be heavy. But although the controller was thinking that the weather looked bad, the transcript actually shows him appearing to downplay its severity: "No real complaints of anything that bad . . . it looks like it's going to be not too bad . . ." The only indication that the storm line might be deadly is the controller's "there's about a 10- or 15-mile band of it that's pretty thick." His subsequent "you got about 15 more miles, sir, and you'll break out" can even be construed as encouragement to continue straight ahead, although he clearly didn't intend it that way.

Controllers are not expected to make basic decisions for pilots. The innocuous phrase "VFR not recommended" was added to the vocabulary of weather briefers only after many pilots protested that anything stronger would be an infringement upon their authority by

mere groundlings. Controllers, likewise, whatever they may be thinking, can do no more than pass on pilot reports and information about
areas of heavy precipitation; they seldom say. "Personally, I would go
around that if I were you," though that may be what they're thinking.
At most, they will say, "If you want to deviate," which is code for "The
weather looks bad enough to deviate around."

Pilots are repeatedly warned to avoid thunderstorms; and yet
they continue to enter them, either inadvertently or because they
think the danger is overstated. The most fortunate pilots are those
who enter a thunderstorm, get badly shaken up, and emerge un-
scathed. They are not tempted to repeat the experiment. Less lucky
are those who have uneventful flights through mild thunderstorms—
and come to believe that there is nothing to fear. Rainy Jove does not
like to be trifled with; his wrath may yet surprise them.

*When an airplane comes apart in a thunderstorm, the breakup often
doesn't occur until after the airplane has emerged from clouds. In the
next accident, it seems probable that the structural failure took place
only after the airplane had escaped from the heart of the storm.*

Inexplicable Breakup
by Peter Garrison

Ask a pilot what are the worst things he can imagine happening in an
airplane, and he's likely to reply inflight fire, night engine failure, and
loss of attitude instruments in IFR conditions. Ask a passenger, and
he's likely to start the list with "the wings falling off."

Pilots aren't as concerned as passengers are about inflight breakup
because they regard it as fantastically unlikely. We've all heard that
when we grasp the control yoke we hold in our hands the power to
take the wings off the airplane, but we've also heard again and again
that airplanes are stout enough to take more punishment than anything other than a wildly ham-handed pilot is likely to dish out.

Still, airplanes do from time to time come out of the clouds in
pieces. One that did was a Comanche 260 on a flight from Burley,
Idaho, to Burns, Oregon, about 10 years ago. The pilot, a 56-year-old
farmer with 2,250 hours and a commercial ticket with instrument rating, was known to be conscientious about his flying. A progressive
flight log of his final flight, filled in up to the last checkpoint, was
found in the wreckage of his airplane. His Comanche was equipped
with twin aftermarket turbochargers and with a Ryan Stormscope that
he regularly used in his instrument flying.

His weather briefing on the morning of his last flight had called for solid instruments at his filed altitude of 8,000 feet, with a chance of embedded thunderstorms. The flight was a short one, and it was uneventful up to the last moment; his last communication with center was a sign-off to go to the unicom frequency of his destination airport for an altimeter setting.

The pilot never contacted Burns Unicom, and he never returned to center. His target remained on center's scope for another couple of minutes and then disappeared.

About an hour later the manager of the Burns airport took off to look for him; he found the wreckage at the point where center's radar had last shown a target. Parts of the airplane were scattered over a wide area, he noted, and the ground was white with recently fallen hail.

Two thunderstorms had passed through the area at about the time of the accident; residents of Riverside, Oregon, a couple of miles from the crash site, described the storms as "heavy" and "major," with intense thunder and lightning and heavy rain and hail. The occupants of a vehicle that had passed close by the accident site about 15 minutes after the accident said the ground visibility was near zero in rain and hail.

Despite the reported strength of the storms, the controllers working the Comanche said that their scopes had painted no cells near it. High terrain prevented the ATC antenna from picking up weather returns unless the storm built up above 15,000 feet msl.

When an airplane breaks up in horizontal flight, parts are found along the airplane's path in the order in which they parted company with it. In this case the outer panels of the stabilator were found farthest from the main wreckage; both had failed symmetrically downward. The outer wing panels, likewise symmetrically parted at midspan, had also failed downward after an initial upward flexure. The tailless, cropped-wing Comanche struck the ground upright in a shallow dive and cartwheeled, throwing the pilot clear; after it settled, fire consumed the cabin.

The customary autopsy brought out two possibly significant facts. First, the pilot had heart disease, including a hemorrhage in one coronary artery, seemingly not related to impact trauma, which might or might not have indicated that he had suffered some kind of heart attack before the accident. Second, there were no bruises to indicate that his seat belt had been fastened.

The structural failures in the tail and wings suggested that the pilot had caused them by pulling on the yoke. The sequence of events is this. First the stabilator goes to a very high (negative) angle of attack, because the pilot pulls back hard on the yoke. If this takes place at a speed lower than the maneuvering speed, a violent pitch-up will ensue, but nothing should break because at those airspeeds the wing will stall before reaching its design limit load. Above the maneuvering speed, however, one of two things may happen, depending on the airplane: either the wings may be overstressed and fail upward, or the stabilator (or stabilizer) may be overstressed and fail downward.

In this case the stabilator failed downward, as indicated by tensile rupture of the top spar cap. (The Comanche stabilator has a midspan spar splice; if it fails, it fails there.) Without the stabilator, the airplane is at the mercy of the nose-down pitching moment of the wing, and noses over violently. At this point unrestrained passengers are tossed against the cabin ceiling and, with any luck, knocked unconscious so that they don't have to attend to the rest of the accident sequence.

As the airplane pitches over, the wings go to a negative angle of attack. The motion is divergent; the angle of attack continues to increase negatively until the wings fail, possibly leaving behind a characteristic signature: a compressive distortion of the top spar cap, produced before the stabilator failure, followed by a decisive tensile failure.

If the message of the airframe failure is straightforward, the pathologist seems to be hedging his bets; he won't go so far as to say that the pilot had a heart attack. If that were the case, the thunderstorm would be merely coincidental, unless some event connected with it, like an encounter with hail or with violent turbulence, triggered a rush of adrenalin and an accelerated heartbeat, and that in turn undid a diseased heart.

I think it more likely that the thunderstorm, which is the smoking gun in this case, set the accident sequence in motion. That this conscientious and Stormscope-equipped pilot flew into an embedded cell is inexplicable. Once he got there, it seems fairly certain that he overcontrolled the airplane to the point that it broke apart, although recovering to level flight from an accelerated spiral could produce the same kind of failure as overcontrol.

In a chaotic situation, what actually happened was not necessarily the thing most likely to have happened. If he didn't have his seat belt buckled, he may have been thrown against the ceiling and briefly stunned by a violent downdraft. For that matter, he may have had a slight heart attack and briefly lost consciousness; on recovering he may have found his airplane in an unusual attitude and losing altitude, and, knowing he was close to mountainous terrain, he may have reacted too abruptly to the perceived danger.

It seems a bit callow, when one is sitting in one's rather comfortable office and not bouncing around in the black heart of a thunderstorm, to pontificate about how undesirable and unnecessary it is to overcontrol that badly. Nevertheless, here goes. The rules for avoiding overcontrol are simple; note that following them *in extremis* may not be simple. First, know your airplane's maneuvering and turbulence-penetration speeds and trim for the lower of the two in a severe turbulence encounter. Lower the landing gear, adding drag to avoid rapidly picking up speed. Keep the wings level. Ride the up- and downdrafts without trying to maintain altitude. Don't turn back; even at reduced speed an airplane is moving very fast, and once you're well into a cell it will probably take no longer to get to the other side than it would to go back the way you came.

There's another lesson here, too: When you hear the words "embedded thunderstorm," think twice before filing IFR.

Possession of a big, expensive airplane and a lot of electronic equipment sometimes makes a pilot overconfident. In the next account, a pilot had the equipment to avoid a thunderstorm encounter, but apparently didn't know how to use it.

Radar Trap
by J. Mac McClellan

Traffic separation is the controller's first and primary responsibility. Heaped on top of that is a responsibility to aid pilots in any way possible. Providing any information available about possibly severe weather is right at the top of controller responsibilities, subordinate only to IFR traffic separation. Yet controllers can only issue warnings and pass on weather advisories about the location of precipitation echoes they see on their radar. The final decision to deviate course remains where it belongs—in the cockpit.

A Cessna 414A pilot listened to a controller's advisory of heavy precipitation ahead, flew into the weather, and lost control. The private pilot and three passengers planned to fly a Cessna 414A pressurized piston twin from Fort Wayne, Indiana, to Atlanta, Georgia, on a July morning. The pilot had been licensed for more than 16 years but had not flown a great deal. As a result there was much confusion about his actual experience, particularly in recent years. The NTSB has determined that he had about 650 total flying hours, about 200 of which were logged in the 414A.

The pilot called flight service for a forecast early in the afternoon before the fatal flight. The briefer described a slow-moving cold front over the Ohio River Valley that was forecast to move little by the next morning. Waves were expected to form along the front, creating reduced visibilities, showers, and the possibility of thunderstorms. The briefer explained that waves on a front are low-pressure systems. The briefer said the Atlanta area was expected to be hot and hazy, with no weather problems anticipated after the showers and thunderstorms forecast for southern Ohio and Indiana. The pilot said "sounds like IFR to me" and filed a flight plan.

The next morning the 414A pilot checked weather with Fort Wayne FSS and found that the previous day's forecast had been remarkably accurate. The cold front stretched from Lake Erie to a low centered in Texas. At seven a.m. the radar summary depicted showers and widely scattered thundershowers over the Ohio River Valley. The briefer emphasized that the possibility of buildups existed and noted that tops were reported as high as 37,000 feet. Fog and obscured ceilings were widespread from Indiana to Kentucky, and towering cumulus were being reported as far south as Knoxville, Tennessee. Atlanta weather, however, was just fine. There were radar reports of precipitation and visual reports of cumulus buildups, but both were either scattered or broken. The conditions probably sounded manageable for a radar-equipped twin.

The flight did not get off to a good start. One witness reported "mass confusion" in the cockpit while the 414A's engines turned at high power for 15 minutes on the ramp. All the time the pilot appeared to be fumbling with checklists in the cockpit. Several times the big twin slipped forward in its spot. Witnesses recall being concerned for the safety of other airplanes and people on the ramp.

The transcripts of radio conversations also indicate that the 414A pilot was not well organized. The pilot said he didn't have a pencil and paper on which to copy his IFR clearance, and made several other requests for controller repeats throughout the short flight. The controllers involved, however, did not report anything unusual in the pilot's actions and control of the airplane once he understood their instructions.

As far as the pilot knew, takeoff and handling of the flight proceeded in a routine fashion. The controllers, however, were busy on their land-lines coordinating the 414A's climb profile with the flight path of another airplane that was deviating to avoid precipitation and cumulus buildups. Chicago Center had Fort Wayne Departure assign the 414A a 180-degree heading to maintain separation between the

414A and the deviating traffic. The heading allowed the Cessna to continue climbing to the pilot's requested cruise altitude of 17,000 feet. The controllers issued two more heading changes to the 414A pilot and told him that the vectors were to avoid an airplane deviating for weather.

The 414A pilot never asked the controller what the other pilot was deviating around. With thunderstorms forecast and reported on the radar summary, the 414A pilot indicated no curiosity about other pilots' actions in the area. The controller did his job by telling the 414A pilot, without an inquiry, that "radar shows an area of precipitation at one o'clock and it begins in about 10 miles and extends to the southwest from there." The 414A pilot responded with, "I just turned on the radar." Apparently he had been flying with the weather radar turned off.

The controller advised "deviation at your discretion is approved." He had fulfilled his responsibility by telling the pilot what precipitation he saw on radar and by clearing him to deviate as necessary. One minute and 45 seconds later the 414A pilot said, "Where did you see that precip? I'm not reading a thing on my radar." The controller repeated that the precipitation was at one o'clock and 10 miles. The pilot responded, "I still don't see anything, it must be pretty light." The controller then handed him off to the next sector.

Over the next three and a half minutes the new controller and the 414A pilot had a lengthy discussion about the Cessna's route of flight. Victor airway numbers had apparently been scrambled on the flight strip at the ATC center. After a total of 15 different transmissions, the routing was established. During that period no mention was made of the precipitation ahead that the previous controller had reported.

At 17,000 feet the 414A would have had a true airspeed of between 175 and 190 knots. The FSS had forecast a southwesterly wind aloft. During the three minutes, 30 seconds the controller and pilot discussed the routing, the 414A must have closed the 10-nm gap between the airplane and the weather that had been on the controller's radar.

What happened next is uncertain, except that the 414A pilot lost control. Center radar showed the airplane entering a right turn and descending before radar contact was lost. The NTSB's post-accident weather analysis determined that the Cessna had flown into an embedded thunderstorm, probably of level-two intensity, which contained at least moderate turbulence and at least moderate icing.

Witnesses on the ground reported hearing loud aircraft engine noise and then seeing the 414A emerge from the clouds at about

1,000 feet above the ground. The airplane appeared to be flying in a nearly level attitude when the wings inboard of the engines and the horizontal tail broke off, leaving the fuselage to plummet to the ground inverted.

The NTSB could find nothing in the wreckage that indicated the airplane or its systems suffered any failure other than being over-stressed by the pilot. This sequence of events is common when pilots lose control in the clouds. The airspeed builds well beyond maximum limits during the ensuing dive. When the pilot emerges from the clouds he tries to recover, but the airframe is stressed beyond its design limits and fails.

The question raised is not why the pilot lost control—he flew into a thunderstorm. Nor is the question why the airplane failed in flight—its design limits were exceeded by the pilot after control was lost. The real question is why this pilot didn't take action to avoid the thunderstorms he knew were forecast and reported. Why didn't he ask the controller for help in avoiding the precipitation showing on ATC's radar? We can only assume that he elected to believe his own airborne weather radar and continued on into the weather reported by the controller.

Why didn't the weather radar in the 414A show the precipitation ahead? The NTSB doesn't discuss that issue, noting instead that one of the probable causes of the crash was "flight into known adverse weather—initiated—pilot in command." There is no way to know for certain why the pilot did not see the precipitation ahead on his weather radar, but there are many possible explanations. Effective use of a weather radar requires skill and understanding. This pilot may not have possessed that knowledge. He may have operated the radar's controls improperly or, more likely, the radar may not have had time to warm up. Less than two minutes elapsed between the time the pilot reported that he had just turned on the radar and when he said it was showing no precipitation.

Weather radars use a vacuum-tube-like device called a magnetron to generate the electronic pulses transmitted in search of precipitation. Magnetrons need time to warm up to operational temperature. Because of this required warm-up period, weather radars should be kept in standby mode so that the magnetron is warmed up and ready for instant use. The 414A's weather radar should have been turned on and operating from takeoff, given the weather conditions, but apparently it wasn't.

The weather forecasts and briefing had been accurate, the controller did a good job of warning the pilot about precipitation indicated ahead, but it wasn't enough to save him or his three passengers. Controllers do not have the authority to vector us away from weather conditions when we choose to fly through them, and that's the way we pilots want it to be. But why would any pilot not recognize and use an offer of help?

The pilot in the preceding account had radar but didn't use it. In the next, a jet crew decides to press on even though its radar isn't working. They hope a controller's guidance will get them through a line of major storms.

Blind Alley
by J. Mac McClellan

A Westwind business jet crew flew into an area of severe thunderstorms, lost control and crashed. The important question is not why the airplane crashed—it flew into an extremely strong thunderstorm—but why this crew did not avoid the severe weather.

The Westwind crew had planned to depart Redbird Airport in Dallas, Texas, at about 3:30 p.m., bound for home base at Teterboro, New Jersey. The pilot called Dallas Flight Service at about 11:30 to file a flight plan and check the weather. It was early April, but hot and humid weather combined with a stationary front to kick up thunderstorms in northern Texas, Oklahoma, and Arkansas. The briefer copied the flight plan, discussed several areas of thunderstorm activity and told the pilot he expected the storms to continue to build in the heat of the day.

As so often happens in business aviation, the departure was delayed as passengers completed their business in town. The planned 3:30 departure slipped, and it was nearly five p.m. when the pilot asked Dallas FSS to change his proposed departure time to seven p.m. The flight would now depart after sundown, and bad weather is always worse in the dark.

Though he didn't expect to take off for nearly two hours, the Westwind pilot received his last briefing on the continuing thunderstorm situation. The briefer concentrated on the radar picture of "a pretty good line of weather in the Dallas area that's probably going to move through before the time of your departure."

"So basically the only thing you're showing on your radar is in the general area of Dallas?" the pilot asked.

"Well," the briefer said, "the general area here, and it does run, like I said, up across Blue Ridge, then the northwest corner of Arkansas, and movement only about 15 [knots]; and hasn't really been moving very much—it's been sort of redeveloping, so I don't really think it's going to have time to move across your route of flight other than right here in the Dallas area." The briefer later reminded the pilot to recheck the conditions before takeoff. The pilot didn't call again.

The National Transportation Safety Board places great importance on the fact that the FSS briefer did not relay details about sigmets for severe weather issued for the Westwind's proposed route. The briefer's failure to mention sigmets may be important, but even more important is the fact that two additional sigmets for thunderstorms were issued after the pilot's last call to FSS but before the crash.

The crew did use WSI computer service to obtain an automated weather briefing at 5:28 p.m. The briefing contained valid sigmets at that time, but another convective sigmet, Number Two Charlie, was issued before the crew called for a clearance at 6:45 p.m. Ten minutes later another sigmet warned of an area of severe thunderstorms across the Westwind's intended route. Tops were above 45,000 feet, hail to one inch. The sigmet forecast the possibility of tornadoes, hail to 3.5 inches and wind gusts to 75 knots. There is no indication the crew received this sigmet at any time during the flight.

Departure from Redbird was routine until the Westwind crew asked Regional Departure Control, "You painting anything out in front of us?"

"Well, about your 11 o'clock, 10 miles, I'm showing an area everybody's been going to, then turning northwestbound," the controller said.

"Sounds real good to us. Would like vectors around these buildups. We would appreciate it; our radar is not doing very well this evening," the Westwind crew responded.

The NTSB interprets that statement to mean the onboard weather radar was not functioning and had not been operating properly at takeoff. The controller later said he did not understand "our radar is not doing very well" to mean that the radar had failed totally. Even with onboard weather radar, most pilots ask for weather information from controllers as well, so the request for help was entirely normal, even if the Westwind's radar had been working perfectly. The controllers had been conferring with pilots on the best weather-avoidance deviations all afternoon, so it's understandable if the controller placed no special emphasis on this statement from the crew.

While the Westwind crew was talking to departure controllers, the Fort Worth Center controller read the new convective sigmet Two Charlie, warning of the severe weather ahead. Four minutes later the

Westwind crew was handed off to Fort Worth Center, unaware of the new sigmet. The crew did, however, repeat its request for help in avoiding the weather, but made no mention of onboard weather-radar problems. The controller suggested a heading of 055. "That looks like it will get you up to the north side of some [weather] area around Lades intersection. If you see anything you need to deviate off that heading, just go ahead and do it."

Airplanes were deviating at a furious pace, keeping Fort Worth Center controllers busy coordinating the unanticipated requests. The Westwind crew could not hear the discussions among controllers but could hear the many deviation requests on the frequency. The controller suggested a heading of 090 to the Westwind, but the crew asked for and received permission to continue on 055.

No further mention of the weather was made by the Westwind crew as it was cleared to climb to Flight Level 330, and later to FL 370 for cruise. About seven minutes after the clearance to FL 370 was issued, the controller asked for a ride report. "Oh, some light bumps every now and then, but we've topped it," the crew responded. The controller asked for the tops. The crew reported building tops at FL 380 to 390 to the left and tops at FL 360 to 370 to the right.

One minute after its report of "some light bumps" the Westwind crew told center, "We need to maintain the heading we're presently on and would like to request 390 if you can." The Fort Worth controller needed to coordinate the new altitude request with Memphis Center because the Westwind would soon enter that center's airspace. Also, FL 390 is a standard westbound, not eastbound, altitude. One minute after the initial request the Westwind crew said, "We need to get up." The controller had just completed the coordination and issued the clearance to climb. That was the final communication with the Westwind crew.

The desperate climb was apparently an attempt to top giant thunderstorms that surrounded the Westwind. The NTSB determined that at the time the crew made its final communication it was flying in an area of weak level-one precipitation. Just eight miles ahead was a strong storm of at least level four. Off to the right at about 11 miles was an intense storm of level five. Worst of all, a level-six storm was just seven miles ahead on the left. Level six is the most intense weather-radar measurement of a storm, and this enormous cell topped at 45,000 feet.

Even at FL 370 the sun had already set, and the moon was still below the horizon. Without weather radar the crew relied on visual information to avoid the storms, and in the darkness it would have been impossible to see building clouds at great distances. Other pilots and witnesses on the ground reported continuous lightning, which would have been an additional distraction for the crew.

The NTSB determined that the severe turbulence of the huge storms, especially the level-six monster, caused the crew to lose control. After control was lost and the jet headed down out of control, it penetrated the level-six storm, where it encountered extreme turbulence and severe icing. It was determined that both engines flamed out as a result of the upset and thunderstorm penetration.

The Westwind emerged from the clouds at about 4,000 feet in a nearly vertical descent. The NTSB believes that as the pilots attempted to recover from the dive they overstressed the airframe. The left main landing gear door is believed to be the first component that failed, and as it blew away it apparently struck the left horizontal tail, causing it to fail. The airplane hit in an 82-degree nose-down attitude. It was estimated the airplane may have reached speeds well above 500 knots in the dive.

The NTSB researched what the crew would have experienced during the upset and ensuing dive. The double engine failure would have shown the crew a host of warning lights, caused the cabin altitude to begin climbing, and overloaded the pilots. The airplane was out of control, neither engine was running, and there was no hope of restarting them until the airplane was below 30,000 feet. The NTSB calls this kind of terror "excessive workload," or "task overload." A pilot calls it his worst nightmare. The NTSB even includes a report of a pilot who survived an upset and double engine flameout in a Jet Commander, the Westwind's predecessor. That upset was also caused by thunderstorm turbulence, but the crew—after giving up all hope of survival—flew into visual conditions and was able to recover even though the landing gear was distorted by the G-force of the pullout.

The real cause of the Westwind accident was not the loss of control but the crew's apparent lack of awareness of the size and nearness of the thunderstorms. The NTSB blames the crew for deciding to take off with a known weather-radar malfunction and flight service for not issuing all hazardous weather information available. The pertinent convective sigmet was not broadcast on the VOR voice channel as it should have been. And the controllers did not pass along to other controllers—if they in fact ever understood—that the Westwind's radar was not working.

There is certainly plenty of blame to go around; but unless we wish to give up control of our cockpits, the major blame must rest with the crew. The captain elected to take off into an area of thunderstorm activity without a properly functioning radar, and then failed to make it crystal clear to controllers that he was operating without radar and needed more than the normal amount of help. Through some procedural failures by FSS, the crew did not have the latest weather information; but the crew took off almost two hours after its last contact with a briefer—a long time in the presence of convective weather.

The NTSB issued recommendations to ensure timely dissemination of severe-weather information and to require that crews report immediately the failure of important safety equipment, such as radar. But we're back to that same old problem of freedom to fly versus enforced safety. Airliners must have a functioning weather radar to take off legally; general aviation airplanes, even business jets, do not. If that requirement had been in force the accident almost certainly would have been prevented. Good operating practice and judgment dictated a need for weather radar on this particular day, but the rules did not. Most of us in general aviation reject the straitjacket of such rules, but in turn we must accept the responsibility for our decisions.

As always, many factors conspired against the Westwind pilots, but none was nearly as important as their own decision to face thunderstorms at night without radar.

5

Mechanical Problems

Mechanical causes are underrepresented in this collection for the same reason that pilots' decisions are overrepresented: They seldom teach a useful lesson to pilots. To the extent that mechanical difficulties make "good" Aftermath columns, they usually involve some inappropriate response by the pilot. In four of the following five reports, the crisis began with some sort of malfunction of the airplane—in the first instance, not even a true malfunction, only an unsecured door. In each case, however, the pilot failed to respond properly to the problem. The final crash—that of a DC-8 bringing soldiers home from the Middle East for Christmas—remains, and will probably always remain, unexplained.

Door Open to Disaster
by Nigel Moll

Shortly after 5:30 p.m., a Beech H35 Bonanza took off from Phoenix Sky Harbor Airport in Arizona, headed for Mesa. Visibility was seven miles, and there were scattered clouds at 6,000 feet. The pilot was alone, having flown two friends from Farmington, New Mexico, and dropped them at Sky Harbor at about 5:19 p.m. The airplane, which belonged to the pilot's fiancé, was flying in a northwesterly direction at low altitude when it suddenly pitched downward in a 45-degree, nose-down, wings-level attitude; it continued in this attitude until crashing into the backyard of a house and exploding.

The pilot was killed instantly. Worse, though, the airplane had plowed into a family of three sharing a barbecue with three friends. The homeowners' 10-year-old daughter was killed instantly, along with two adult friends. The parents suffered serious injuries, and a nine-year-old friend of their daughter escaped with minor injuries. The house was destroyed by fire. Just before the airplane hit, the daughter's grandparents had pulled into the driveway.

Witnesses' accounts were peppered with the usual inconsistencies: Some said the engine sounded fine, others said it didn't. One captured the sound of the dive on videotape, and the National Transportation Safety Board deduced from this that the engine sounded loud and steady throughout the descent until impact. A pilot witness who had been working in his backyard nearby said the engine was running at high power, and he estimated that the airplane dove into the ground from about 1,200 feet at more than 200 knots. The grandfather said that as he pulled into the driveway he saw the Bonanza in a slight nose-down attitude at between 100 and 200 feet agl. Within two seconds, he said, the right wing banked down, followed by a "violent nose pitch down" before the airplane crashed. The witnesses and the NTSB were in agreement, however, that the airplane was intact until impact. The NTSB decided the Bonanza hit at a 45-degree, nose-down angle, wings level, at between 90 and 120 knots.

In its report on this particularly gruesome tragedy, the NTSB points the finger at what might, on the face of it, appear to be a relatively bland malfunction: At some point after takeoff from Sky Harbor, the Bonanza's door popped open. When the airplane hit the ground, the pilot's seat belt was not fastened and her right arm was outstretched to the right, presumably attempting to secure the door. Examination of the door frame and latching mechanism showed them to be relatively free from deformation, which the Board interpreted as meaning that the door was free at the time of the crash. (Investigators compared the same components on a G35 Bonanza that had been flipped on its roof at the airport by a violent windstorm and found them to be heavily deformed from the forces of overturning.)

A door popping open might seem to be among life's blander emergencies, until it happens to you. It is sudden, noisy, and totally unexpected. Papers can fly around and even out of the cockpit, and you might suspect initially that the airplane is coming apart. But in the vast majority of cases—and certainly in a Bonanza—the airplane remains perfectly flyable as long as the pilot makes flying the first priority. A door hinged along its forward edge will open only a few inches before the force of the slipstream halts its progress. A Bonanza's door finds this equilibrium when it is ajar about three inches. When an airplane is in flight, the slipstream serves to decrease the relative pressure of the air immediately outside the fuselage; this weak pressurization effect pushes, normally to no avail, against doors and hatches—it's the same principle that creates lift and makes the ragtop of a convertible taut and bowed out at speed. It's also the force that makes it extremely difficult to close an airplane's door in flight.

The airplane's owner told investigators that his fiancée had flown the Bonanza for nearly 150 hours in the preceding two years, and that she was very proficient in flying it. He also said that on two or three occasions while flying with her in the accident airplane, the door had opened unexpectedly and that she was able to handle the situation and land at an airport without any problems. The instructor who checked her out in the accident airplane said she was a good pilot. This instructor also told the NTSB that she had trained the pilot to open the door in the event a forced landing was imminent.

The statement by the controller at Phoenix Tower who cleared the Bonanza for takeoff seems to indicate that the pilot was distracted by something shortly after takeoff from Runway 26R. He instructed her to turn right to 300 degrees, and although he saw the airplane turn to that approximate heading he received no acknowledgment. He then told the pilot to reset her transponder, since he was not receiving a return. This time she acknowledged. Twice he instructed her to contact departure but received no acknowledgment. He noticed smoke about three miles northwest of the departure end of Runway 26R, and then the hand-off facility said it had lost radar contact and had had no communications with the Bonanza.

The NTSB did not attempt to recreate what happened on board the Bonanza in the final stages of the flight, other than to say that the door opened, the pilot's attention was diverted, her right arm was outstretched, and her seat belt undone. The fact that she was five feet tall might have played a role, in that her small stature could have kept her head down in the cockpit as she leaned over to secure the door.

Reports of door openings are nothing new on Bonanzas or their multiengine stablemates, the Barons. In March 1987, some 14 months before this accident, Beech published a safety communique that was sent to owners of Bonanzas and Barons, including the owner of the accident airplane. On the first page, three phrases stand out in bold caps: THESE ACCIDENTS NEED NOT HAPPEN . . . DO NOT ATTEMPT TO CLOSE THE DOOR . . . ALWAYS MAINTAIN CONTROL OF THE AIRPLANE. Beech says that in each accident the pilot failed, first, to make sure that the door was properly latched before takeoff (this check should include a firm push on the top rear area of the door); and, second, failed to continue flying the airplane, thereby losing control or allowing the airplane to stall at low altitude. When a Bonanza's door has stabilized at approximately three inches ajar, drag increases, but not drastically enough that the airplane and its occupants are condemned immediately to an untimely end.

The Bonanza's handling characteristics remain unchanged, but climb performance is decreased. Beech determined in flight tests on an A36 with its front door open that the greatest reduction in climb performance was about a 160-fpm drop compared with the POH value. At higher-density altitudes, though, the resulting percentage reduction in climb performance with the additional drag of an open door is more significant. Service ceiling is also reduced, although this would normally pose less of a threat than the degraded climb performance.

Airspeed and altimeter indications can also be affected at airspeeds close to the stall. The altered pressure field sensed by the static system due to the open door will cause the airspeed indicator to read higher than the actual airspeed at the stall. That said, though, Beech also found that airspeed indications at the normal approach speed and above are accurate to within one knot. The drag of the door can also increase the altitude lost in a stall and recovery.

In its findings on the accident, the NTSB lists the probable causes as an unlocked door, an inadequate preflight by the pilot, and "altitude—not maintained—pilot in command." Above all, though, is what the NTSB calls a "related factor": "diverted attention—pilot in command."

The advice offered by Beech in its communique holds good for all pilots. If a door pops open on takeoff, abort the takeoff if there is sufficient runway remaining. If this is impractical or the airplane is in flight, fly the airplane first and do not allow the door to distract you. Continue to climb, straight ahead if possible, to pattern altitude and accelerate to normal pattern speed. Turns should not exceed 30 degrees of bank. Land as soon as you can, but there's no mad rush. Maintain at least the approach and landing speeds recommended in the POH to provide an adequate margin above the stall. You will likely need to carry more power than usual to counter the added drag. Once the airplane is safely back on the runway, then and only then should you turn your attention to the door itself.

In the next case a doctor, perhaps accustomed to dealing with chronically ill patients, allowed himself to grow so accustomed to the chronic illness of his airplane that when the illness became acute, he had no remedy.

Loose Needle
by Peter Garrison

The doctor's Geronimo-converted Apache was plagued by an intermittent engine problem. The left engine would run fine for a while, then begin to backfire and run lean. Once the engine lost fuel pressure on climb-out; on another occasion it quit on the run-up pad, and the doctor had a struggle to taxi the airplane back to the hangar on the right engine alone.

The engine problems had begun to appear long after factory-new 180-hp engines had been installed on the airframe. Repeated visits to the mechanic had brought no relief; but the discovery and replacement of a damaged seal in the carburetor four months before the accident gave a temporary and deceptive hope that the problem had finally been fixed.

One winter Saturday in 1989 the doctor went to the airport for a local flight. The weather was clear—a good day for the doctor, who had not flown in the past 13 weeks, to brush up on his take-offs and landings.

A pilot who was in a nearby hangar described the takeoff:

"As he passed the hangar his engine began afterfiring. He said on the radio, 'I've lost my engine, I'm coming back.' I turned to watch. He turned toward the airfield and the airplane rolled over and descended vertically to the ground."

Another witness wrote:

"My attention was drawn to the aircraft as it lifted off because of the heavy and continuous amount of backfiring, which sounded as though both engines were contributing to the backfiring. Also I was somewhat astounded that the pilot continued to take off, as he had ample time to put the aircraft down on the remaining runway."

The pilot did not spin out of a desperation turn back to the airport. He had identified the malfunctioning engine and feathered the propeller, had successfully completed a 180-degree right turn to the crosswind leg, and was apparently preparing to enter a left downwind leg for the takeoff runway when he lost control of the airplane.

The pilot had obtained his multiengine rating in 1979, when he and a partner bought the freshly reengined twin. At that time he had 424 hours of single-engine time. He flew 9.2 hours getting the rating. Since then, he had flown 10 hours in single-engine aircraft and 83 hours in the twin—an average of about 10 hours a year. His last work on single-engine procedures with an instructor had been in 1983, though he had demonstrated them as recently as 1988, eight months before the accident, while renewing his BFR.

The real cause of the engine trouble was discovered too late. A complete teardown revealed a metering needle rolling around loose in the carburetor float bowl. It had been there long enough to leave polished spots on the grainy surface of the casting—presumably since the engine was built. The needle was a spare; the carburetor had a complete metering assembly, including needle, properly installed. Occasionally, the loose needle would obstruct the fuel mixture metering assembly port, causing rough running.

Why did the pilot continue the takeoff after the engine started to backfire?

We don't know a great deal of detail about the history of the pilot's problems with his left engine, but he had mentioned several occasions of faulty operation to friends; possibly there had been others as well. Perhaps there had been occasions on which the problem had spontaneously cured itself; in fact, from the pilot's point of view it must have seemed as though it *always* did so, until the "final" repair of the damaged seal. But if the problem had been persistent and seemed to defy diagnosis, the pilot-owner of the airplane had probably made a mental accommodation to it. After all, if the engine works fine most of the time, and the airplane does after all have two of them, and you don't want to just give up flying altogether, then there's nothing to do but accept that the problem may occur and be ready to deal with it. That attitude was the mainstay of the early days of aviation, and it still has wide currency today.

If the pilot had lulled himself into accepting the problem as an irritating but constant companion, like a bunion, then his failure to abort his last takeoff may have been due to a reflex underestimation of the danger. Most likely, he was aware of the backfiring and thought it would clear up, as it had done on other occasions; probably he debated whether to abort the takeoff, but his hesitation, owing to his habitually minimizing the gravity of the problem, carried him far enough down the runway that he no longer felt he could safely abort.

At this point, he was the lone occupant of a small twin with an engine out. The field elevation was 4,700 feet, and the density altitude was about the same. The airplane should have been able to climb—and climb it did. But the pilot let it get too slow, and it departed and crashed.

In retrospect several things about this accident seem clear that may not have been so clear before it happened. The engine's symptoms suggested intermittent fuel starvation, and hinted at some kind of abnormality, possibly dirt, in the carburetor. Why did the owners not order a complete teardown of the carburetor? We don't know.

More nebulous, but equally important, is the fatal combination of a low-time pilot without recent experience and an unreliable airplane. A short hop around the patch on a clear day doesn't sound like "life on the edge." But it can be: The lack of recent experience, the high density altitude, and the very uncertainty about the severity of the engine's problems all combined to narrow the margins of safety around the pilot. He felt that everything was under control; he performed correctly at first; but a slight misstep was his undoing.

Many factors—weather, illness, fatigue, darkness, even slight and seemingly insignificant mechanical problems—nibble away at the edges of the platform of safety upon which a pilot stands. As the margins shrink, missteps, however slight, take on larger and larger significance. It is important for pilots to recognize that it is not enough to be safe as long as you make no mistakes; real safety means being safe even if you *do* make a mistake.

It's often said, only half jokingly, that twins are more dangerous than singles because, to start with, they have double the chance of an engine failure; and, whereas when the engine of a single fails you can only do one thing, with a twin you have several choices, most of them bad. The reasoning isn't strictly true: You can make bad choices in a single as well. The classic bad choice is to turn back to the runway when the engine fails soon after takeoff, rather than land straight ahead.

You Can Go Home Again
by Peter Garrison

It was a perfectly classical example of what they always tell you not to do.

The corporate Bonanza A36 took off and had a partial power loss after liftoff. The pilot, a 5,000-hour ATP, had sufficient time and composure to call the tower and say he "might" have to turn back. He climbed a little more and then attempted to make a 180 back to the field. In the perfectly classical way, the airplane spun out of the turn and crashed into a golf course. The pilot, the only person aboard, died instantly.

A flight instructor who happened to be standing beside the takeoff runway gave as detailed and probably as reliable a report as any other witness. "I first detected a loss of rpm," she wrote, "as if he was reducing power. Seconds later the engine started running rough. All this happened about 100 feet in the air. He continued climbing to about 500 feet, then started a shallow right turn, still with the engine partially operating.

"Slowly the angle of bank increased to a steep angle, and it looked as if he was getting eager to complete the turn back to the runway. Possibly using rudder to get it around. One hundred to 110 degrees around, the airplane dropped and exploded immediately."

The post-crash investigation revealed that the probable cause of the power loss had been a complete failure of the engine-driven fuel pump. Because the wreckage was consumed by fire, it was impossible to tell whether or not the electric fuel boost pump had been running.

But the aspect of this accident that concerns other pilots is not the failure of the engine. It is the failure of the pilot to complete the turn back to the airport. From the flight instructor's account, it seems that running out of altitude was not the problem here; it was spinning out of the turn, possibly because of overzealous use of the rudder.

It's proverbial that if the engine fails just after takeoff, you should land straight ahead (more or less) rather than attempt a return to the airport. The proverb unfortunately lacks a footnote explaining at what altitude it ceases to apply. Obviously there must be some altitude from which you *can* safely turn back.

A few years ago I exchanged a series of enlightening (to me) letters with Bernard H. Carson, professor of aerospace engineering at the U.S. Naval Academy. At one point he sent me a paper by one of his students, then Midshipman First Class Brent W. Jett. Jett's paper, written in 1981, is sonorously entitled "The Feasibility of Turnback from a Low Altitude Engine Failure During the Takeoff Climb-out Phase." By chance, it tumbled out of my file cabinet just as I was studying the National Transportation Safety Board report on this accident.

Jett made a theoretical analysis of the aerodynamics of the power-off turn and concluded that the ideal strategy was to make the turn at a bank angle of 45 degrees and a speed just above the stall. He then tested 28 pilots, ranging in experience from 40-hour students to a 5,000-hour military veteran, in a simulator. Initially, the pilots were not told the purpose of the experiment; they only knew that at some point in their simulated flight an emergency would occur. In six subsequent flights, they were given increasingly detailed instructions for various techniques to be used in turning back to the field. In every case, the engine failure occurred at 500 feet agl.

Of 20 subjects who made the first flight, 17 heeded the proverb and landed straight ahead. Of the other three, two stalled and spun while attempting to return to the field. (The one who succeeded in turning back and landing was a private pilot with less than 100 hours.)

All straight-ahead landings were considered "successful" by the somewhat abstract criteria of the test, which did not take terrain into account; the main requirement was that the pilot arrive at the ground under control, with a comfortable rate of descent, and land in a more or less level attitude.

On subsequent tests, subjects were told first to make a 180-degree turnback, then to make it in various specific ways—with 45-degree and 30-degree bank angles, for example, and with "full rudder," in recognition of the fact that a desperate pilot might try to hurry his airplane around a turn with extra rudder.

On the turnback without a specified technique, only 12 of 28 pilots "landed" safely. Success correlated strongly with experience level. The success rate with a prescribed angle of bank of 45 degrees was 75 percent, while with a 30-degree bank it was 95 percent (some allowance has to be made for learning; the 30-degree-bank flight was also the last test in the series).

The tests requiring full rudder, which involved cross-controlling the airplane, were inconclusive, but a lot of pilots crashed out of a 45-degree banked turn with crossed controls. This is hardly surprising; crossed controls, a steep bank and low speed are practically a standard spin-entry technique.

The difference in altitude loss between the turns made with 45-degree banks and those made with 30-degree banks was insignificant, but pilots emerged from the lower bank angle with a lower rate of descent. They also had, presumably, a little more time for communication or for trying to restart the engine; but they finished their turns 12 percent farther from the runway centerline than did the pilots who used the steeper bank.

Jett concluded with the proverb, that "if engine failure occurs just after takeoff and there is a suitable landing area ahead somewhere—continue straight ahead to an emergency landing."

He then added his own codicil to this ancient wisdom: "Turning back to the airfield after engine failure is feasible under proper circumstances. Turning with 30-degree bank, coordinated rudder, at an airspeed slightly above the stall, will yield the best combination of performance and safety."

So far, so good; but not far enough. I wish that Jett had used his conclusion, which had the support of both mathematical analysis and common sense, as his starting point, and investigated further questions that immediately pop into any pilot's mind. What is meant by "just above the stall?" Two knots? Ten? How is gliding performance in the turn affected by speed? How do wing loading and cleanness affect the outcome? (One would assume that since the issue here is minimum sink rate, not L/D ratio, heavier airplanes would require a higher starting altitude for a safe turnback.) Would pilots provided with angle-of-attack indicators do much better than those who rely on their airspeed indicators?

Jett very sensibly suggested that pilots go out and test their airplanes for themselves, measuring altitude loss in a 180-degree turn (or a 240-degree teardrop turn) and assessing the difficulty of making the maneuver safely at various speeds and bank angles. (Obviously, this needn't be done at low altitude, but it should be done below 3,000 feet so that the results are nearly representative of normal take-off elevations; it should also be done at a fairly high weight.)

Several operational issues cloud the question of whether or not to turn back. First, the quality of the terrain ahead or to the sides has to be weighed against the perceived chance of a successful turn and the pilot's often quite powerful (and reasonable) reluctance to damage the airplane. Returning to the airport may not be much help in itself; Jett's subjects emerged from their 180s 1,400 or 1,500 feet to one side of the runway; they still had to get back to the runway or a taxiway or find some other clear place to land.

Another factor, itself rather obscure and the subject of a vast number of misconceptions, is the fact that the turn back is a "downwind" turn. Many pilots erroneously believe that turning from upwind flight to downwind flight entails a loss of airspeed. It doesn't.

But if a downwind turn is combined with a rapid change of altitude it can expose an airplane to wind shear, which can be strong close to the ground, and which in some situations definitely *can* produce a loss of airspeed. But in this case wind shear would normally be in the pilot's favor, because the tailwind would diminish as he descended. More significant, perhaps, is the fact that a turn performed close to the ground in a stiff wind also produces strong visual illusions, and can lead a pilot to fumble his rudder coordination.

Finally, if you take off into a strong wind, make a rapid initial climb, and then try to turn back, you may actually overshoot the runway on the return.

A rational approach to this puzzle would be first to perform a few simple tests to find out the critical altitude for turnback for your airplane. (Remember to add at least a couple of hundred feet for positioning after the turn.)

When preparing to take off, mentally review the airport layout and the surrounding terrain, and decide what you will do in the event of an engine failure.

Finally, practice flying steadily and smoothly in low-speed maneuvers. The inexorable laws of aerodynamics don't care about your *average* speed and bank angle—only about the one momentary excursion that triggers a stall and spin.

The next case in this group involves a phenomenon called "aileron snatch." It took the crew so completely by surprise that they were briefly paralyzed. When they reacted it was too late: The airplane was upside down and heading for the ground.

Misrigged and Rolling
by Peter Garrison

The Hawker Siddeley 748 is a 46,000-pound airplane with a wingspan of almost 100 feet and a cruising speed of around 240 knots. Today, an airplane in this class would be likely to have powered controls— that is, movement of the yoke would meter hydraulic boost to the control surfaces, just as movement of the steering wheel does to the front wheels of a car equipped with power steering. In 1959, however, when the design of the 748 was laid down, purely manual controls still seemed preferable because they were simpler, lighter, and on the face of it, more reliable.

Tailoring the control forces of an airplane this size to human proportions is a complex job. The 748's ailerons have considerable aerodynamic balance, in the form both of an aft location of the hinge line and of a horn balance at the outboard end of each aileron. In addition, each aileron carries a so-called "lagging tab," or servo tab, which is geared to the aileron in such a way that deflection of the larger surface causes the smaller one to deflect in the opposite direction. The effect of this arrangement is to apply a little extra push in the desired direction to the trailing edge of the aileron.

The aft position of the hinge line lightens control forces by putting some of the air pressure acting on the aileron ahead of the hinge. A hinge at 25 percent of the chord of the aileron would give a neutral balance—no control resistance at all. The hinge line on the 748 is at 22.5 percent of aileron chord.

The trouble with a lot of aerodynamic balance is that what's just right at small deflections turns out to be too much at large ones, when the nose of the aileron pokes out of the wake of the wing and into the airstream. Ailerons of this kind consequently have a peculiar force gradient, rising to a maximum at about half travel and then decreasing again. There is still a centering force at all times; but it doesn't increase steadily with deflection, as you would expect. Mindful of this quirk, the designers of the 748 provided springs that come into action at large aileron deflections to increase the control forces.

Now, it happens that the 748's roll forces can be reduced by rigging the ailerons to float upward slightly, and this is routinely done. Reducing roll forces, however, also reduces the margin of protection against control force reversal.

All this would be of merely academic interest had not an HS 748 flying at 3,000 feet on a cargo-carrying run from Montreal to Ottawa in September 1988 suddenly rolled and plunged into the ground.

The airplane was equipped with both a cockpit voice recorder (CVR) and a flight data recorder (FDR), the first storing cockpit conversation and the second a number of aircraft parameters, including control surface positions. It was therefore easy to establish that, apparently without warning, the ailerons had suddenly gone to a full-left roll position, where they remained for about 10 seconds before returning to neutral. By the time they were neutral again, the airplane had made one complete roll and 100 degrees of another and entered a steep dive. It struck the ground three seconds after the ailerons were neutralized, but before the crew could regain control. The plane was in a 90-degree bank when it hit, with the pilot pulling back hard; the FDR recorded a maximum acceleration of 4.7 Gs.

Investigators from the Canadian Aviation Safety Board (since renamed Transportation Safety Board of Canada) determined that the cause of the accident had been a slight misrigging of the ailerons, which had caused them to go to their stops when the captain, either because of turbulence or because he wanted to show the first officer something on the ground, moved the yoke sharply to the left. The thing that's startling about the accident, however, is that in 13 seconds the crew was unable to regain control of the airplane. The forces holding the ailerons to their stops were high, but not too high to overcome; they were of the same order of magnitude as the forces normally encountered in maneuvering the airplane. Why did the captain not apply full right ailerons immediately? And why, once he had arrested the roll, did he not level the wings?

Company records indicated that the captain was an average pilot. He was cautious, reliable, quiet, and well-liked. It had sometimes been noted by examiners that he was slow to anticipate problems on check rides and during instructional flights; but his performance was good enough for his company to offer him the position of training/check pilot. He declined it, explaining that he disliked the sensations of positive and negative G forces that some training exercises would entail.

Not surprisingly, there was no record of his ever having received any aerobatic training.

The first officer was outgoing, hardworking, and a skillful pilot who consistently drew favorable comments on check rides. He, too, was not known to have had any aerobatic training.

Fatigue could have been a factor in their failure to cope with the uncommanded roll. The two men were on the third day of a grueling series of shuttle runs between Ottawa, Montreal, and Dayton that had begun on the evening of September 12. Each day required two round trips, with more than eight hours of flying and another eight hours spent attending to turnaround operations—cargo loading, refueling, paperwork, and so on. The crew took sleeping bags and mattresses with them and slept during irregular stretches of ground time. At the time of the accident on the morning of September 15, the crew had been on duty for 16 hours. The captain had slept seven hours in the past two days, and the first officer nine and a half hours.

When the captain applied left ailerons only to feel the yoke snatched from his hands, his first reaction must have been to apply right ailerons. At this point to free the ailerons would have required a force of at least 38 pounds at the yoke. To the startled pilot it may have appeared that the ailerons were jammed solid.

As the airplane went over on its back and began to descend, the pilot pulled back on the yoke, applying about three degrees of up elevator and making the airplane pitch into a steeper descent. Now the pilot saw the ground coming up at him in the windshield—not a sight that engenders cool reflection. Rolling at nearly 50 degrees per second, the 748 went though wings-level and on to a wings-vertical left bank, nose-down and picking up speed. Rising speed increased the overbalance loads; at 250 knots a 68-pound force was necessary to free the ailerons. Nevertheless, the captain—or the captain and first officer working in concert—managed to unlock them and arrest the roll. But now the visual cue of the onrushing ground was too strong and the crew's single instinctive reaction seems to have been to pull up. Singly or together, they applied a pull of more than 100 pounds to the yoke.

Given the magnitude of their physical efforts at this point it perhaps isn't surprising that they failed to apply right ailerons as well. In any case it would have been too late; the 748 could not have recovered from its 90-degree bank and 30-degree dive in the three seconds that remained before impact.

The important elements in the captain's reaction to the emergency are two. First, he was unprepared for it. The sensitivity of the

HS 748's ailerons to misrigging was known to the manufacturer, but was not strongly emphasized in maintenance manuals—which did not clearly make mandatory an inflight ailerons check after rigging—or in the pilot's operating handbook. A crew trained to recognize aileron overbalance, as HS 748 crews now are, would probably have dealt with the problem easily.

Second, there was a lack of situational awareness on the part of the captain once the uncommanded roll began. The FDR indicated a slight reduction in the deflection of one aileron during the roll, indicating that some antiroll pressure, but not enough, was being applied to the yoke; but the CVR recorded no effort by the pilot to explain to the first officer what was happening or to enlist his help in moving the control yoke.

The application of back pressure on the yoke when the airplane was going over onto its back, whether reflexive or intentional, was completely inappropriate, and was the single action that more than any other made the situation unrecoverable. But a pilot with no aerobatic experience, taken completely by surprise and without time to think, could hardly be expected to act otherwise.

Unexpected gyrations can have a peculiar effect on a pilot's perceptions. His objective sense of the airplane's position in space—the sense one has when seeing an airplane from outside—vanishes. The swirl of motion in the windscreen cannot be translated into action. The pilot may simply not know what's happening, and may be unaware of his own reflexive actions.

Aerobatic training is supposed to help pilots cope with this kind of situation. Certainly to have done a few aileron rolls, and to have practiced the coordination of rudder and elevator necessary to maintain a steady altitude while rolling, might have helped in this case. The pilot's automatic response to seeing the ground overhead would have been to push on the yoke, not pull on it.

But one should not put too much faith in a short exposure to aerobatics, or to the rote performance of "unusual attitude recoveries" required on check rides. Pilots have shown again and again that conditions that should not be life-threatening, like a door or canopy popping open in flight, often are. The missing elements in practice are surprise and fright; and these are elements that regularly prove more powerful than knowledge, training, and common sense.

The last accident in this chapter involved a particularly terrible human toll, but remained frustratingly inscrutable to investigators.

Unsolved Mysteries
by J. Mac McClellan

The Arrow Air DC-8 crash at Gander, Newfoundland, was one of the most disturbing major aviation accidents in recent years. The stretched DC-8 carried 248 soldiers of the 101st Airborne Division, who were being rotated home from the Middle East to spend Christmas with their families. The airplane had stopped at Gander to refuel for the second leg of the trip from Cairo, Egypt, to Fort Campbell, Kentucky.

A description of the accident is uncomplicated; but details of the investigation are complex, contradictory, and confusing. So little hard evidence survived the crash that the Canadian Aviation Safety Board—that country's equivalent of our National Transportation Safety Board—was unable to come to a detailed conclusion about the probable cause. In fact, several members of the board disagreed with the majority so strongly that a dissenting opinion was published along with the standard report.

What *is* known is that the DC-8 was heavy. Investigators determined that the basic operating weight—the weight of an airplane with crew, crew baggage, and cabin stores, ready to fly with everything but payload and fuel—was understated by about 1,000 pounds because Arrow Air failed to include the weight of potable water and removable galley equipment that was actually on board. But a more important miscalculation in weight was caused by the makeup of the payload—soldiers, all men, who each weighed on the average much more than the standard 170-pound passenger-weight estimate. Arrow Air procedures called for use of "actual" passenger weights when carrying troops, but the weight-and-balance numbers for the ill-fated takeoff were calculated using standard estimates. Combine higher passenger weight with some small errors in cargo weight and Canadian investigators calculated the DC-8 actually weighed 344,540 pounds, which was about 12,000 pounds more than the crew believed. But even that weight was about 11,000 pounds below maximum certified takeoff weight, and the actual CG was near the center of the envelope.

The weather is another factor, but what effect it had is impossible to know. Gander weather that day was dominated by a deep winter low over the North Atlantic. The low generated overcast skies that spit occasional light snow, very light snow grains, and very light freezing drizzle. All precipitation was very light during the entire period the DC-8 was on the ground for refueling. At the time of the early-morning accident, conditions were 700 feet scattered, measured ceiling 1,200 feet broken, 2,500 feet overcast, with 12 miles visibility in very light snow grains. Air temperature was 25°F and wind was less than two knots.

The airplane was near maximum certified takeoff weight, but conditions were in fact excellent for a heavy takeoff. The air was cold, the airport elevation only 496 feet and the runway selected was 10,500 feet long. But something went wrong. The DC-8 appeared to accelerate and rotate in a normal fashion, but it failed to climb after rotation. In fact, the airplane began to descend in a more level attitude than normal. The landing gear was never retracted.

The airplane crossed the Trans-Canada Highway about 900 feet beyond the departure end of the runway at a very low altitude and struck trees just beyond the highway. The terrain dropped away from the departure end of the runway, so the DC-8 first struck treetops 146 feet below runway elevation. Witnesses reported seeing the nose raised to a higher deck angle just before initial impact.

Because of the icy winter weather—and the frequency of large-jet crashes caused by ice-contaminated wings—early speculation about the cause of the crash centered around the possibility of ice or frost on the wings. The airplane's obvious lack of sufficient lift would have been consistent with ice-contaminated airfoils.

Early in the accident investigation, however, the wing-ice theory ran into difficulties. As the dissenting minority of the investigation board points out, nobody saw any ice on the airplane before takeoff. Two refuelers had to duck under the leading edge of the wing to connect fuel hoses, but from this vantage point, inches away from the leading edge, they reported they saw no ice.

Human-factors investigators found that the DC-8 crew had a history of professionalism and meticulous attention to detail. The flight engineer made a walk-around inspection of the airplane before takeoff and would have seen ice if it had been there. And other airplanes flying in and out of Gander around the time of the accident had not required deicing on the ground. If ice had been there, it seems somebody would have seen it.

But the investigators pressed on with the wing-ice theory and include many charts and graphs to show how ice contamination degrades the performance of an airfoil. The ice theory ultimately led the majority of investigators to postulate that the lack of lift led to a stall when ground effect could no longer support the airplane. A minority of investigators argue that there was no ice and the airplane did not stall. Again, witnesses reported the airplane to be in an unusually level attitude as it crossed the highway. Only at the very end, as it was about to strike the trees, did witnesses see the nose rise, and that certainly can be explained by the instinctive reaction of a pilot trying to reduce impact forces.

In defense of the investigators it must be pointed out that the DC-8's cockpit voice recorder did not operate, so no crew conversation was recovered. Also, the flight data recorder (FDR) was the old-style mechanical "trace on a graph" type that yields little precise flight information compared with the multichannel digital electronic FDRs in newer air-carrier airplanes. The final difficulty for investigators trying to place events in sequence was the devastated condition of the wreckage, which was consumed by an intense post-crash fire.

What was left of the airplane gave conflicting clues as to what caused the accident. Indications were that the number-four engine was producing low, if any, power. Also, marks on the flap tracks and flap lockout cylinders gave contradictory evidence of different flap settings among the flap panels on the DC-8's wing. The flap-position indicator in the cockpit read 38 degrees instead of the expected 18-degree takeoff setting. And there were indications that the thrust reversers were not locked in the stowed position. Impact marks on the wreckage indicated that the reversers had moved back at least a little from their forward locked and stowed position.

The majority says that impact damage jolted the reversers out of lock. The minority presents evidence that impact would in fact have driven the reversers forward, not aft, if they had been locked at impact. The evidence in the minority's report indicated most strongly that the number-four engine may have been in at least partial reverse. And that was the engine that was also operating at low power on impact.

The contradictory and multiple failures indicated by the wreckage could possibly be explained by a massive failure of major hydraulic and electrical systems in the airplane. Such a failure could have been caused by an explosion.

Several witnesses who saw the DC-8 take off reported seeing bright lights, or an orange glow, or an explosion, on the lower right side of the airplane. If there was an explosion or intense fire in that portion of the airplane, it could have destroyed all hydraulic lines, for example, and caused the loss of control of flaps, spoilers, and reversers, as the wreckage investigation suggests.

At least one explosives expert believed there was evidence of an inflight explosion in the right side of the fuselage. Loss of major systems could also explain why an experienced crew flying an airplane that was not climbing would have failed to raise the landing gear.

So we are left with two opinions. One—the majority's—is that tiny amounts of undetected ice on the wing's leading edge and upper surface destroyed the lift necessary for the DC-8 to climb out of ground effect. The ice effects may have been intensified by an underestimation of actual takeoff weight and a resulting miscalculation of takeoff rotation speed.

Or we can believe that the airplane had no ice (or so little ice it was undetectable), that the relatively minor miscalculations in weight had no meaningful effect, and that an explosion shortly after liftoff led to multiple system failures that rendered the airplane unflyable.

I have no reason to doubt the reported professionalism and integrity of the crew. And I cannot believe that we fly with so little margin that an amount of ice so small as to be undetectable by several observers can bring down a transport airplane. The hard evidence pointing to a bomb or some other cause of an onboard explosion is slim, but so is the evidence indicating that the crew failed to notice ice on the wings. The majority of the Canadian Aviation Safety Board elected to blame the crew. The minority argues just as vehemently that the crew was the victim of an inflight explosion. We pilots certainly make our share of mistakes, but there is much that is beyond our control.

6

Human Error

To err is human, to forgive divine. Cases involving divine forgiveness, however, don't find their way into the accident statistics.

Until something other than a human pilot drives airplanes, human error is bound to be an element in many accidents. The errors in this section are not so much errors of judgment as errors of execution. In the first, an airline captain lets his attention stray during an approach in the murky borderland between instrument and visual conditions.

Danger Zone: IFR to VFR
by Peter Garrison

Graphic artists sometimes use Mylar overlays to separate elements in an illustration. Color, for example, may be on one transparent sheet, lines and ink shading on another. When the two sheets are in perfect register, the picture jumps out at us; when one is shifted with respect to the other, bewildering ambiguities develop, and we may not be able to make sense of what we see.

When we fly visually, the world is like that perfectly registered image; sense perception fits exactly with the reality outside. The sight of a tilted horizon, the sensations of rolling or leaning, meld into a seamless and unambiguous reality.

In instrument flying the overlays slip apart, and we experience two worlds. One is the world of bodily, or kinesthetic, sensation: confused impressions of leaning, turning, rising, or falling coming obscurely from the vestibular mechanisms of the inner ear. The other is the synthesized world in the brain. Instrument flying requires that intellect triumph over sensation; we must ignore physical cues in favor of information compiled from instruments, charts, and rational processes. In effect, we put one of the Mylars aside—the one with color and shape and space depicted on it—and look only at the one with the inked lines and printed captions.

What is difficult, and occasionally deadly, is to dwell for long on the border between the real world and the synthetic one: to keep the two Mylars, misregistered, before our eyes at once. This is the situation that occurs at that moment in an approach to minimums when we lift our eyes from the security of the instrument panel and search the windshield for a clue about the reality outside. If the eye finds nothing, it returns to the instruments and we fly the missed approach. If it finds a runway, the brain instantly seizes upon the new reality and all is well. But if it finds something uncertain—a flash of pavement, two or three lights, an orange girder momentarily glimpsed— then the mind wavers as it searches for meaning in the scene. It is in that moment of uncertainty, suspended between the real and synthetic worlds, that flights are sometimes lost.

A Fairchild Metro III operated by a British Columbia regional carrier was such a flight. It was carrying a crew of two and five passengers on a scheduled flight from Vancouver to Terrace, B.C., a valley airport surrounded by high terrain. At Terrace the weather was an innocuous-seeming sky obscured, 12,000 and 25,000 broken, with two miles visibility in fog and smoke except to the south, where the visibility was half a mile in fog. A dense fog bank was rolling over the airport from southwest to northeast at the same time as scattered clouds at 600 feet and 3,500 feet were disappearing.

The weather looked worse from the air than it did to ground observers. The pilot of a Learjet that landed on Runway 15 as the Metro was beginning its approach reported that the leading edge of the fog bank sloped upward from ground level at the midpoint of Runway 15 to a height of about 200 feet above the threshold, but that there was a hole over the LDA transmitter through which an approach was possible. From the north side of the airport, where weather observations were taken, the threshold of Runway 15 could be seen; but it might not have been visible to an airplane on final approach.

The accident sequence was simple. The Metro crew flew the LDA approach to Terrace from the south. The approach course lies about a mile east of the center of the triangular airport on a heading of 342 degrees. The final approach course of an LDA does not align with a runway centerline; that is the primary difference between an LDA (localizer-type directional aid) and a standard localizer. The signal quality and guidance precision of an LDA is essentially the same as that of a standard localizer.

The circling approach to Runway 15 required a left turn of 195 degrees. Shortly after reaching the MDA, the pilot called for a missed approach; he brought the power levers forward, called for flaps up, and began to trim nose down. Initially the airplane climbed; then it stopped climbing and began to descend. The first officer twice said "Descending," with increasing concern in his voice; but the captain continued to trim nose down, and the airplane collided with terrain 22 seconds after initiating the missed approach.

The Metro was equipped with both a cockpit voice recorder and a flight data recorder, and the Transportation Safety Board of Canada was able to reconstruct the final seconds of the flight in detail. It appeared that there had been no mechanical malfunctions; the accident was a simple case of pilot error. Incidentally, the airplane also carried an altitude alert system, but it was apparently turned off.

The TSBC hypothesized that the captain had fallen prey to the "somatogravic illusion." This is something akin to "the leans," except that the leans (which for the purposes of ponderous speech are called the "somatogyral illusion") go from side to side, and this goes front and back. The basic idea is that, as Einstein once noticed in an elevator, one cannot distinguish between gravity and an acceleration due to motion. Manufacturers of simulators capitalize impressively upon the fact that accelerating forward and leaning backward produce the same set of bodily sensations. In the case of this accident, the Board surmised that the captain experienced the rapid acceleration of the missed approach as a pitch-up and trimmed accordingly, presumably while looking out the left window trying to discern the airport through the mist. The first officer, who was on the wrong side of the cockpit to see the airport and so was probably looking at the instruments, twice warned the captain that the airplane was descending, but the captain does not seem to have registered the information. You might have expected the first officer to grab the controls and pull up, but the Light Brigade were not the last to go to their ends under the influence of higher authority.

The airplane was equipped with a new flight director with which the crew had little previous experience and concerning which they had received no training or reference materials. The presentation of information on the FD was different from that on attitude indicators in the company's other Metros, and it is possible that if the captain glanced at the FD during the missed approach, he failed to take in what it was telling him.

Clearly the crew did not expect weather as bad as they encountered, and the captain's inattention to the flight instruments might be attributed to a lingering conviction that there was, as the Learjet crew had reported, a hole over the airport through which they would be able to land. The captain had repeatedly called out visual contacts with the ground during the approach, and twice referred to seeing a runway threshold. But the runway he was seeing may not have been the one on which he intended to land. In the vicinity of the localizer transmitter the captain called for full flaps, evidently committing to a landing, and perhaps having found the "hole" referred to by the Learjet. At some time during the ensuing turn, however, he must have lost sight of the landing runway in conditions of such visual ambiguity that he failed to switch back to instrument flying even after he called the missed approach.

The captain's state of mind emerges as an important factor—the most important factor—in the accident. The crew began the approach somewhat casually from a holding pattern at 16,000 feet struggling to bring the airplane down rapidly and crossing the final approach fix more than 1,000 feet above the published altitude. Throughout the approach the captain seems to have been preoccupied, repeatedly asking the first officer questions to which he should have known the answers had he been listening to the radio communications. "All these queries," write the TSBC investigators, "illustrate a certain confusion in the mind of the captain . . . and an inability to fully assimilate all the information being presented to him." On reaching the MDA the captain even said to the first officer, "Okay, yours," but then did not relinquish the controls. "The captain," the Board blandly comments, "appeared to be saying this to himself."

The captain was not a deficient pilot. The Board developed evidence that he might have been fatigued; one company employee described him as "exhausted" on the night before the accident. He had probably gotten six hours' rest that night, however, and was in good spirits the next morning. The Board finally decided that fatigue did not play a part in the accident after all. Nor were there any drugs or emotional stressors to which to attribute his apparent distraction during the final approach.

Most likely the fundamental cause of the accident was the crew's expectation of landing and lack of mental preparation (and failure to brief) for the missed approach. This could be attributed to the peculiar nature of the weather. Remember that the crew had arrived with a forecast of two miles visibility and high ceilings, and had expected an essentially visual approach. Having once caught sight of the airport and deciding to descend below the MDA (which the captain believed to be 1,240 feet, 527 feet above the surface, though it was actually 1,600 feet for the Metro's approach speed), the captain most likely continued to search the environment for visual cues while circling, and relied, as pilots do when flying by outside reference, on his bodily sensations to know if he was going up or down. The aircraft's rapid acceleration, combined with the ambiguity of visual cues in the fog, persuaded the captain that he was going up when in fact he was going down.

The accident vividly illustrates the perils of the borderland between instrument and visual flying. Its moral is, stay with instruments until you have solid visual orientation. There is no ambiguity in the instruments; but in the visual and kinesthetic world, when cues are scarce, there can be a great deal.

The next report concerns an accident that occurred under circumstances similar to those of the last: marginal visual conditions beneath a ragged low overcast. In this case, however, the pilot had ground contact; in fact he had the field in sight.

Low and Slow
by Peter Garrison

An unforecast fog hung over the hamlet and airport of Sachs Harbour, Northwest Territories. Located on Banks Island in the Beaufort Sea, Sachs Harbour lies about 400 miles north of the Arctic Circle. Although it was only September there was already thick ice on a lake near the airport, and the treeless tundra was blanketed with recently fallen snow. The fog was local; a few miles away the weather was clear. A moderate northeast wind was blowing.

At around four in the afternoon a Cheyenne approaching the airport requested weather, and the airport radio operator passed on a pilot report from a Britten-Norman Islander that had just taken off. The visibility was then one to one-and-a-half miles, with a ragged ceiling 200 to 300 feet above the ground and tops at 1,300 msl. The visibility was extremely variable, shifting from six miles down to a quarter mile at times. The sun could occasionally be seen glowing through the low stratus layer. The ceiling was higher to the west, and the visibility better. Above the stratus deck there were no other clouds.

The pilot of the Cheyenne reported that he was inbound from the NDB, which is located less than a mile from the threshold of Runway 8. Shortly after, he asked for verification of the visibility; the radio operator reported that visibility to the southwest was now four miles.

The Cheyenne pilot missed the approach and came around to try again. The report was now one-quarter mile visibility, and he missed a second time.

The pilot radioed that he would hold until 1625, and if the weather did not improve he would continue to his final destination of Inuvik. The airport radio operator continued to pass weather updates on to the pilot.

At 1625 the Cheyenne was seen flying in an easterly direction a mile or less south of the runway and at an altitude of about 200 feet. It turned left and flew across the east end of the runway, then turned again onto the downwind leg. On the turn to base the nose suddenly dropped. The airplane rolled and plunged into the ice-covered lake just northwest of the runway threshold. It sank in 35 feet of water. All five people aboard died.

The wreckage was recovered and examined by Transportation Safety Board investigators. There was no indication of mechanical failure; all evidence pointed to a stall-spin on the downwind-to-base turn.

Accident analysts like to believe in a sort of *karma*—that is, in a connection between present events and a kind of burden of past responsibility borne by the pilot. It is abhorrent to suppose that fatal catastrophes are randomly inflicted upon the innocent; much more comfortable to reconstruct a chain of misjudgments or even indiscretions that leads to the final retribution. Then it is possible to say, "Only do not do this and this, and the same fate will not be yours."

The pilot, in this case, was 25 years old. He had about 2,200 hours, with 321 in type, and 327 hours in the last 90 days. He had been on duty seven hours prior to the accident, and had had 11 hours of rest before that. He had been flying the accident aircraft for the last three days, logging 15.3 hours.

His colleagues described him as cautious, not prone to take risks, and not averse to canceling a flight because of weather conditions. He had flown into Sachs Harbour 17 times in the past year (including once the previous day); he had aborted one flight because of bad weather conditions.

Unlike some employers that turn up in accident reports, the operator of the Cheyenne did not pressure its pilots to make approaches regardless of weather conditions, and responded favorably when pilots requested copilots for airplanes that were approved for single-pilot operations.

So the pilot was under no particular external pressure to complete the landing at Sachs Harbour. He may have been motivated to try the visual approach, however, by the clear visibility in nearby areas; most likely, he may even have caught a glimpse of the runway while holding, and decided that there was sufficient space between the stratus and the ground for a circuit. He was right, furthermore, since the visibility below the clouds was sufficient for witnesses to observe the Cheyenne throughout its approach.

Investigators were puzzled by the pilot's failure to announce the attempt at the visual approach, since up to that point he had maintained communication with the airport radio station. He had given his two position reports at the beacon when the approaches were already in progress, however, and so it is perhaps not so remarkable that he didn't feel a need to inform the ground operator that he was coming down to take a look.

In trying to find a reason for the stall, investigators focused their attention upon the visual conditions at the time of the approach. The ground was a uniform, featureless, gently undulating white. The only contrasts in the area were provided by the gravel runway, the small frozen lake near its threshold, and the buildings of the nearby hamlet. In order to maintain his attitude in such an environment the pilot would probably have had to shift his scan rapidly from objects on the ground to his attitude indicator and back.

While the Cheyenne was circling the airport and on the early part of the downwind leg, visual references were ahead of the pilot and to his left. Correlating the outside view with an instrument scan was easy. Once he had flown past the threshold, however, he had to look back over his shoulder to see the runway or the town.

Evidently reluctant to go too far past the runway on the downwind leg, the pilot began his downwind-to-base turn very shortly after passing the threshold. He was about 750 yards from the centerline, and was evidently trying to turn tightly; witnesses reported that the angle of bank just before the stall seemed to be about 45 degrees.

In a 45-degree banked turn a load factor of about 1.4 Gs is necessary to maintain altitude, and the stall speed rises by about 20 percent. In the case of the Cheyenne with 15 degrees of flap, the stall speed is 74 knots in level flight and 88 knots in a 45-degree banked turn. The stalling speed is also slightly influenced by power; a sudden reduction of power might precipitate a stall in an airplane flying just on the verge. But in this case a power reduction is not particularly likely, since the airplane was slow and already below the normal altitude for a turn to base.

It's worth noting, however, that we don't generally pull 1.4 Gs on turns in the pattern, precisely because we are aware of flying slowly and of the increase in stalling speed brought about by increased wing loading. Instead, we let the nose drop a little, and the rate of descent increase. Since pattern turns are short—only 90 degrees—the airplane does not have time to build up an excessive rate of descent.

There are two situations, however, in which we cannot permit this relaxation of stick force in pattern turns. One is a tight approach in which we have to make a continuous turn of 180 degrees; another is a pattern flown at abnormally low altitude. In this case, at least the latter situation existed, and possibly the former as well.

Finally, it's possible that there is a tendency to get a little slow in patterns flown at very low altitude, because of the exaggerated impression of speed produced by flying close to the ground. Only a regular instrument scan can guard against this tendency.

Is there a chain of responsibility here? Not a very strong one, certainly. It appears that the pilot's decision to try the visual approach may have been perfectly reasonable. In the end what caused the accident was just a small but critical technical error: He got too slow.

We may say in retrospect that his getting too slow was due to the lack of visual references in the vicinity of the airport, and to his consequent inability to make his instruments a sufficiently prominent part of his scan. But was it a misjudgment to continue the approach once the pilot saw what the conditions looked like? No more, I suspect, than it becomes a misjudgment to descend a flight of stairs, if one happens to trip along the way.

A small improper movement of the controls is all that separates a low, slow approach from a fatal stall-spin. In formation flying, too, small movements of the controls make all the difference. In the next case, a landing-gear glitch leads, almost incredibly, to a midair collision.

Formation Disaster
by Peter Garrison

On April 4 of last year, a Piper Aerostar and a Bell 412 collided in midair. That was already bad enough, but by an almost incredible twist—since this is exactly the situation that is always mentioned, with grim humor, in discussions of aircraft liability insurance—they did so over a schoolyard. And as if Nemesis were not satisfied that she had arranged her calamities conspicuously enough, the sole passenger in the Aerostar was a U.S. Senator—John Heinz, of Pennsylvania.

The accident occurred seven miles from the Philadelphia International Airport (PHL). The Aerostar was operating as an on-demand charter (Part 135) from Williamsport, Pennsylvania, to Philadelphia, on an IFR flight plan; the weather, however, was clear. There were two pilots aboard because, although only a single pilot was required, the senator's staff had requested a copilot. All aboard both aircraft died, along with two people on the ground.

It was noon. The helicopter, with only the captain and first officer aboard, had just taken off from PHL and was leaving the TCA as the Aerostar was inbound on the approach. The crew could hear the radio communications between the tower and the arriving Aerostar, which had reported trouble with its nose gear.

The helicopter made a dogleg to pass beneath the Aerostar, and the first officer in the Bell reported to the tower that the gear appeared to be down. "I can tell it's down," said the pilot of the Aerostar, "but I don't know if it's locked." The Aerostar, like many other twins, had chrome-plated propeller spinners to allow the pilot to verify gear position. The gear appeared down in the curved wide-angle view provided by the spinner; but was it down and locked? Was the problem a stuck drag link or a burned-out lightbulb?

The tower cleared the Aerostar to land and alerted the airport firefighting and rescue units. Approach control routed arriving aircraft to other runways to give the Aerostar and the Runway 17 local controller a clear communications frequency.

The tower offered to inspect the nose gear if the Aerostar cared to fly by; shortly after, the captain of the helicopter said that he could "take a real close look at that if you wanted." The helicopter turned back toward the airport.

The Aerostar flew past the tower and the tower controller repeated the observation that the helicopter crew had already made— that the nose gear appeared to be down. The pilot repeated that he could see the gear reflected in the spinner, but that the problem was that the indicator light was not on.

At this point the controller instructed the Aerostar to make a left downwind leg for Runway 17, and advised the pilot that the helicopter could take a close look at the nose gear. "Okay, I appreciate it," returned the pilot.

The tower controller helped the helicopter crew locate the Aerostar, which was now at 1,100 feet, northbound on an extended downwind leg for Runway 17. Talking on the tower frequency, the pilots of the two aircraft agreed to join up at 125 knots. "Aerostar," said the first officer of the helicopter, "we're gonna pass around your right side now, take a look at everything as we go by."

About 45 seconds later, the first officer of the helicopter was heard to say, "Everything looks good from here."

"Okay, appreciate that. We'll start to turn in," said the pilot of the Aerostar. The transmission ended abruptly, with a loud noise.

Many people on the ground observed the collision, their attention initially attracted by the unusual spectacle of two noisy aircraft flying close together at low altitude. As is often the case, the reports of witnesses differed about the details; the movements and positions of aircraft are hard for untrained observers to interpret.

They all agreed, however, that the helicopter had been below and to the right of the airplane. Both aircraft were flying straight-and-level on parallel flight paths. Some thought the airplane veered to the right and collided with the helicopter; others saw the helicopter climb and collide with the airplane. The pilot's "we'll start to turn in" isn't as significant as it sounds, since the airport was to the left. All that is really known is that the two aircraft somehow collided.

National Transportation Safety Board investigators found no evidence that any of the four pilots involved had any formation-flying training or, except for one instance in which the helicopter's pilots had flown close to another helicopter, formation experience. This doesn't mean none of them did—formation flying does not produce a large paper trail—but on the other hand if either pilot had had military or airshow experience or had recently done much formation flying, it would have been known.

There are no legal recency or training requirements for formation flying, and most pilots probably imagine they could formate perfectly well if the need arose. My own experience in setting up air-to-air photography is that most pilots believe they can formate safely. Not all actually can; yet very few ever decline on grounds of their own incompetence or, for that matter, attempt to probe *my* qualifications for the job. Many pilots seem to assume that formating is part of the repertory of any good pilot, and certainly any professional.

Usually, formation flights begin with a briefing on the ground; if they are set up in the air, it is between pilots who have worked together before and have a good idea of what to expect. Close-formation operations are seldom set up on the spur of the moment, as this one was. But it is not unusual, in an emergency of this type, for one aircraft to come up to have a look at another.

In all formation flying, there is a lead pilot whose job is to fly his airplane without doing anything abrupt or unexpected, and at least one "wingman" whose job is to maintain separation and position. Navigation and obstacle avoidance are the responsibilities of the lead. In this case, it was clear enough to the participants, though the formal terminology wasn't used, that the Aerostar was the lead. It isn't necessary for the lead to see the wingman; in this case, since the helicopter was below, behind, and to the right, he couldn't. In such a situation, obviously, responsibility for avoiding collision lies entirely with the wingman.

The trailing pilot flying in the lead's blind area commonly gives regular position reports—"Okay, we're about a hundred feet behind you at about 5:30 now, coming up . . ."—both to reassure the lead pilot and to remind him not to do anything silly. In this case, however, there was very little radio contact between the two crews during the formation sequence. The pilot of the Aerostar flew along in silence, taking on faith that the whirling rotor approaching from behind him would not come too close.

Regardless of who made the maneuver that finally brought the two aircraft into contact, the helicopter obviously did come too close. It's possible that an aerodynamic interaction was responsible for the collision—when one aircraft flies close behind and below another, it tends to pitch up and the lead airplane tends to pitch down—but if the aircraft were close enough to one another for that interaction to take place, they were far from having safe separation.

Yet the NTSB criticizes the judgment of the pilot of the Aerostar as much as that of the helicopter pilot.

The NTSB report emphasizes that the Aerostar pilot had minimal experience in the aircraft and an incomplete knowledge of its systems. In addition, the Aerostar operating handbook did not address gear problems in the emergency procedures section; those instructions were grouped with a description of the hydraulic system. If the pilot had been more familiar with the airplane, he might have realized that the nose landing gear retracting linkage cannot be seen when the nose gear is down; partial doors close and conceal it. Therefore he had, as soon as he looked at the reflection of his nose gear in the spinner, all the information anyone could get: The nose gear was down. Whether the drag link had locked overcenter could not be determined by an observer at any distance from the aircraft.

It was unlikely, furthermore, that the helicopter could have given the pilot an absolute assurance that his nose gear was locked. So in the end he would have had to make the same kind of soft-field landing whatever the helicopter crew reported. And other than some bent sheet-metal, that landing entailed little risk.

Why did he accept the offer, then? Diffidence, perhaps; it came to him through the tower controller, whom, for no reason other than the force of habit, he may have been reluctant to contradict. Furthermore, he may have felt that if he declined the helicopter's offer of help and then damaged the airplane or its occupants, he would appear not to have taken every possible step to ensure the safety of his flight. He probably thought that there was at least a chance that some help would come of the closer inspection.

Yet the NTSB report states, "Therefore, the captain should have rejected the offer for the close inspection by [the helicopter]." This statement is colored by knowledge of the outcome; the pilot of the Aerostar had no reason to suppose that the helicopter would approach so close as to collide with him. A man with a tumor may as well reject the services of a surgeon because there is a chance that the scalpel will slip.

Ironically, one reads from time to time of people doing crazy things to get stuck landing gear down; you may have seen pictures of a pickup racing along the runway while somebody yanks on the wheel of the airplane hovering overhead. And there was another one involving a 310 and two cars and a rope in some weird combination. And yet these stuntmen survive, and the Aerostar pilot, who did nothing more foolish than agree to let a corporate helicopter crew take a look at his airplane, ends up the victim of, among other things, a damning NTSB report.

There's no justice.

Usually, the airplanes involved in a midair don't see one another until it's too late—or not at all. Our basic tool for ensuring separation between airplanes in visual conditions is a common vigilance. But is that enough? Some people don't think so.

"See and Avoid" or Blind Faith?
by J. Mac McClellan

The National Transportation Safety Board used the investigation of a midair collision just east of Kansas City, Missouri, to issue its most damning evidence yet against the "see and avoid" concept of collision avoidance. The NTSB says pilots may not be able to see other traffic in time to avoid collisions without some outside help—either controller assistance or automated collision-threat warning equipment in the cockpit.

The accident in question was about as simple as an accident can be. A Piper Navajo departed Kansas City Downtown Airport climbing eastbound VFR. While still climbing at 7,000 feet, the Navajo collided virtually head-on with an Army U-21 flying northwest on an IFR clearance.

The weather was nearly perfect, with thin clouds at 25,000 feet and visibility of 20 miles. The sun was not a factor for the pilots of either airplane. The lone pilot in the Navajo and the two pilots in the

U-21, an unpressurized version of the Beech King Air, all had ATP certificates, exemplary piloting records, and medical certificates issued without limitations, indicating they had good vision. No equipment failed, and the pilots were better trained and more experienced than most involved in general-aviation accidents.

The cause of the crash was obvious from the outset. The pilots were required to see and avoid each other but didn't. A reconstruction of the radar track of both airplanes didn't reveal any course or altitude deviation, which indicates that neither pilot attempted to avoid the collision. It's clear that none of the three pilots involved spotted the threatening airplane until it was too late.

With the actual cause of the crash being so obvious, the NTSB focused its attention on the viability of the "see and avoid" concept and on the Kansas City approach controllers who were handling the IFR Army U-21. The controllers watching the radarscope said they never saw the Navajo's VFR target with Mode C altitude readout climbing out of Downtown Airport directly into the path of the U-21.

The scary part of this report is how little opportunity the pilots had to see and avoid. The NTSB quotes research data indicating the human eye can reasonably see and accurately recognize a target when it subtends at least 12 minutes of arc. Visual perception is expressed in minutes or degrees of arc because our eyes can only detect objects that occupy a small portion of our total viewing angle. A small object up close, or a large object in the distance, can occupy the same portion of our total viewing arc and thus both can be identified by the human eye.

The NTSB calculated that a Navajo occupies 12 minutes of viewing arc when it is 11,000 feet away. The larger U-21 would appear the same size at 14,000 feet. But that calculation is based on the wingtip-to-wingtip size of the airplanes. If the U-21 crew had seen the Navajo at this maximum theoretical distance, it would have had 19 seconds at the airplanes' 350-knot closure rate to avoid the collision. In theory, the Navajo pilot had 24 seconds to see and avoid the U-21.

But the NTSB found it unlikely that pilots can see the leading edges of a wing of an airplane flying directly at them at the maximum theoretical distance. The Board thought it likely that visual identification of a threat would be possible only when the frontal area of the fuselage occupied the minimum viewing arc. When that calculation was made, not enough time remained for either pilot to see and avoid the collision.

Military research shows that pilots need a total of 12.5 seconds to see a threatening airplane and take action to avoid a collision. One-tenth of a second is needed to see the airplane, and an additional second is required to recognize the object as an airplane. But after recognition, a pilot needs another five seconds to perceive a collision course. Four more seconds are used up deciding how to avoid the collision. Finally, the pilot needs four-tenths of a second to move the controls, and the airplane doesn't fully respond for another two seconds. After a pilot has seen and identified an airplane on a collision course, he needs another 6.4 seconds to actually avoid the collision. The Board believes the pilots in this accident had no more than four seconds to respond after they could possibly have seen and identified the collision threat.

Using a model developed for the FAA by Lincoln Laboratory, the NTSB found that the Navajo pilot had a 27-percent chance of seeing the U-21 in time to avoid a collision, and the U-21 crew had no more than a 33-percent shot at staying alive. The model is based on an in-flight study of real pilots flying a Bonanza. The pilots flying in the project were told the study was focused on VFR pilot workload and that they were to call traffic as soon as they saw it. Unbeknownst to the pilots in the study, a Cessna 421 "threat" airplane was intentionally flown at the Bonanza.

The same study found that pilots' abilities to see, identify, and avoid threatening airplanes jumped remarkably when they were alerted to the presence of the threat airplane. Using the same model, the NTSB determined the odds of avoiding the Kansas City collision would have jumped to 96 percent if the U-21 crew has known the Navajo was in the vicinity, and the Navajo pilot would have had a 91-percent chance to avoid the collision if traffic had been called.

Why didn't the controllers see the two targets converging on their radarscopes? The NTSB has no answer. A developmental controller and a supervisor delivering on-the-job training were both watching the scope but reported they never saw the Navajo's beacon target. Yet when the NTSB replayed the recorded radar data the Navajo's target—complete with Mode C altitude—was there.

The weather was excellent, and traffic was light. The NTSB believes that scenario fits a pattern of controller mistakes. Light traffic workload may have "lulled both controllers into a reduced state of vigilance." The Board reported it had investigated five midair collisions in the last 12 months involving "light to moderate" workloads for controllers; in no case did the controllers see or perceive a collision threat. But the Board also points out that pilots suffer from the same reduced vigilance when flying IFR or when receiving radar traffic advisories in the belief that controllers are watching out for them.

The computers at the Kansas City terminal radar are equipped with a program that warns controllers when the continued track of airplanes will create a collision threat. But the conflict alert only works for airplanes being "tracked." (An airplane is "tracked" when the controller identifies it and commands the computer to begin tracking.) The radar displayed the position and altitude of the Navajo but did not track it because the pilot had not communicated with the controllers. The NTSB believes the collision could have been avoided if the Navajo had been tracked. The collision could also have been prevented if the conflict-alert logic was extended to all Mode C-equipped airplanes, not just those being "tracked."

Even after pointing out the severe limitations of the "see and avoid" concept, the NTSB still refuses to abandon it. Without "see and avoid" our air traffic system could not function. But the Board does demand supplements to "see and avoid," including automated conflict-alert computers to back up controllers and an airborne collision-avoidance system. For those reasons the NTSB found the probable cause of the crash to be "failure of the radar controllers to detect the conflict and to issue traffic advisories or safety alert to the U-21 crew," along with the "deficiencies of the see-and-avoid concept as a primary means of collision avoidance."

The NTSB is saying we can't "see and avoid" without a lot of help from the ground or automated equipment. That's a bitter pill for many an independent-minded pilot to swallow, but the NTSB certainly has a preponderance of evidence on its side this time.

The passing years have seen a steady increase in the amount of airspace kept under radar control for the sake of traffic separation. Radar control is not a panacea, however; until better collision-avoidance computer software is widely disseminated, radar still requires the vigilance of controllers who, being human like pilots, can make mistakes. It also relies on the compliance of pilots—and that's not absolutely assured either.

Flight of the Intruder
by J. Mac McClellan

Imagine the chaos that would result if we never expected other drivers to halt for a red light. Or if we wouldn't land because we refused to believe another pilot would hold short as directed. We must carry on expecting others to perform reasonably and supplement our faith in the reliability of others with constant vigilance. But that doesn't always work. It didn't work over Salt Lake City when a Mooney pilot intruded into the ARSA without a clearance and hit a Sky West Airlines Metro IV, killing all aboard both airplanes.

The Sky West Metro was inbound to Salt Lake City International Airport from Pocatello, Idaho. Salt Lake was landing to the north, using the parallel 34 runways. The Metro was being vectored on a left downwind for Runway 34L, while other air-carrier traffic was being vectored from the south for both runways. The weather was good VFR, and visual approaches were in progress.

Though visibility was unrestricted, pilots were having difficulty picking out other traffic. It was winter; the sun was low in the southern sky. Snow covered the ground and the mountains that surround Salt Lake, causing airplanes to blend into the background. The controller called the Sky West crew several times, pointing out traffic to follow and other aircraft heading for the right runway. The controller's objective was to obtain visual separation between the airplanes on final so that he could clear pilots to space themselves on the visual approach. The final-approach controller was "moderately" busy, according to his own assessment, but the several calls he made to pilots to help them find traffic increased his workload.

As the Sky West Metro was being vectored to base leg it disappeared from the radar. An expletive was transmitted on the frequency. The controllers had no idea what happened to the Metro; the final approach controller called the tower asking if local control knew the whereabouts of the Metro. None of the controllers saw the VFR radar target merge with the Metro's radar return. The wreckage of both airplanes was spread over two square miles of Salt Lake City, killing eight people in the Metro and two in the Mooney. Luckily no one on the ground was injured.

When the National Transportation Safety Board pieced together the recorded radar data, it discovered that the Metro and the Mooney had collided at 7,000 feet, about 2,400 feet above the surface. The Mooney struck the right forward section of the Metro's fuselage. The NTSB believes the Sky West crew saw the Mooney seconds before the collision, pulled up and rolled left, but it was too late to avoid impact. The expletive was transmitted on approach frequency just as the radar targets merged and is believed to be the final transmission from the Metro's crew.

The Mooney was based at Salt Lake City Municipal 2 Airport (SLC 2), located just 10 miles south of Salt Lake City International Airport. The pilot who owned the Mooney was in the left seat, and his instructor was in the right. This instructor had trained the pilot for his private certificate, and the NTSB believes the fatal flight was the start of his instrument training. The Mooney remained in the SLC 2 pattern doing touch-and-goes for about 20 minutes before departing the traffic pattern to the south.

Analysis of radar recordings shows the Mooney flew about 25 miles southeast of SLC International before turning back to the northwest. The Mooney headed straight for SLC 2, overflew that airport, and came within nine miles of SLC International before starting a turn to the left. It struck the Metro in the turn.

SLC 2 is an uncontrolled airport outside the SLC International's ARSA. The ARSA was designed to allow pilots to use SLC 2 without establishing communications with Salt Lake approach controllers. To remain clear of the ARSA, pilots using SLC 2 need to stay below 5,800 feet. Traffic pattern altitude for the airport is 5,408 feet.

The instructor owned and operated his own airplane, based at SLC International. The Mooney owner had learned to fly in the area and was based at SLC 2. The NTSB could find no reason why these two qualified pilots would not be aware of the location of ARSA boundaries. For that reason the board assumed the illegal ARSA intrusion was unintentional. The Mooney illegally flew in the ARSA for about one minute before the collision, and the NTSB believes the left turn may have been an attempt to exit the ARSA airspace.

A major question in the investigation was why the controllers didn't see the Mooney on radar and warn the Sky West crew. The Mooney was equipped with a transponder but had no Mode C altitude-reporting capability. The Mooney's "1200" VFR target was clearly recorded on the radar tape up to the point of impact.

The controller working the Sky West Metro reported that he saw a VFR target about three to four miles southwest of SLC 2, flying northwest, while he was vectoring Sky West on downwind. Salt Lake approach controllers routinely see VFR targets in the traffic pattern of SLC 2 and generally assume the airplanes are operating below the floor of the ARSA. Airplanes would be lost from radar at SLC 2 when they descended below 400 feet agl. An airplane flying touch-and-goes would disappear and reappear on the controller's display. The Mooney was in about the same place that this "normal" SLC 2 pattern work takes place and did not look unusual on the radar.

Another problem for the controller was that the unidentified Mooney VFR target had no radar data block. The computers that drive the radar display generate data blocks identifying all airplanes a controller is working. The data tag contains the identity, code, and altitude for each airplane being tracked. The computer positions the data blocks to avoid covering up data of other aircraft being tracked. But the computer will put a data block over a VFR target that is not being tracked, and that's what happened here. The data block of a Boeing 737 covered the triangle that indicated the presence of the VFR Mooney. When the Mooney's target became clear, about 48 seconds before the collision, it was directly over SLC 2. Without altitude reporting, the controller would expect the VFR target to be in the pattern at SLC 2 and under the ARSA.

The final question in the investigation is why the pilots of each airplane didn't see the other. "See and avoid" is still the primary means of collision avoidance in visual weather conditions. The NTSB determined that the airplanes collided on an angle 117 degrees relative to each other, meaning the Mooney was approaching from the right and slightly behind. Closure rate was calculated at 272 knots, or 461 feet per second.

Cockpit visibility studies of both airplanes demonstrated that the Metro pilots had about a 14-second opportunity to see the Mooney, but the Mooney pilots had 27 seconds when it would have been physically possible to see the Metro. At the time, the Mooney was approaching from the right, while the Metro crew was being directed by the controllers to look left to find traffic to follow. The Mooney pilots had the better chance to see the other airplane, but all pilots were having difficulty spotting traffic that day. When it's hard to find a Boeing 737 at three miles, it's almost impossible to see light airplanes.

In the end, the NTSB determined that the probable cause of the collision was the lack of navigational vigilance by the Mooney instructor pilot, which led to the unauthorized intrusion into the ARSA. Contributing to the accident were the absence of a Mode C transponder on the Mooney and the inability of the ATC system to provide collision protection under the circumstances of this accident.

The Mooney pilots broke the rules and died. The Metro pilots obeyed the rules and trusted in their vigilance to protect themselves from pilots who break the rules. The ATC system was busy keeping IFR airplanes apart and proved, once again, that it can do little to separate airplanes from those that break the rules and do not participate in the system.

The next accident involves a place of absolute positive control—Los Angeles International Airport—and a simultaneous failure of vigilance on the part of a controller and two aircrews. Are such failures rare or unlikely? The NTSB didn't think so.

Don't Blame Us

by Peter Garrison

In a recent period of little more than one year, there were three airline accidents in the U.S. involving collisions on a runway.

One took place at Detroit Metropolitan Airport on December 3, 1990. It involved two Northwest Airlines jets. The crew of a taxiing DC-9, disoriented and lost in heavy fog, wandered onto a runway, and had just reported to ground control that it was "stuck" when a 727 taking off on that same runway hit it.

The other two accidents took place in darkness, but with good visibility. In both cases a landing airplane struck another on the runway. At Atlanta International Airport on January 18, 1990, a 727 on roll-out overtook a King Air clearing the runway. The wing of the 727 struck the King Air, killing the pilot and severely injuring the copilot. And on February 1, 1991, a 737 landing at Los Angeles struck a Metroliner that was holding for takeoff on the runway, demolishing it, killing its 12 occupants, and igniting a fire that eventually claimed 22 more lives.

In its finding of probable cause for the Detroit accident, the National Transportation Safety Board blamed the DC-9 crew and the ground controllers for their failure to properly manage the airplane's movements as it attempted to locate its departure runway by way of a confusing series of taxiways. In the Atlanta accident, controllers ended up shouldering the blame; but, in a novel twist, the NTSB then went on to shift responsibility for controller errors to the FAA. The agency, it said, failed "to provide air traffic control procedures that adequately take into consideration human performance factors." In other words, controllers can't be expected to do everything right all the time, and so procedures must be immune to a standard level of blundering.

A finding like this would have been unlikely a few years ago. Then the NTSB did not hesitate to name as a probable cause any error by a pilot or controller, however slight or understandable. We seem now to have a kinder, gentler NTSB; its new motto is "To err is human." I suspect that in a future era, when human pilots and controllers have been phased out and robot airplanes ply the airways among automated airports, some historian will note this shift in attitude at the NTSB as an early symptom of the "mere humans" attitude that paved the way for the acceptance of machines as a superior alternative.

One of the beneficiaries of the new clemency was the controller who was working the 737 and the Metroliner that collided at LAX.

The NTSB found systemic causes for that accident too, mainly casti-
gating the FAA for failing to provide the required redundancy in air
traffic control, notwithstanding that there were not one but at least
five human beings who, under the NTSB's stringent old regime, might
have been faulted for a contributory lack of situational awareness.

The captain of the 737 first contacted the local controller at the
outer marker at 1804:44. Skywest 5569, the Metroliner, had checked
in with her a little more than a minute earlier. The essential communications during the period that all three participants shared a common frequency were as follows. (USA = USAir Boeing 737 Flight
1493; 569 = Skywest Metroliner Flight 5569; TWR = the local controller. Numerous transmissions by the tower and other aircraft have
been omitted for the sake of clarity.)

TIME: 1803:38
569: Skywest 569 at [Taxiway] 45, we'd like to go from here if we can.
TWR: Skywest 569, taxi up to and hold short of 24 Left.
569: Roger, hold short.
TIME: 1804:33
USA: USAir 1493 inside of Romen [the outer marker for Runway 24L].
TWR: Skywest 569, taxi into position and hold Runway 24L, traffic
will cross downfield.
569: 'Kay, 24L position and hold, Skywest 569.
TIME: 1805:29
USA: USAir 1493 for the left side, 24 Left.
TIME: 1805:53
TWR: USAir 1493, cleared to land Runway 24 Left.
TIME: 1806:55
TWR: Southwest 725, position and hold 24 Left.
At the time of the last transmission the 737 had already crossed the
threshold of Runway 24L. The collision was seconds away.

Flight tests conducted on a subsequent evening made it apparent
that the Metroliner holding on the runway about 2,500 feet from the
approach end was all but invisible to an approaching aircraft because
its exterior lights (which number 11 in all) simply disappear into the
general clutter of a big airport. The crew of the 737 might have dis-
cerned the lights on the runway if they had known an airplane was
there, because in ambiguous situations what the eye sees can be
strongly conditioned by what the brain expects to see.

That the controller could have become distracted and forgotten
that 569 was holding on the runway is not surprising. The airport and

surrounding airspace were swarming with airplanes (although the traffic level at the time was merely moderate for LAX). Several of them were Skywest Metroliners. The controller was distracted for some time by one taxiing commuter airplane's temporary disappearance—it had selected the wrong frequency. The data strip for the airplane on the runway had been mislaid. And, finally, the intersection of Taxiway 45 and Runway 24L was invisible from the controller's position.

It is a little surprising that of all the airplanes taxiing around the airport none noticed—or at least none noticed and reported to the tower—that an airplane was parked on the runway as the landing lights of another approached the threshold. But it may be that no crewman happened to be in a position to take the situation in.

What is more surprising is that neither the crew of the 737 nor that of the Metroliner detected the impending conflict from the sequence of radio transmissions. In the edited transcript the problem is quite evident. It is much less so in the complete transcript, because there are so many transmissions instructing other Skywest aircraft to taxi here or there or to hold short. Nevertheless, the clues are all there: One aircraft is instructed to taxi into position and hold on Runway 24 Left, and no aircraft is cleared to take off from that runway during the entire period of the 737's descent from the marker.

Pilots perform a mental editing function as they monitor the radio, highlighting certain transmissions and discarding others. "Taxi into position and hold" is a transmission that your mind might highlight when it refers to the runway on which you intend to land. Likewise, when you are parked at midfield on Runway 24L and nearly two minutes have passed since a jet reported *inside* the outer marker behind you, the phrase "cleared to land Runway 24 Left" might be expected to get your attention.

Unfortunately, pilots in busy environments often also make use of another, even more powerful kind of mental filter: They ignore all transmissions that do not begin with their own identifier.

The Metroliner did not carry flight data or cockpit voice recorders. The 737's voice recorder shows, however, that the crew was unaware of the airplane holding on the runway. They were not distracted by idle cockpit conversation; the cockpit was, in fact, "sterile," as it's supposed to be, throughout the approach. Apparently, however, both crews were operating in the maximum-filtration mode, preoccupied with their own aircraft and alert only for their own call sign in the stream of radio talk.

In the Atlanta accident, the controller failed to advise the approaching jet that the King Air was landing just ahead, even though the separation between the two aircraft was below standard; nor did he instruct the King Air to expedite his departure from the runway. Given the controller's reticence, neither pilot could have been expected to recognize that the 727 would overtake the King Air on the runway.

In Los Angeles, on the other hand, the pilots *could* have recognized the conflict if they had adjusted their mental filters to pass not only transmissions including their own call signs, but also ones pertaining to their runway. To have done so would have supplied the redundancy that the NTSB found lacking in the tower. In the past, under the rubric of situational awareness, the NTSB would have expected that kind of attention, and would have faulted pilots who did not display it. The new, more tolerant NTSB no longer demands such a high level of performance from pilots. Henceforth, we will simply have to demand it of ourselves.

Instrument flying is a matter of rote procedures; there's not much feel to it. The important thing is to adhere to the procedures; many deviations—such as being above the glideslope early in an approach—may be perfectly harmless, but others can be suddenly fatal. In the next accident, a crew used a nonstandard entry to an approach, with the permission of Air Traffic Control. That deviation was all right. It was the next deviation, which no controller would have approved, that led to disaster.

Snow Storm
by Peter Garrison

In February 1988, a corporate pilot staying in a hotel in Phoenix met a woman who, in the course of conversation, told him that she had been the fiancée of a pilot who had recently been killed in the crash of a commuter airliner at Durango, Colorado. She went on to say, casually and somewhat incautiously, that she was glad they had buried him right after the crash, because the night before the crash they had "done" a bag of cocaine, and she was worried that the autopsy would find there were traces of it in his system.

The pilot to whom the woman divulged this tidbit may have looked to her like the sort who would get a chuckle out of it, but he was, in fact, a former military drug counselor who, after getting the woman's address and phone number, called the National Transportation Safety Board to report the conversation.

The burial of the indiscreet woman's fiancé had not, however, been so precipitate as to forestall the usual toxicological tests, and the Board already knew that the captain of the Metro III that had crashed in the course of a night VOR/DME approach had had significant residues of cocaine and cocaine metabolites in his system. The captain, however, had not been flying the airplane; it was the first officer's approach that ended with the airplane striking a ridge five miles short of the runway.

The weather at Durango was an indefinite ceiling of 800 feet with sky obscured, one mile, dew point and temperature both 25°, wind calm. The flight from Denver was running late, but it had enjoyed a 15-knot tailwind and would make up more time if, as such flights often did, it skipped the time-consuming DME arc portion of the approach. Denver Center knew the routine. "If you want to proceed direct to the zero-two-three radial one-one-mile fix, that's approved," the controller volunteered, and the captain acknowledged.

That was at 7:01 p.m. local time. Twelve minutes later, center cleared the flight to cross the "zero-two-three-zero [sic] one-one-mile fix" at or above 14,000.

The VOR/DME Runway 20 approach at Durango was a special private-use approach approved for a particular carrier and not for general use. (There are more than 300 such approaches in the U.S.) The published crossing altitude for the 11-mile fix inbound was 10,400 feet. An airplane would reach the MDA (7,200 feet) in about nine miles. The descent gradient was unusually steep; a waiver of normal gradient standards had been required for its approval.

Durango is situated on a plateau at the foot of a line of high mountains lying to the northeast, and all of the normal instrument approaches are from the southwest. The MEA on V95, the airway connecting Durango and Denver, is 16,100 until a point 15 nm from Durango, where it drops to 12,000. Thus, a flight approaching Durango along V-95 practically could not be at 10,400 feet at the 11-nm fix; it would have to descend 5,700 feet in four nm. The approach therefore provided a seven-mile-long DME arc from the 096-degree radial to the 023-degree radial (the final approach course) to give airplanes a chance to descend to 10,400 feet.

But pilots and controllers are permitted to use shortcuts, and, in this case, despite the fact that the approach required a waiver even if begun from 10,400 feet, center positioned the flight to begin the approach at 14,000 feet, and the crew accepted the clearance.

Now, the crew presumably knew from their groundspeed en route that although the wind was calm on the ground at Durango, they would be flying most of the approach with a tailwind. The company operations handbook specified a 135-knot speed on nonprecision approaches; given the altitude and the tailwind, this would correspond to a groundspeed of something like 165 knots on this approach, and they would cover the nine nm to the MDA in three minutes, 16 seconds. The rate of descent on the approach would be 2,079 fpm.

In fact, however, the crew allowed the airspeed to drift up during the approach, and the groundspeed averaged around 180 knots. The required rate of descent was actually close to 2,300 fpm.

Nevertheless, they did it. Descending initially at 3,000 fpm, they reached the glidepath about 6.5 miles out—and kept on descending. They were at the MDA, probably about 300 feet below the overcast, when they struck a low hill, bounced and struck again, spreading wreckage over a 1,000-foot path. Both crewmembers died, as did seven passengers; there were eight survivors.

The minimum altitude for the segment of the approach on which they crashed was 7,600 feet, 400 feet above the MDA. The crew's final error, then, boils down to its failure to level out at 7,600 feet from the "slam-dunk" descent.

The NTSB blames the error on two factors: the first officer's flying skills and the captain's use of cocaine.

The first officer, who had logged 8,500 hours, had begun professional flying in 1974 as an instructor. After six years he moved to a job as a first officer with a commuter airline, which terminated him after a year because he displayed a lack of proficiency in his attempts to upgrade to captain. According to a flight instructor with that airline, he "demonstrated periods of inaction as the flight regime required changes in the aircraft's configuration or attitude . . ." This proved to be an eerily prescient critique.

He returned to flight instructing for another five years, then moved to Alaska, where he worked as a charter pilot until he failed a Part 135 flight check in 1986. The unsatisfactory areas were ILS and NDB approaches.

When he went to work in 1987 for the Colorado commuter airline for which he was flying at the time of the crash, the first officer was asked about his employment history for the last five years, and so he did not have to divulge his earlier termination. He did reveal on his application for a first-class medical certificate, however, that he had a record of two alcohol-related traffic convictions; but he was now an active member of Alcoholics Anonymous, so he was not disqualified.

Unlike the first officer, the 4,200-hour captain was an excellent pilot. Everyone praised his intelligence, good nature, and flying skills, and he had a reputation for being able to make up time on behind-schedule flights. The only criticism anyone made of him was that he tended to taxi too fast.

The Board's investigation revealed, however, that he had been involved in various minor scrapes that could be interpreted as indicating a certain disregard for rules and regulations. He and a woman traveling as his wife (she wasn't) had once made an angry scene over baggage at an airline service counter in Denver. They had been traveling as nonrevenue passengers. Bogus wives and angry scenes are both in violation of company and industry rules.

He had also, in his zeal for saving time, once fueled an airplane himself, and once allowed a passenger to board while an engine was running—both infractions of company rules. On his medical history questionnaire he had failed to reveal a series of traffic violations that included a license suspension and two accidents. Finally, he had once destroyed a Cessna 182, injuring a passenger, while attempting a downwind landing.

But his big problems involved cocaine. From the testimony of a close acquaintance of the captain, it appeared that he had become involved in 1987 with a woman—who has already appeared in the story as the bogus wife and the fiancée—and that his use of cocaine was connected with her. "She's like a sickness," the captain allegedly told his friend. "It's all a disease and there is no cure."

According to the close acquaintance, the captain's behavior had changed radically between 1986 and 1987, though the acquaintance thought it might not have been apparent to someone who did not know him very well. Indeed, airline personnel and the medical examiner who had performed the captain's recent medical examinations were unaware of anything unusual.

Readers of NTSB accident reports who have become accustomed to considering nasal decongestants as plausible contributing factors to aircraft accidents will have no difficulty believing that cocaine might have played a part in the captain's failure to notice that the first officer was descending below minimums. Nevertheless, a refresher on the pharmacology and sociology of the drug may be in order.

Cocaine is an extract of the leaves of a South American plant called coca. When ingested, the extract has a tonic effect, and in Latin American countries the leaves are chewed or made into a tea. The substance found its way to Europe in the sixteenth century along with other novelties and treasures from the New World; it was used both medically, especially as a topical anesthetic, and recreationally as a stimulant, and not regarded as particularly pernicious. In fact, coca extract was an ingredient of the original Coca-Cola recipe; hence the name.

Cocaine became a "controlled substance" early in this century. It disappeared from Coca-Cola, but entered the pharmacopoeia of the recreational drug user. Always expensive, it became the prestige drug of the 1970s. Some of the bloom went off the rose when various sports and entertainment figures incinerated or inadvertently killed themselves with cocaine, and the profile of the "average" user has changed in the 1980s. Although coke is still the pause that refreshes among many moneyed non-squares, the big issue today is the traffic in and use of the drug among the poor in the more potent form of "crack."

Authorities on these matters distinguish between cocaine, which is a "reinforcer," and, say, heroin, which is addicting. Cocaine does not produce physiological dependence. Instead, like some kind of infinite chocolate, it makes those who have it want more. Dope-snorting apes in laboratories have been found to choose cocaine over both sex and bananas, no matter how long they have been deprived of the wholesome alternatives. Humans are no different.

Unfortunately, the drug wears off quickly, and the debt to mortality must be paid. Fatigue returns in the form of a "cocaine crash." Heavy users find the crash depressing and escape from it by taking more cocaine.

While the captain's use of cocaine makes this accident memorable, no one asserts that he was the victim of some sort of "reefer madness" during the flight. He did not mistake a mountain for a runway or an artificial horizon for his mother's arms. The drug residues in his system did not in all likelihood directly affect his behavior; what affected it, if anything, was the fact that he had been up all night. Indeed, if the element of cocaine use were removed from this accident, it would remain very similar in outline to at least two other recent commuter airline accidents in which the inexperience or incompetence of a first officer and the failure of a captain to monitor the other pilot properly led to an accident.

Is a pilot who is exhausted because he stayed up all night taking cocaine (how much, we don't know) different from a pilot who devoted the night to amorous endeavors or who was kept up by too much coffee or by the aftermath of a visit to a Bactrian restaurant? The NTSB doesn't know. It has asked the DOT to study the effects of various drugs upon specific tasks involved in the operation of vehicles, and such studies are now underway. Whether they will be successful in drawing a clear line between the effects of drug use on piloting skills and those of fatigue, stress, illness, anger, or age remains to be seen.

The subtlest kind of error is one in which the pilot does everything right, but in terms of some wrong assumption about the circumstances. The basic error may be one of forgetfulness or, as in the next accident (whose crew fortunately survived), of a subtle misinterpretation of a chart.

Mistaken Identity
by Peter Garrison

I'm driving my car. The top is down, the sun is shining, the radio is playing. I'm daydreaming. I reach down to turn on the radio.

This is a common enough experience, like calling your son by your daughter's name or your dog by your husband's or wife's. Psychologists debate the deeper significance of mixing up names, but I think a good many of these errors come about because life situations bear various structural resemblances to one another, and one often acts in accordance with the general structure of the situation, and not its fine detail. Utterances involving tones of endearment or condescension, for example, may be associated in your mind with certain names, and so you may use the wrong name when addressing another person with those tones. Likewise, a vague sense of restlessness or boredom in a car may be associated with a desire to turn on the radio—even when it's already on.

The common structural threads among life situations are the stuff of habit. They simplify our lives, freeing our minds to do something other than constantly cross-check the accuracy of our assumptions about the present situation. They save us a lot of trouble—and sometimes get us into a lot.

Because of the same kind of inappropriate automatism that makes me turn on a radio that's already on or makes you address your dog as "Kim, darling," a Boeing 737 collided with terrain during a daytime localizer approach to an airport at Unalakleet, Alaska. The jet struck a hill seven and a half miles from the runway threshold and broke apart. There were no passengers aboard; one flight attendant was seriously injured, while the flight crew and the other flight attendant survived with minor injuries.

The captain was baffled by the crash, since he was certain that he had flown the approach according to the specifications on his Jeppesen approach plates. The first officer, who was new to 737s and who was flying with this captain for the first time, was likewise unaware of the cause of the accident. Only after reviewing the cockpit voice recorder (CVR) tapes did the crew understand the mistake they had made.

The localizer approach calls for crossing the VOR, which is about three and a half miles from the airport, and proceeding northwestward to intercept the localizer at Drige Intersection, the final approach fix five miles from the threshold. You then fly the localizer outbound, make a procedure turn within 10 miles and above 3,000 feet, and track inbound on the localizer, crossing Drige again at 1,500 before descending to 500 at the NDB 2.3-mile fix. The MDA is 360 feet.

The weather at Unalakleet was 500 overcast with one-and-a-half-miles visibility. While approaching the VOR, the captain, who would be the flying pilot, briefed the first officer as follows:

"Plan the localizer 14, you got it out, via Unalakleet which we're heading to the feeder fix, 291, 6.1 miles, which takes us to Drige. Drige, I'll just do a quick procedure turn headed back in, so I'm not going to straighten out on the thing, the localizer, just teardrop and come right back around and land. Three thousand 'til we're inbound. Drige at 15. Five at the 2.3-mile fix, then down to 360, which is corresponding to 339 above. We got good enough viz . . .."

All of this was correct. After briefing the first officer on the missed-approach procedure, the captain encouraged him to speak up if he saw anything he didn't like or had any questions.

The 737 crossed the VOR at 4,500 feet and passed over Drige outbound about 90 seconds later. The captain continued to descend while the first officer lowered 10 degrees of flap. Two minutes after crossing the localizer, the captain began a right turn. During the turn, the following rather elliptical exchange took place:

FO: Going to 1,500 inbound.
Captain: Fifteen 'til 10 DME.
FO: You got the 10 in right.

The first indication of the error that would lead to the crash was the captain's reference to "10 DME." In fact, Drige, with a crossing altitude of 1,500 feet, was at five DME, not 10. (The DME in question is the localizer DME, not that of the Unalakleet VOR; at this point the airplane was about 13 miles out.)

The meaning of the first officer's "you got the 10 in right" is unclear; in any case the captain did not respond to it, but merely called for landing gear a few seconds later. About halfway through this turn, the airplane, which had been holding level slightly above 3,000 feet, began a descent. This was a procedural error, since they should not have descended below 3,000 until completing the procedure turn; but it was inconsequential, since the captain, who had flown into Unalakleet before, probably knew that during the procedure turn the airplane was over the sea.

About a minute later the captain said, "Fifteen hundred to 10, that's what we're shooting for." Shortly afterward the airplane intercepted the final approach course, and the captain said, "Eh, comin' up on 10, let's go flaps 30 . . . There comes the 10 to 1500, 500 is what we're shooting for." At this point the airplane was descending through 1,740 feet. "Two point three DME," the captain said, referring to the next fix.

There was little further conversation. The first officer called a thousand feet, verified "altimeters and instruments cross-checked," and then said "Ground contact," apparently in a normal tone of voice. "Okay," the captain said. The 737 hit rising terrain two seconds later.

The NTSB's investigators tried hard to figure out what had given the captain the idea that Drige was at 10 miles rather than five. Their hypotheses center upon some differences between Jeppesen and NOS approach plates.

One difference is the typography and phraseology of the notation limiting the distance from Drige within which the procedure turn must be completed. Jeppesen reads "10 NM from DRIGE," while the NOS charts say "Remain within 10 nm." The Board surmised that at a quick glance the Jeppesen text, which has the word "from" in small type, might have caused the captain to associate the "10" with Drige. This is unlikely, however, since the format of the approach profile is familiar to all pilots who use Jeppesen charts, and even if the text were in Greek they would know that the subject of the notation is the procedure-turn distance.

More convincing, I think, is the observation that Jeppesen and NOS put circles on their charts, but the sizes and purposes of the circles are different. Jeppesen's "reference circle," five statute miles in radius and centered on the airport, is intended, according to the legend, "to emphasize obstructions and other information close to the airport."

The NOS, on the other hand, provides "distance rings," generally 10 nm in radius, centered on the IAF, not the airport; their purpose is to inform users that everything within the ring is mapped to correct cartographic scale. (And I'll bet you thought the whole NOS approach plate was to scale.)

The captain flew Air National Guard C-130s as well as airline 737s. For his ANG flying he used NOS plates, but for his civil flying he used Jepps. Now, Drige happens to lie exactly on the Jeppesen reference ring, the difference between the "center" of the airport and the location of the localizer DME antenna exactly compensating for the difference between statute and nautical miles. The Board suggested that the captain could have unconsciously identified the Jeppesen ring as the NOS one, whose radius would have been 10 nautical miles rather than five statute ones, and so began to think of Drige as a 10 DME fix.

Neither the Board nor the pilot himself would blame his error on fatigue, stress, or the vagaries of instruments. The captain, and I think this very honorable of him, simply could not understand how he made the mistake, and offered no excuse for it.

An important sidelight to this remarkable case of mistaken identity is the role of the first officer. In principle he is supposed to watch the pilot's actions for just this type of mistake. Both pilots had taken their cockpit resource management courses. But because the first officer was new to 737s and by his own admission was still kept extremely busy by his lack of familiarity with the airplane, his position was not that of a coequal with the captain; he was an apprentice, and to some extent he may have felt himself to be learning the approach rather than criticizing it.

The ability to catch subtle errors can be affected by one's sense of one's position vis-á-vis the object of one's criticism. Obviously, people are willing to believe all kinds of crazy things uncritically on the say-so of various specious authorities; but the copilots of airplanes have to cultivate a more thoroughgoing skepticism. They need a kind of *ad hoc* hostility that makes them react to every move of the flying pilot with a mental "Oh yeah? Sez who?"

The next accident is similar to the last, but involves, rather than a misread chart, a mistuned radio and a somewhat lax approach to cockpit resource management. As in many cases of errors of situational awareness, the clues are there, but the mindset of the crew prevents their noticing them.

Tuned for Disaster
by Peter Garrison

On a February evening, a little after seven, a Cessna 421 took off from Missoula, Montana, for a charter flight to Helena, Montana. The route of flight was direct Missoula, Victor 2 via the Drummond VOR to Helena, with an assigned altitude of 17,000 feet. The weather at Helena was deteriorating, but it was still good—15 miles visibility in snow flurries, with broken clouds at 3,000 feet and an overcast layer at 20,000—when, 40 minutes later, the airplane slammed into a mountain 12 miles southeast of the Helena airport.

The following transcript of ATC communications covers the last minutes of the flight. (17S = the 421; APP = Helena Approach Control; 272 = a National Guard aircraft.)

TIME: 1945 MST

17S: Helena Approach, this is 517S with you descending to 13,000, we're 36 DME.

APP: Twin Cessna 517S, Helena Approach, cleared to the Helena VOR, maintain 13,000, expect no delay, report 15 DME. Altimeter 3020.

17S: Okay, we're cleared to the VOR, maintain 13,000, expect no delay.

TIME: 1948

APP: Twin Cessna 17S say DME.

17S: 7S, 20.6.

APP: Thank you sir.

17S: And 7S level 13,000.

APP: Twin Cessna 17S, roger sir, you can plan on the ILS approach, sir, I have twin traffic outbound underneath you.

17S: 7S.

APP: Twin Cessna 17S cleared to the Hauser radio beacon via the VOR direct Hauser. Maintain 13,000, expect lower upon crossing the VOR.

17S: Okay, we're cleared to the Hauser beacon via the VOR and maintain 13,000.

APP: G51272 report crossing the VOR.

272: 272.

17S: 517S will do.

TIME: 1953:37

17S: Approach, we've crossed the VOR westbound.

APP: Cessna 17S say DME.

TIME: 1953:46

17S: We're showing 4.3.

APP: Twin Cessna 17S cleared for the ILS approach via the VOR direct Hauser. Report Hauser outbound please.

17S: Okay, 517S is cleared for the VOR, pardon me, the ILS approach via the VOR outbound to Hauser and we're to report, report Hauser.

17S: Ibis is 517S, we're leaving 13,000 now for 7,000.

APP: Twin Cessna 17S, roger sir, report leaving 10,000.

TIME: 1958

17S: This is 517S, we're procedure turn now Hauser.

APP: Twin Cessna 17S, so you're procedure turn outbound or inbound sir?

17S: Yeah, we're turning inbound now.

APP: Twin Cessna 17S, say altitude leaving.

17S: We're leaving 11,000 now.

APP: Twin Cessna 17S thanks, report leaving 10,000 and the outer marker please.

TIME: 2000

APP: Twin Cessna 17S, say DME. Twin Cessna 17S, approach. Twin Cessna 17S, approach . . .

The pilot, a 52-year-old ATP with 4,900 hours, was in the right seat and operating the radios. The copilot, also an ATP with 2,020 hours but little multiengine experience, was aboard the flight for purposes of familiarizing himself with the 421; he was in the left seat and was flying the airplane.

It didn't take long to figure out what had happened. For the intended approach, the radios would be set up as follows: number-one nav, Helena ILS; number-two nav, Helena VOR, 88 degrees outbound course; the ADF on Hauser NDB; and the DME on the Helena VOR. In fact, the number-two nav was set for the Drummond VOR, 51 nm west of Helena. The outbound course was set for 88 degrees. The Helena VOR frequency is 117.7; Drummond's is 117.1.

Presumably one would navigate the route by starting outbound from Missoula with the Missoula VOR in the number-one nav and Drummond in the number-two; then switch the number-one to Helena after passing Drummond. This all works naturally and provides a nice economy of effort until it's time to start the approach; then you have to reset number-one to the ILS and the number-two to Helena.

Once you're near Helena, mistaking Drummond for Helena doesn't necessarily get you a lot of dramatic needle swings; the bearing from Drummond to Helena is 073 degrees, and so if you set the number-two nav course to 088 you just appear to be a bit to the right of course—the same indication you would have if you slightly overshot the Helena VOR before turning to a heading of 088.

To judge from the reconstructed radar records, the flight must have tracked outbound from the Drummond VOR all the way to Helena. The track is straight, and coincides perfectly with the Drummond 077 radial; it's the track an autopilot would make while following the 073 radial with a four-degree error in the VOR receiver.

Possibly the two pilots didn't make a clear division of labor on the tuning of radios, so that the pilot thought that the copilot had changed the number-two nav frequency. Or perhaps some discussion—a fair amount of peripheral talk might be expected on a flight like this—interrupted the pilots' radio-tuning routine. In any case, the pilot, sitting in the right seat in the darkened cockpit, misread the frequency on the number-two radio; investigators pointed out that the radio installation made it difficult to see the top third of the frequency readout from either pilot's seat.

When the pilot selected the 088 course on the number-two nav, the needle swung right and the copilot turned the airplane to a heading of about 105 degrees to intercept. Before he could intercept the Drummond 088—it lay 10 or 15 miles to the right—the ADF needle swung slowly abeam, indicating that the Hauser beacon, which lies on the ILS, was off the left wing. At this point the copilot began a procedure turn to the left. The airplane hit a mountain a few seconds later.

You're supposed to verify the audio identification of VORs after tuning them, but few pilots do. (I remember a dull voice in a Cessna 175 from years ago: "Hector . . . VOR . . . Hector . . . VOR. . .") With modern electronic tuning, misidentification is considered a remote risk; if you have the right frequency in the window, you should have the right VOR. That the pilot mistuned the VOR was probably due to a combination of factors; lack of a precisely prescribed crew routine may have been one of them. No situation is more conducive to error than that of a pair of pilots flying an airplane together, improvising their cockpit resource management strategies as they go along.

Given, however, that this kind of mistake is bound to occur from time to time, can pilots be expected to detect it and recover before it's too late?

Judging from its position report at 1953:46, the flight apparently missed the Helena VOR by about four nm. At this point they must have realized that they had been tracking outbound from Drummond when they should have been inbound to Helena. The pilot now presumably looked at the number-two nav and read the frequency as 117.1—that of Helena. Perhaps he supposed that the copilot had already switched frequencies; in any case, it was probably now that he set the OBS to 088. The needle swung right.

What did the pilot, or pilots, now think? They must have concluded that they had passed north of the VOR, not south of it as they had in fact done. So they turned to intercept the outbound radial that led to the NDB. The ADF now pointed ahead and to the left. It was more to the left than it should have been, but that was a rather subtle point; as far as the pilots were concerned, the navigational picture made sense. As they flew along, the needle swung more to the left; that was logical, too. In principle, if the NDB stayed on the left they should start the procedure turn when the NDB was about 20 degrees behind the left wing, and that's exactly what they did.

There's only one flaw in this picture. If they hadn't crossed the radial by the time they were abeam the VOR, the NDB ought to have been off their right wing, not their left. On the other hand, if the NDB went by off the left wing, they would have to have crossed the radial (the localizer, too, for that matter). And they hadn't.

You practically have to draw a map on a piece of paper to see the geometry of the situation; and instrument flying is not done on a mental map, but rather by a chain of steps that, if properly executed, are sure to get you where you want to go. The pilots can hardly be faulted for failing to discern the inconsistency between their supposed position and the indications on the instruments; after all, they had, so far as they knew, made all the right moves, touched each of the links in the chain, and so, except for the error introduced by their failing to pass overhead the Helena VOR, they had to be where they thought they were.

In a nonradar environment, the IFR chain can be unexpectedly fragile. Did the public servant who assigned frequencies to the Drummond and Helena VORs ever stop to wonder whether their similarity could lead to confusion? Probably not; a one is a one and a seven is a seven. Did the installer of the avionics take note of the fact that a one and a seven might look the same from the pilot's viewpoint? Probably not; the installation, no doubt, was of some approved and standard variety. So everything came down in the end to the two pilots routinely fingering the rosary of IFR procedures, and making a tiny slip of the kind pilots make every day, but for which few pay so dearly.

The next two reports involve forgetting to set flaps for takeoff, an oversight that would be inconsequential in a light airplane, but is significant in a jet, where certain takeoff procedures and speeds are strictly adhered to. In each case, checklists and warning systems failed to do their jobs.

Flap Trap
by Peter Garrison

On August 31, 1988, a Delta Air Lines 727 taking off from Dallas-Fort Worth International Airport crashed at the end of the runway, taking out a localizer antenna, destroying the airplane, killing 14 people and seriously injuring 26. The National Transportation Safety Board concluded on the basis of physical evidence, and despite contrary testimony by the crew, that the flaps had not been extended for takeoff.

This was not the first jet airliner to attempt a takeoff with its flaps up, nor even the first to do so recently. Such accidents invariably raise issues of system design, and, more important, of crew performance; and so, despite their superficial similarities, each is worth studying for what it reveals about the chinks in our armor against error.

It may seem strange to pilots familiar only with light airplanes, which take off equally easily with or without flaps, that taking a jet airliner off without flaps can have such a disastrous effect.

The reason is that jets generally, because they are eating up runway very rapidly as they accelerate, perform a strictly ritualized kind of takeoff, with rotation coming at a particular speed, which is calculated for each loading, and with a specific target pitch angle for initial climb. A jet takeoff is a maximum-performance takeoff, roughly corresponding to a short-field-with-obstacle takeoff in a small airplane.

A 727, or any other jet, is capable of taking off with its flaps retracted, but the required rotation speed and initial pitch angle are quite different from the usual ones. The danger arises when the no-flaps takeoff is inadvertent—which is invariably the case. A no-flaps takeoff performed with the speeds and pitch angles required for a flaps takeoff is almost certainly doomed to failure.

Jet airliners are provided with warning systems that are supposed to alert the crew when the airplane is on the ground, the engines are spooled up beyond a certain power setting, and the flaps are retracted. On the accident airplane, the warning failed to sound; investigators traced the failure to a single microswitch in the throttle assembly. The switch showed some evidence of corrosion and, more important, its triggering arm had been slightly bent, so that from time to time, in a random way, the switch failed to operate.

The warning system on this airplane had previously been squawked for intermittent operation; service personnel had replaced the horn, which was the most accessible item in the system and so the first to get replaced when an intermittent problem of uncertain origin turned up. The defective switch had gone undetected.

There was one other mechanical system on the airplane that could indicate, in an indirect way, that the flaps were not down: the auto pack trip arming indicator light. The cabin air conditioners—called "packs"—are designed to shut down in the event of loss of power on an engine during takeoff; the idea is to conserve maximum power on the remaining engines by shutting off bleed air. The auto pack trip system automatically arms as power is increased with flaps extended and the gear struts compressed—in other words, at the start of the takeoff roll.

The second officer (flight engineer), who sits behind the captain and first officer and monitors the airplane systems, noted that the auto pack trip arming light did not come on during the takeoff roll; but since this was not a no-go item for this takeoff, he did not announce it to the captain. Even if he had, the captain might very likely have assumed, as the second officer did, that the failure was local to the auto pack trip circuitry, and not that it betrayed something about the flap position. After all, all three crewmembers firmly *believed* that the flaps were in the correct position for takeoff.

How did they come by that belief? Delta crews normally judged flap position from an indicator and from the position of the flap handle. More important, perhaps, flap extension is a checklist item, and if you have completed the checklist it follows that the flaps must be down.

The cockpit voice recorder (CVR) preserved the recital of the checklist. Sure enough, there it was:

"Shoulder harness."

"They're on."

"Flaps."

"Fifteen fifteen green light."

"Flight controls."

"Tops and bottoms are checked . . ."

And yet the flaps were up.

The crew had started engines at 8:32 a.m. CDT. They started to taxi, then held for several minutes at a taxiway intersection. The delay occasioned some joking:

"How about lookin' down our way while we still have teeth in our mouths?"

"Growing gray at the south ramp is Delta . . ."

At 8:36 the captain decided to shut down the number-three engine to conserve fuel. Two minutes later they were rolling again, and the second officer resumed the taxi checklist up to a break that occurs after the stabilizer trim has been checked, but before the flaps. Normally, the flaps would be lowered during taxi, and before this point.

A flight attendant came into the cockpit and several minutes of casual conversation ensued. There was more joking about the long taxi distance and the delays; one crewmember suggested that here at DFW, American Airlines' home base, they let all the American airplanes take off first. There was a discussion of egrets and their reasons for sitting on the backs of cows, and of the comical conduct of the gooney birds on Midway Island.

Finally, at 8:57, the flight was number four for departure. The captain called for restart on the number-three engine. Less than a minute later, the tower cleared the 727 to taxi past several other airplanes into position for takeoff.

Having waited, the crew now had to hurry up. The second officer rapidly ran through the remaining callouts on the taxi checklist, which included the flap-position check. The first officer verified the flap position, but the second officer did not, nor was he strictly required to do so.

The flight started rolling at 8:59:30. It rotated 36 seconds later, and after another eight seconds the stick shaker cut in.

"Something's wrong!" the captain exclaimed. His voice was followed by the repeated, muffled bang of compressor stalls.

"Engine failure!" said the first officer. "We got an engine failure!"

Five seconds later, the captain said, "We're not gonna make it." The airplane was rocking uncontrollably from side to side. Eight more seconds passed, and the captain said, "Full power."

The first impact came half a second later.

Despite the crew's certainty that the flaps had been in the proper takeoff position, the NTSB concluded that they had been retracted all along; that the airplane had pitched up into a stall during rotation, causing the uncontrolled rolling motions; and that the wing stall had disturbed the airflow into the engines, triggering the repeated compressor stalls. Although the captain said that he called out "Full power" only to confirm that he had already applied power, the Board concluded, on the basis of the airplane's performance and of the first officer's testimony that he had seen both of the captain's hands on the yoke, that power had not been increased much before impact. (Maximum power would have exceeded the jet's takeoff power by about 25 percent, and might have prevented the accident.)

The Board further noted that the proper procedure—which the captain knew—for stick-shaker activation at takeoff was to lower the nose to still the shaker. The captain had not done this, presumably because he felt he was too close to the ground to lower the nose. Finally, the Board suggests that if one crewman had checked the airplane configuration on perceiving the stick shaker, he might have detected the flap problem and set the flap handle to the takeoff position. This action would have deployed the leading-edge devices immediately, greatly increasing the wing's stall margin and restoring controllability.

"What might have been" is a famously sad phrase, and a vain one. Speculation about what the crew could have done to salvage the situation in the space of a few frantic seconds is quite idle; for every crew that reacts with brilliant aplomb to an emergency, nine probably hesitate, fumble, or misinterpret the situation. More significant is the analysis of what led to the flap-position error in the first place.

Since the crew did perform the checklist correctly, the NTSB concluded that the first officer must not actually have checked the flap position while responding to the second officer's challenge, or may have looked at the handle and indicator and seen what he expected to see and not what was really there.

The Board connects this lapse with laxity in cockpit discipline, which it in turn lays at the feet of the captain and the airline. Delta, the Board says, erred in allowing captains too much latitude in determining their own cockpit style. In this case, the Board said, "the first officer acted as the social element in the cockpit," while "the captain only occasionally entered the conversation." The first officer's routine of pretakeoff duties was repeatedly interrupted by "nonrelevant conversation." (This cockpit dynamic is curiously similar to that of the Air Florida 737 that crashed into the Potomac; that accident too involved an omitted checklist item.)

"Had the captain exercised his responsibility," the Board concludes, "and asked the flight attendant to leave the cockpit or, as a minimum, stopped the nonpertinent conversations, the 25-minute taxi time could have been used more constructively and the flap-position discrepancy might have been discovered."

While it's probably unrealistic to expect flight crews to act like dormant robots during long periods of delay, it is true that any interruption in routine is potentially disruptive. Even a private pilot holding for 20 minutes for an IFR takeoff clearance is in slightly increased danger of finding, when he finally gets going, that he has failed to latch the door, turn on the fuel pump or activate the transponder. Pilots need to be aware of this danger, and to take special care to neutralize it.

The thick NTSB report on the accident, which runs to 132 wretchedly edited pages, finds its way from the remarkable coincidence of a simultaneous failure of human observation and electrical contact to a broad criticism of Delta Air Lines' management and training procedures and the FAA's oversight of both. The Board did not recommend greater redundancy in the design of cockpit warning systems, although a second microswitch could have prevented this accident, while three (much more expensive) crewmembers did not. Nor did it suggest that other flight crews in the long takeoff queue at DFW might have been expected to notice a 727 with its flaps retracted, and comment upon it.

Whenever an accident occurs, it creates the impression that the events leading to it must have been inexorably linked. The massive official investigation of an accident, and the ponderous documentation it produces, likewise imply that if certain steps are taken, similar accidents will be prevented in the future.

In fact, airline pilots joke with flight attendants during long holds every day and still manage to conduct their flights safely; on the other hand, pilots who maintain silence and uninterrupted concentration also make mistakes.

Stolid, silent crews do not necessarily always perform better than garrulous, sociable ones. Really, human beings are just like microswitches: capable of unpredictable errors. No amount of cockpit resource management and FAA oversight will alter that.

The similarities between the foregoing accident and the next one are remarkable; they could almost be two accounts of the same accident. The NTSB report notes that a crew could fly out of an inadvertent no-flap takeoff; the bigger problem is escaping from the erroneous belief that the flaps are already down. Most likely many other crews have taken off with flaps up, understood the situation before it was too late, and scrupulously avoided reporting their mistake.

Sins of Omission
by J. Mac McClellan

Cockpit errors of omission are doubly deadly. The important item forgotten threatens the safety of the flight, and, maybe worse, the omission disrupts our crisis-solving ability because we assume we have already accomplished the normal and necessary procedures. The crew of a Northwest MD-82's sin of omission: They forgot to set the wing slats and flaps for takeoff from Detroit.

The NTSB expended great effort to be certain the flaps and slats were fully retracted as the stretched DC-9 started its takeoff roll. The digital flight-data recorder showed the flaps were up, the flap handle was found in the up position, and damage marks on the flap tracks indicated the flaps were fully retracted at impact. Most telling of all was the flight path of the airplane. If slats and flaps had been set, the MD-82 should have cleared its impact point by 600 feet. The most shocking aspect of the report is that the crew of Flight 255 could have safely continued the takeoff without slats and flaps if their flying technique had been appropriate.

The crew's first indication that something was wrong came at rotation. The captain began lifting the nose at the calculated VR speed of 144 knots. Normally the airplane would lift off at six to eight degrees nose up, but it didn't. The captain continued to rotate until reaching an angle of between 11 and 12 degrees nose up. The tail of an MD-82 will strike the runway at 11.7 degrees, but there was no evidence of a tail strike.

As the airplane lifted off, it was accelerating through 168 knots. The computed stall speed for the airplane's weight with slats and flaps retracted was 170 knots, so the MD-82 was barely flying. A half second after liftoff the stall-warning stick shaker operated and continued until impact.

Imagine the confusion in the cockpit. The speed was already 10 knots above the engine-out safety speed (V2) of 158 knots, but the airplane wouldn't climb. The stick shaker was rattling both control columns, both throttles were pushed to their stops, and the airspeed was increasing.

The MD-80 series of airplanes have a complex stall-warning and prevention system. When the airplane is in takeoff configuration with the wing slats in their normal "mid-sealed" partially extended position, the stall-warning computers will automatically fully extend the slats to create additional lift when the computers recognize an impending stall. But the stall-warning computers do not automatically extend wing slats if they are not already in the takeoff "mid-sealed" position.

If a near-stall condition persists, the stick shaker is the next warning. The stick shaker activates by vibrating the control column as warning of an approaching stall. Excessive angle of attack (AOA) or a rapidly increasing AOA triggers the stick shaker while the airplane is still flying four percent above its unaccelerated stall speed. The final level of stall warning is called the "supplemental stall-recognition system" (SSRS) which, at stalling speed, annunciates the word STALL on both pilots' glareshields, activates a series of warning tones and calls the word "stall" repeatedly over the cockpit audio warning system. If the stall condition persists for six seconds, or if the AOA increases another three degrees, the post-stall recovery system pushes the control columns forward to lower the nose.

Just 4.5 seconds after liftoff, the SSRS activated with its tones, annunciations, and verbal proclamations of "stall." The captain eased pressure on the wheel until the SSRS ceased and before the stick pusher could dump the nose. But he never relaxed enough back pressure to halt the stick shaker for the 14 seconds of flight, and the SSRS activated three more times before impact.

When the airplane reaches the AOA necessary for SSRS activation, the airplane is stalled; the stick shaker, however, warns at a margin above stalling speed. Because the airplane was actually nibbling at the aerodynamic stall during the SSRS activation periods, roll stability was degraded and the captain could not keep the wings level. The first roll deviation was only eight degrees to the left. But stability was so degraded by flight in the stall region that the captain's correction rolled the airplane right about 16 degrees. The roll oscillations continued until bank angles reached about 35 degrees.

The NTSB measured the MD-82's performance under the same weight and atmospheric conditions over six possible takeoff-climb profiles. With slats in the normal takeoff position and flaps set at 11 degrees—as the crew believed it had done—the airplane cleared Flight 255's impact point by 600 feet. With slats extended for takeoff, but no flaps, and with the crew maintaining a speed of V2 plus 10 knots, the airplane also climbed, clearing the impact point by 600 feet. With slats but no flaps the airplane was allowed to accelerate beyond V2 plus 10 and still had a 400-foot margin over the obstacle.

The slats are critical for low-speed lift in the MD-80 series. Extending slats knocks 40 knots off the stall speed, while setting flaps correctly 11 degrees only lowers stall by an additional six to eight knots.

But the NTSB determined the airplane could have barely made it without either slats or flaps. If the captain had recognized the impending stall just after liftoff and, as set forth in Northwest procedures, had asked for 15 degrees of flaps and full power, the airplane would likely have cleared the initial impact point by 350 feet. Wing slats are controlled by the flap handle and extend with any flap deflection, so extension of flaps would have extended the critical slats.

If the captain had lowered the nose and flown just below stick-shaker speed—instead of flying in and out of the actual stall—the airplane would have cleared the impact point by 80 feet. Finally, had the captain only been able to control the uncommanded rolling motion, NTSB tests show the airliner would have made it by 41 feet. Wing rocking itself expends lift, but even worse, when the captain turned the wheel to counteract uncommanded roll, the spoilers were coming up on the high wing, further killing precious lift. The NTSB believes the Northwest crew suspected they had encountered wind shear. Thunderstorms were in the area, the low-level wind-shear alert systems on the airport had warned of wind shear, and there had been pilot reports of airspeed fluctuation on approach.

The best escape route from wind shear on approach is to fly with a high pitch angle, which converts the stored energy of excess speed into lift to reverse a high sink rate while power comes up to full and the airplane begins to accelerate. But Flight 255 was gaining, not losing airspeed. It was already flying at, or near, the stalling angle of attack. There was no wind shear present. But the forecasts of possible wind shear and the emphasis on wind-shear escape in training may have led the captain to fly at the highest possible deck angle.

Northwest's recommended procedure for wind-shear recovery includes throttles to the stops, pitch attitude high enough to prevent ground contact and to expect possible stick-shaker activation, rotation not beyond the point the stick shaker is activated. In contrast, the recommended procedure for stall recovery calls for "max power, flaps to 15." The captain certainly appeared to be flying the wind-shear recovery profile instead of the stall-recovery procedure.

As to why the slats and flaps were never set, the NTSB determined the flight crew neglected the step because checklists were not performed in accordance with prescribed procedures, and the takeoff warning system was inoperative.

The automatic takeoff warning system was inoperative, the NTSB determined, because electrical power was cut off at one of three circuit breakers that supply power to the entire cockpit warning system. The key circuit breaker was so badly damaged in the accident that it was impossible to determine how it failed.

What can be added about poor cockpit discipline? It happens. Nobody knows how to eliminate it, and all of us who fly are guilty of it at one time or another. The crew was qualified and experienced. They made a mistake.

There is no warning system to warn the crew that the takeoff warning system is not working. During certification of the MD-80 series it was determined by the FAA that the takeoff warning system is a "Class I" risk, so it is safe to fly the airplane without the system functioning.

But maybe this crew had grown dependent upon the sophisticated warning systems of the MD-82. The NTSB's human-factors experts have identified a phenomenon they call "primary backup inversion, where the primary system, which is the human and human vigilance, becomes the backup." Thousands of instructors over decades have shouted the same thing at hapless students: "Fly the airplane, don't let it fly you."

We all make mistakes, and if we're lucky, we live to fly another day. But this crash reminds us that what we don't do can be more deadly than our actions. The epitaph, "They never knew what hit 'em," is too frequently true. Any of us who fly could fight the airplane all the way to the ground wondering what was going wrong, when the real problem was not what we were doing, but something that we forgot to do.

In the next accident, a captain aborts a takeoff when the engines begin to misbehave. The abort goes badly—but only afterward does the crew realize what a minor error was at the root of their troubles.

Control Conundrum
by Peter Garrison

On May 26, 1987, Air New Orleans Flight 962, a British Aerospace Jetstream with nine passengers and two crewmembers aboard, crashed after an aborted takeoff at Moisant Field in New Orleans. No one was killed, but two passengers were seriously injured and the $3.7-million airplane was destroyed.

The captain described the sequence of events leading up to the accident:

It was a busy afternoon at Moisant. The flight was holding short with all checklist items complete except for advancing the engine-speed levers from taxi to flight setting, a step which is delayed in the Jetstream until just before takeoff. The tower controller instructed the crew to be ready for an immediate takeoff following an MD-80. As the MD-80 started rolling, the tower cleared the Jetstream onto the runway with instructions to "be ready to roll as soon as the [MD-80] rotates." A few seconds later the tower again cautioned the crew to "be up on power" and ready to go. Immediately afterward, the flight was cleared for takeoff.

When the airplane had climbed to an altitude of about 200 feet, its two Garrett TPE331 turboprop engines began misbehaving: The torque meters fluctuated wildly, and the airplane started to yaw back and forth. At first the pilot thought he might be in the MD-80's wake turbulence; he quickly discarded that thesis, however, and tried another: that the fluctuations were due to the engines' temperature/torque-limiting (TTL) system. He thought the engine-power levers were advanced too far, and pulled them back somewhat. But the situation got worse.

The captain now made a fateful decision. He concluded that something inexplicable had gone wrong with both engines. He pulled both power levers back, pushed the nose down toward the runway, and when the airplane touched down he applied full braking and reverse thrust. It was too late to stop; the airplane went off the end of the runway, through a chain link fence, and halfway across a highway, striking several cars.

National Transportation Safety Board investigators decided, after considerable testing of engine components by Garrett, that there had been nothing wrong with the engines or the propellers, and that the accident was the result of a pilot error.

Although both the captain and first officer testified that they specifically remembered the captain pushing the rpm controls forward before beginning the takeoff roll—the first officer remembered it because the captain had done it, and normally it was not his job but the first officer's—the Board concluded that the rpm controls had been left in the taxi position, or had not been fully advanced.

Applying flight power at less than 100 percent rpm can produce a feedback loop in Garrett's turboprop engines; the engine fuel supply begins to be driven not by the normal fuel-controller schedule but by the propellers, which in turn are being driven by the fuel supply. This happens in Garretts because the propeller is geared to the gas generator.

The instability is similar to the "bootstrapping" that occurs in turbocharged piston aircraft when the wastegate is completely shut. If the TTL system (which is not present on all Garrett turbine engines) cuts in, it adds a third destabilizing element to the loop. In fact, it may be a nudge from the TTL system—or even some other disturbance, like a bit of turbulence—that sets off a previously latent oscillation when the engine is running "on the governor."

If you didn't have the rpm controls at 100 percent and you reduced the power, the oscillations might or might not disappear; it would depend on how much you reduced the power and where the rpm controls were. But there would be no reason to expect surging to diminish in proportion to power; the captain's observation that the oscillations increased when he backed off on the power levers was therefore not inconsistent with the hypothesis of insufficient rpm.

In distributing blame the Board did not spare its usual targets: the airline's operations manual and the FAA surveillance of the operator. But it attributed the crew's alleged failure to set the rpm controls properly—the final item on the before-takeoff checklist—to their having been accustomed to flying Pratt & Whitney-powered Beech 99s, whose engine-rpm controls are set to the takeoff position at the beginning of taxi. The Board's report did not explain the discrepancy between its analysis of the accident and the crew's testimony regarding the rpm levers.

It appeared during the investigation, however, that this crew and others flying BAe Jetstreams were hazy about the effects of the Garrett engines' TTL systems and about how to deal with power fluctuations if they occurred. The NTSB found that British Aerospace "was in possession of a procedure to alleviate TTL problems in flight," but had not passed it on to operators or to the FAA. The procedure was simple: check for 100 percent rpm, reduce power, and switch off the TTL computers if instability persists; so simple, in fact, that the conspiratorial overtone of the Board's phrase "in possession of a procedure" seems out of place.

According to a Garrett spokesman, checking for 100-percent rpm—which is attained within seconds of advancing the power levers—is a basic part of the takeoff procedure with Garrett engines. If you don't have 100 percent, and the rpm controls are where they should be, you abort. The engine and airframe manufacturers consider this a reasonable demand upon the pilot, and so do not install a low-rpm warning system or a mechanical system that would make it impossible to run the power lever to flight power without simultaneously pulling the corresponding engine-speed lever forward.

What the engine manufacturer considers a standard and basic practice may not seem so to pilots, however. The pilots of the Jetstream were not the first to encounter engine-power oscillations after takeoff. Others, however, looked at their engine instruments and controls, noticed that rpm were low, and pushed the engine-speed levers forward. So we come to a human-factors question. Should an airplane or an engine be designed so that forgetting a single item could lead to a spurious but convincing appearance of a life-threatening malfunction—not immediately, but once the airplane is airborne and the omission has faded from memory?

Computer programmers face this kind of question constantly; they never know what the novice user will come up with, and so they design their programs to survive any kind of abuse. But airplane designers are dealing with a different kind of user: a highly trained professional in many cases, and never an untutored tinkerer. But a computer crash is one thing, an airplane crash is another. Do airplane manufacturers have to take the same precautions as computer programmers? Many a lawsuit has sprung from the idea that they should: that human beings, however well trained, will sooner or later make mistakes, and that the manufacturers of their tools should make every effort to ensure that mistakes do the least possible damage. The test of the manufacturer's duty must in part be whether safeguards detract from the function of a device or add disproportionately to its cost. Another question concerns the multiplication of safety devices: Eventually more and more bells and whistles in the cockpit produce more confusion than information for pilots.

Manufacturers consequently resort to the most inexpensive of fixes: the cockpit placard or the flight-manual amendment. As a result of the New Orleans accident, Jetstream manuals now contain explicit warnings about fluctuating torque, a list of remedial measures to be taken (which include verifying that the problem is in the engines and not merely in the torque meters), and a specific requirement that pilots verify 100 percent of rpm when the power levers are advanced for takeoff.

A momentary distraction may have combined with the "somatogravic illusion"—confusion of the sensation of acceleration with the sensation of climbing—to produce the next accident.

Pushed to the Limit
by Peter Garrison

In outline, the accident was a simple one. It was night, and the weather conditions at Raleigh-Durham International Airport were IMC with a low ceiling, sky obscured, and a runway visual range of less than 2,500 feet in light drizzle and fog. The Fairchild Metro III, with 10 passengers and two crewmembers on board, was cleared for takeoff on a regularly scheduled flight from Morrisville, North Carolina, to Richmond, Virginia. The tower had asked the crew to turn right 60 degrees as soon as feasible after takeoff, to clear following traffic.

About 22 seconds after the takeoff roll began the Metro III lifted off. Ten seconds later, at about 200 feet above the runway, it began a turn to the right. Five seconds later it was 260 feet above the runway, but its rate of climb had diminished to zero. Then it began to descend.

In the next 15 seconds, the Metro III accelerated to 209 knots from 150 and descended more than 400 feet, ultimately crashing into a reservoir less than a mile from the runway. There was no indication of power loss; it appeared that the airplane had simply been flown under control—of a sort—into the water.

Investigators found evidence in the wreckage to indicate that the stall avoidance system (SAS) clutch power had been manually switched off—it is normally checked in the ON position prior to take-off—and that the SAS fault warning light had been illuminated at the time of the crash. The implication was that the warning light had come on during the takeoff sequence and that the crew had responded, as suggested by the operations manual, by switching off power to the stick-pusher clutch.

The SAS warning light is a red light, not a yellow one, on the theory that the stall avoidance system is a safety-of-flight item, and so its loss is an "emergency" of sorts. Actually, however, the red light coming on does not imply an imminent crisis, but just a fault in a backup system. Nor does the light have a clear meaning. When it blinks, power to the SAS clutch has been lost, and so switching off the clutch really does nothing except turn off the light. A steady light, on the other hand, is ambiguous, indicating an unspecified internal fault in the SAS computer. In this case, turning off clutch power protects against an inappropriate stick-pusher actuation. Even if the stick pusher is improperly actuated, however—it had happened 15 times on other Metro IIIs up to the time of this accident—it can be overpowered by the pilot. Illumination of the SAS fault light is not, therefore, a critical occurrence in any sense.

Because the airplane appeared to have been under control up to the moment of impact, the National Transportation Safety Board hypothesized that the crew had been distracted by the SAS fault light, and in the process of reacting to it had failed to notice that the bank angle was increasing. The first officer, who was flying the airplane, did nothing to correct the bank or to increase back pressure (four times as much pressure is required for a 45-degree bank as for a standard-rate turn), and so the airplane began to descend. Investigators considered, but rejected on evidence, the alternative possibilities of a trim runaway and a wake-turbulence encounter.

When it appears that a flight crew has failed to observe the most fundamental of rules for an emergency—fly the airplane first—one naturally wonders why. After all, this was scarcely such an emergency as should even put one's deodorant to a test. The answer arrived at by the NTSB in this case was that the captain wasn't feeling well—he had an upset stomach and sinus trouble—and the first officer had a history of difficulty in instrument flying.

The Board readily admits that the captain's health problems, which were minor, did not necessarily have anything to do with the accident; it is merely *possible* that his performance was slightly below par. "Certainly," the Board intones, "the sinus congestion and gastrointestinal discomfort . . . could have reduced his concentration and, possibly, his reaction time, in the environment which placed the highest demands on these very skills." Since the captain was merely called upon to flick a switch and had 15 seconds or more to do it, the demands on his skills were actually quite modest.

The first officer had had trouble with instrument approaches during her training with the airline. Some at the airline considered her performance typical of a new trainee; one captain, however, thought her abilities were "less than what he expected of a 'new-hire.'" At least four different captains who flew with her found that she was chronically "behind the airplane." One pilot who gave her a check ride recommended to the company that it terminate her. Furthermore, the Board writes, "an examination of her difficulties suggests that her performance may have deteriorated when she was under stress. The first two check airmen . . . with whom she attempted to qualify . . . were described as demanding pilots who could be critical and . . . create a tense cockpit environment . . ."

Having broached the theme of "stress," the report makes the most of it. The flight was "highly stressful." "Additional stressors to this potential stress [sic] included a last-minute change in ATC's clearance . . . the perceived need to initiate a right turn almost immediately after takeoff, and the knowledge that a . . . jet was taking off right behind them." Furthermore, the first officer had just come back from a temporary layoff due to financial difficulties at the airline, and this was her first instrument flight in more than a month. Adding disorientation to stress, the report goes on to characterize a climbing turn into IMC as a "vertigo-inducing maneuver."

The NTSB's analysis of this accident leans heavily on rhetoric. Few professional pilots would agree with its characterization of this takeoff as highly stressful. In fact, all night takeoffs, whether under a high ceiling or in near zero-zero conditions, require continuous attention to the attitude instruments from the moment of liftoff. Other airplanes are always rolling into position behind you as you advance the power levers; no pilot would break a sweat over that. The Board suggests that the crew should have climbed straight ahead to 500 feet before turning; but a shallow turn immediately after takeoff is not unusual, and in fact is recommended under certain circumstances to avoid wake turbulence. Nor is it likely, if the first officer was indeed as incompetent as the report suggests, that the captain would have let her make her first takeoff into the soup in more than a month without himself keeping an eye on the attitude instruments. While the report comes down hard on the first officer, one must bear in mind that she was a 2,000-plus-hour ATP flying twin-turboprop airliners, and also that she was a woman in a profession dominated by men, a few of whom still take umbrage at the invasion of their province.

In reference to the stick pusher the Safety Board asserts that "the potential benefit the [stall avoidance system] provides to airplane stability in the early stages of a stall may be outweighed by the potentially adverse consequences of a system fault during critical phases of flight. Since the Metro III airplane with its larger wingspan, more powerful engines and more efficient propellers is inherently more stable than its Metro II predecessor, the need for such a system on the Metro III is questionable."

The second sentence is odd, since a larger span may or may not influence airplane stability, and more powerful engines and more efficient propellers almost certainly influence it for the worse. In fact, the larger and more powerful an airplane is, the more likely it is to have a stick pusher. On airplanes of the Fairchild Metro III class—14,500 pounds gross weight—a stick pusher is typically installed because without one the airplane does not meet certification requirements for stall behavior. This was the case with the Metro III; although its stall is generally benign, it did not meet the Part 23 requirement of less than 15 degrees of roll during recovery. Efforts to correct the problem by aerodynamic means were unsuccessful, so the stick pusher was installed under the regulation's "equivalent level of safety" provision.

The idea that a stick pusher should be removed because it might be dangerous if it malfunctions reminds me, at least at first glance, of the logic of a chronically sick person who, feeling better after taking palliative medication for a while, decides he didn't need the medicine after all; or of a government that, noting that after decades of operating under regulation an industry runs smoothly, decides that regulation is unnecessary. Since stick pushers have been installed in many aircraft, stall and departure accidents have become less common; in the face of this efflorescence of safety, the stick pusher now begins to look superfluous.

In short, the Board is at pains to convince the reader that the takeoff was particularly difficult; that the crew's abilities, compromised by this or that, were barely up to the task; and that the illumination of the SAS fault warning light threw the pilots into a tizzy. It backs up this interpretation with the suggestion that the airline, which had experienced a period of rapid growth followed by a Chapter 11 reorganization, was sloppily run and had hired a lot of new, inexperienced pilots. Finally, lax FAA "oversight" is mentioned.

From a pilot's standpoint, however, the case is weak. One is simply not convinced that two ATPs couldn't fly an airplane and flip a switch at the same time. In fact, two Board members dissented from the finding of probable cause, arguing that the information available to the Board was only enough to make the causes *possible*, not *probable*.

The distinction between possible and probable in this context is not perfectly clear. Certainly the sequence of events envisioned by the Board is no less possible than some alternatives one could imagine—for example that both crewmembers were terrorists on a suicide mission to eliminate an important CIA functionary traveling incognito on the flight. But it is more probable.

The effort to find an explanation for the Metro III accident at least shed some light on the mystifying conflicts that can sometimes arise between the mechanical elements of a flight and the human ones, as well as between the NTSB's mandate to find the causes of accidents and its limited ability to do so.

Certain maneuvers, such as a landing from a fast approach on a wet runway, require the pilot to do everything just right. In the next accident, minor deviations from correct technique result in a 737 going off the runway.

Too Hot to Handle
by J. Mac McClellan

A Piedmont Airlines Boeing 737 landed long and fast at Charlotte, North Carolina, and ran off the end of the wet runway. Nobody was killed, and there were only three serious injuries. The airplane was a total loss. End of story; no mystery here. As in most aircraft accidents, however, the story isn't that simple.

Piedmont Flight 467, a Boeing 737-222, operated from Newark, New Jersey, to Charlotte. The flight was routine for an October evening, with the 737 arriving in the Charlotte area just after eight o'clock. There were rain and fog at the destination, and a 500-foot ceiling and half a mile visibility were being advertised on the ATIS frequency.

Piedmont was in the midst of an arrival surge at Charlotte, with several company airplanes in line ahead of Flight 467 awaiting their turn for the Runway 36 Right ILS approach. On the first vector the approach controller advised "vectors for a close-in base leg." The controller then advised all pilots on the frequency that conditions at Charlotte were "measured ceiling 400 overcast, visibility two, light rain and fog, temperature and dew point remain the same, winds 090 at eight." Visibility had improved by 1.5 miles, but the ceiling was down to 400 from 500 feet. Light rain continued.

A Piedmont airplane ahead of Flight 467 had reported a "right to left wind of 20 to 25 knots on the final approach course." The controller relayed this information and it was recorded on Flight 467's cockpit voice recorder, though neither pilot commented on the information. Winds at the surface remained light.

Although the controller was vectoring a stream of arriving airplanes for right traffic and turning them onto final about three miles outside the outer marker, and although he warned the Flight 467 crew of a "close-in" base leg, the crew of the 737 fell behind the airplane. Evidence of this shows up in the 737's airspeeds recorded on the flight data recorder during approach and landing. The VREF approach speed for Flight 467's landing weight was 131 knots, but the Boeing didn't manage to slow to that value until more than half the available runway length was behind the airplane.

Piedmont's procedures called for an initial approach speed of 210 knots, slowing to 190 knots and flaps at position one on base leg. The flaps were supposed to be set to position five and the airplane slowed to 170 knots before the turn to final. After localizer interception, the landing gear was to be lowered and the flaps were to be set at position 15 with an airspeed of 150 knots. At the final approach fix the flaps were to be extended to the final landing position and speed stabilized at VREF plus wind-correction factors. Piedmont used the common procedure of adding half the steady-state wind speed and all of the gust value to VREF (but under no circumstances should a pilot add more than 20 knots for wind). The wind on the surface was reported to be no greater than eight knots but, because he said he was concerned about the reports of changing wind direction and velocity, on final, the captain decided to add the maximum 20 knots to VREF, yielding a target approach speed of 151 knots. Even when extra speed is carried through the final approach, normal procedures dictate that the excess speed be bled off near the runway so the touchdown occurs near VREF.

The NTSB determined that the 737 actually crossed the final approach fix at 195 knots indicated, crossed the runway threshold at 165 knots and finally touched down at 147 knots. The captain did not call for landing-gear extension until the airplane was inside the outer marker and he did not call for the landing flap setting of "30" until the airplane was less than one mile from the landing threshold and still indicating 173 knots. The captain, who was flying, commented that "George didn't do me any favors there," which the NTSB interpreted as meaning that the autopilot did not perform as expected. The ground proximity warning system (GPWS) issued its "Whoop, whoop, pull up" command just before touchdown. The system measures several conditions at low altitudes to warn of unsafe closure rates with terrain. One of those conditions is rate of sink, and the NTSB believes the warning sounded because the sink rate in the final few hundred feet of the approach exceeded the GPWS parameters.

Based on eyewitness reports and reconstructions of the approach using the onboard flight-data recorders, the NTSB determined that the 737 landed about 3,200 feet down the 7,845-foot runway. Although landing that long violated Piedmont procedures and good operating practices, all was not necessarily lost. The NTSB examined data from four Piedmont flights that landed within 11 minutes before Flight 467 and found none had any problem with the approach; all of the other four airplanes stopped in 3,450 feet or less after touchdown. Boeing calculated that even with the high touchdown speed and the wet runway, a 737 at Flight 467's weight could have stopped in 2,200 feet, using spoilers and reverse thrust, or in 3,480 feet with reverse thrust but no spoilers.

Clearly, additional factors were at work in this accident. The 737 left the runway while still moving at a speed of about 72 knots and quickly hit a concrete culvert and then a railroad track embankment, which halted the aircraft. The airplane's deceleration devices did not work as they were supposed to.

The Boeing 737 is equipped with ground lift spoilers (speed brakes), as are all jet transports. The 737 ground spoilers consist of four panels on the upper surface of each wing that pop up and disrupt airflow, eliminating about 70 percent of the wing's lift at touchdown. The ground lift spoilers are a primary component of the airplane's deceleration system, along with the wheel brakes and the engines' thrust reversers.

Ground spoilers and thrust reversers are wonderful on the runway, but no pilot wants them to accidentally deploy in flight, so Boeing designed several logic systems to prevent accidental deployment. Before all the deceleration devices can operate, the landing-gear struts must compress to indicate that the airplane is on the ground, the wheels must spin up to a minimum value, and the thrust levers must be at idle, or some combination of all of those factors. Under normal operating conditions the ground spoilers automatically deploy as soon as sensors detect 60 knots of tire rotation plus some other conditions that indicate that the airplane is on the runway.

The crew operation and performance of the deceleration devices was central to the NTSB investigation, because if all had worked normally—or been operated by the crew correctly—the airplane could have stopped on the runway, or at least left it at a lower speed. On short final the copilot noted "spoilers manual" and got no response from the captain. The spoilers should have been armed for automatic deployment, and the captain later said they were. The NTSB couldn't determine how the spoilers were armed before touchdown and finally decided that factors other than the position of the spoiler handle may have been more important in determining if the spoilers operated.

The captain told the NTSB that he tried to pull the thrust-reverser "piggyback" handles immediately upon touchdown but noticed that the ground-spoiler speed brakes had not automatically deployed. He manually deployed the speed brakes and moved his hand back to the reverser levers, but said he still couldn't get full reverse. He applied the wheel brakes but got "no sensation of stopping, not a sensation of antiskid, a cycle, there was nothing." He then said he released all pressure from the brake pedals and reapplied foot pressure. Normal procedure, however, calls for firm and steady pressure on the brake pedals. The airplane was using up the wet runway at a ferocious rate, but neither the brakes, spoilers, nor reversers seemed to be working properly.

The NTSB found that the airplane touched down in a nearly level attitude, followed by three seconds of oscillation in vertical acceleration (bouncing). Boeing said that a touchdown speed of only 15 knots above V_{REF} generates enough wing lift to equal roughly the weight of the airplane. This almost "weightless" condition on the wheels could last four to six seconds without ground spoilers and with the forward stick pressure the captain said he applied to hold the nosewheel on the runway. With most of the airplane's weight off the main wheels, the gear-strut squat switch would not close and thrust reverse would not be available, which is consistent with the captain's recollection. The light weight on the wheels and wet runway surface could also explain why the ground spoilers did not receive a signal of sufficient wheel-rotation speed to deploy automatically.

The wet pavement and delayed gear-strut compression could also have disrupted normal braking. The antiskid braking system compares rotation speeds of the four main landing-gear wheels and reduces hydraulic pressure to a wheel that is turning slower than the others, based on the assumption that the slow-turning wheel is skidding. The antiskid system also looks for rapid deceleration of a wheel, indicating that it is locked in a skid, and releases pressure on the wheel brake. In addition, the system prevents the airplane from landing with the wheels locked by preventing braking until the main gear strut compresses and closes the squat switch, indicating that the airplane is on the ground. The spoilers, wheel brakes, and reversers could not operate properly until the airplane "knew" for sure it was on the ground. The fast touchdown speed and wet pavement may have prevented this 737's systems from switching from air to ground mode until it was too late.

The NTSB determined that the probable cause of this accident was "the captain's failure to stabilize the approach and his failure to discontinue the approach to a landing that was conducted at an excessive speed beyond the normal touchdown point on a wet runway." Contributing to the accident was "the captain's failure to optimally use the airplane decelerative devices." The Board also complains about "poor frictional quality" of the final 1,500 feet of the runway and of the dangerous obstruction presented by the concrete culvert located only 318 feet beyond the end of the runway.

One of the most basic requirements of instrument flying is mental calm. Fear produces growing confusion and may eventually make a pilot unable to perform the simplest tasks. In the next accident, a pilot seems to become frightened by something—possibly a faulty instrument, possibly an attack of vertigo—and eventually loses control of his airplane in relatively light IFR conditions.

What Failed, Gyro or Pilot?
by Peter Garrison

"We've still got flight precautions for the IFR conditions and thunderstorm and rainshower activity across your routing, also occasional moderate rime icing forecast below 12,000 to the freezing level, and then also we do have an airmet out now for occasional moderate turbulence below 25,000 across the routing. As far as your conditions in Springfield, they're measured 500 overcast, six miles with light rain and fog, 43 degrees, 41 dew point, and northeasterly winds at 17 knots."

It was a few minutes after seven on a gloomy November evening in Norman, Oklahoma, near Oklahoma City. The sun had set at 4:55. The pilot and his 13-year-old son were bound for Springfield, Missouri, 180 nautical miles away, little more than an hour's flight in their A36 Bonanza.

"Out of the Oklahoma City area right now," the briefer continued, "we're reporting ceilings around 300 to 500 overcast, but your visibilities are running a mile and a quarter to three miles with light rain, light ice pellets and fog."

"Ice pellets," the pilot repeated.

They discussed the temperature and dew point, and the pilot requested pilot reports on icing. He then said, "Okay, so if it's 34 on the ground the freezing level's gonna be real low."

"Yes sir, it's going to be right around a thousand feet, two thousand feet. Will Rogers radar is showing a 70 percent coverage of light rain with ice pellets and snow, max tops at 17,000 . . . Springfield's forecast up until midnight tonight's for 600 overcast, four miles light rain and fog, occasional ceiling 300 overcast one mile . . . they're expecting a gradual decrease on their ceilings throughout the rest of the night through tomorrow morning."

Half an hour later the Bonanza was airborne, cleared to climb to 7,000 and proceed direct to Tulsa.

A few minutes after takeoff the pilot called, "Departure, 39R, I'm having trouble with my vacuum and I'm a little disoriented."

The airplane was in a turn to the right and already heading back to the southwest.

"39R . . . I'm gonna try to level and get my climb control, I'm doing all right, I'll worry about my direction in a minute if you can just bear with me."

Departure asked the pilot to maintain 4,000 for traffic. "Bonanza 39R, right now your heading is about 220, you're just about a mile east of Norman now. What would you like to do, come back to Norman or what, sir?"

"I think my best bet is to make a slow turn to the right and try to head on home for a familiar airport. I've got my right wing down and turning around to my right, my compass is working, I'm just gonna try to make a real slow turn and get on a 030 heading."

"All right, Bonanza 39R, roger, and 39R can climb and maintain 7,000. Do you want a different altitude than that? Will 7,000 be okay for you?"

"I'll try to get up to seven, but I want to get this turn established before I try to do any big altitude changes."

Departure soon saw that the Bonanza seemed unable to hold a steady heading. First it completed a 360-degree turn and briefly headed northeast, then it swung back around to the west. It was climbing slowly, and had reached 4,800 feet when the pilot asked whether there were any VFR weather to be found within a couple of hundred miles.

"Let me check. I doubt it," said the controller. "And 39R, would you like to stay around the area here or just continue on up to the northeast? If you want to I can just give you no-gyro vectors around the area here before you get away from us too far."

"Head me toward Springfield, Missouri," the pilot replied.

The controller began giving the pilot no-gyro vectors, and reported that there was no VFR weather anywhere in the state of Oklahoma. He offered the pilot a surveillance or an ILS circling approach to Runway 35 at nearby Oklahoma City, where the weather was 700 overcast, one and a half miles in light rain and fog, and the wind was 310 at 15. The controller noted that the pilot was still having great difficulty holding a steady heading.

Ten minutes after first contacting departure the pilot called, "I'm beginning to pick up a little ice, and I'm having a little trouble climbing. I'm maintaining okay so I'm gonna let you take me back to Will Rogers on the ILS."

The pilot requested a straight-in approach to Runway 17 on the ILS, despite the strong tailwind; he did not feel ready to circle under the 700-foot ceiling.

"I'm a little shook up here and I don't think I can look up that localizer frequency, can you find it for me?"

The departure controller handed the pilot off to another controller for the approach. The controller continued giving no-gyro vectors, and the pilot seemed more able to comply with them now. He maintained 4,000 feet, swinging to the northwest to join the localizer. But his command of the situation was still precarious. The controller asked at one point whether the pilot had the approach plate.

"Yes sir, I have one, I just hadn't wanted to take the time to look at it. I'll try to do that now."

The pilot successfully complied with the vectors to establish himself on the ILS. The controller read him the ILS course and minimums and repeated the wind. Twenty minutes after he first reported trouble the pilot was inbound from the final approach fix and cleared to land. It looked as though everything was going to be all right.

But now a problem began to develop, at first subtly. The Bonanza was too high, and it wasn't coming down.

The crossing altitude at Tuloo, the FAF, is 2,700 feet. The middle marker is 3.4 nm from Tuloo, and the minimum altitude is 1,482 feet at the MM. The threshold elevation is 1,282 feet. The cloud bottoms were somewhere around 2,000 feet.

Given the concern about icing, a pilot might be expected to maintain a higher-than-normal speed on the approach—perhaps 100 knots. To this add the tailwind, which may have been 20 knots or more above the surface, and you have a required rate of descent of nearly 750 fpm *if* you cross the FAF at 2,700 feet.

Instead, the pilot reported "out of three" almost 45 seconds *after* passing the FAF. At this point a rate of descent of 1,400 fpm would have been required to bring the airplane to the runway threshold.

Strangely, the controller, even though he knew the pilot was having trouble keeping himself and the airplane under control, did not comment on his failure to make a timely descent until he said, "Bonanza 39R, you're a little high at this point over the approach end at this time, you may need to execute a missed approach at this time. Climb and maintain 3,000 and turn right 260."

The pilot responded, "39R climbing to, uh, three, uh, three thousand and, uh, head 360 . . . "

Those were the last words the controller heard. The Bonanza, whose Mode C readout indicated that it was then 1,200 feet above the runway threshold, continued straight ahead for a few seconds and then began to turn to the left. The controller repeatedly ordered a climbing turn to the right, but the pilot did not respond. A witness saw the Bonanza in a steep descending left turn, and it landed hard, in a nearly level attitude, in the area between the parallel runways. The Bonanza skidded to a halt and burst into flames. The pilot and his son both died of impact injuries.

Photographs of the wreckage taken by sheriff's deputies shortly after the accident showed substantial accumulations of rime ice on the wings. But subsequent examination failed to reveal the nature of the reported vacuum failure. The pump drive was intact and the pump itself undamaged.

In any case, however, the only instrument that relied on vacuum was the attitude indicator, the HSI and turn coordinator both being electrically driven.

The 45-year-old pilot had ceased logging time about a year before the fatal flight, but he had reported 510 hours total time when renewing his medical five months before the accident. According to the year-old logbook, he had flown 185 hours in the A36, including almost 100 hours on instruments, two-thirds of it actual. He had logged 133 landings in the airplane.

A vacuum failure is supposed to be a "routine" emergency. Every instrument-rated pilot has gone through the easy drill of covering up the attitude indicator and maneuvering by reference to the airspeed indicator, compass, and turn coordinator.

Why did an experienced, instrument-rated pilot lose control of his airplane during an ILS approach under controller surveillance, with both an HSI and a turn coordinator to guide him?

The answer has to be fear. The printed transcript of radio communications may convey a touch of confusion and alarm, but never fully illuminates the inner state of the pilot's mind. Someone who has never experienced panic in an airplane cannot imagine the weird incapacity—some people call it "mental viscosity"—that it can produce. The simplest act, like reading and interpreting the face of a directional gyro, slows to a near halt, the eyes staring with a wild surmise at numbers that might as well be in cuneiform, the brain lurching back and forth like a defective toy, unable to remember whether the perceived pattern of needles and digits means to turn right or left, go up or down.

Most likely the pilot felt uneasy about the flight to begin with. A night IFR flight in conditions very likely to entail icing, and in an airplane with no anti-icing equipment other than a heated pitot tube, is a serious undertaking for any pilot. It is especially so for one with only 500 hours in his logbook.

Pilots often take off with a little seed of fear inside them. Usually the flight is uneventful, and the fear dies in the blood. Repeated inoculation with the dead vaccine of fear eventually confers at least a partial immunity. But in this case the pilot was not yet immune, and the rogue vaccine infected and destroyed him.

A similar lapse of instrument-flying technique led to another accident when a California pilot became disoriented on a routine IFR flight. In this case, there was a complicating factor: Valium. In any case, the pilot needn't have died; as with some of the thunderstorm encounters of an earlier chapter, the fatal moment came only after the pilot emerged into VFR conditions.

Just Say No-Go
by Peter Garrison

Drugs are everywhere, and hopelessly tangled signals about them rain steadily upon us. From kindergarten, children are told, "Just say no to drugs"; bumper stickers exhort us to "dare to keep kids off drugs"; and yet on every other street corner there's a store with a big sign proudly proclaiming "DRUGS." The creativity of drug companies is boundless. Drugs proliferate like kudzu. Illness, fatigue, listlessness, sadness, uneasiness, restlessness, exhilaration—almost any condition of the human psyche departing much from a steady mental dial tone is fair game for some drug or other. Alcohol and tobacco, the most commonly used drugs of all, are not even called drugs.

One of the most widely prescribed drugs in the world is Valium. According to the *Physician's Desk Reference*, a thick tome listing every drug on the market together with every effect and side effect that has ever been reported, diazepam—the generic name of Valium—is a "central nervous system depressant" with infrequent side effects of vertigo and blurred vision. As with many drugs, users are cautioned against "engaging in hazardous occupations requiring complete mental alertness." As drugs listed in the PDR go, however, diazepam looks pretty innocuous.

Nevertheless, diazepam was implicated in the crash of an airplane whose 61-year-old pilot was on a short solo instrument flight for proficiency. The visibility was 10 miles under a 1,000-foot broken layer and a 2,800-foot overcast, with no danger of icing. For a southbound flight, the normal departure from the airport, which is located in a valley, involves flying northward to gain altitude, then turning left southward on course. The minimum safe altitude to the west of the departure course is 4,500 feet, and the MEA southbound is 6,000.

The flight began normally. Cleared to climb to 6,000 feet, the pilot flew straight ahead into the clouds. When the airplane was six miles north of the airport at 4,800 feet, the departure controller asked the pilot to verify that he was turning back on course—a polite way of suggesting that it was about time he did so. The pilot acknowledged the transmission and began a left 180-degree turn. At some point during that turn he lost control of the airplane. He made no distress call; his last communication had been to acknowledge the controller's reminder. Witnesses saw the airplane emerge from the clouds in a spiral dive, shed part of a wing, and veer into the ground.

The engine seems to have been running normally, although, with the usual inconsistency of eyewitnesses, some described it as popping—which would suggest a retarded throttle—and others as screaming—which, with a fixed-pitch prop, would suggest a dive under power.

Witnesses also diverged on the attitude of the descending airplane. One couple agreed that it had been spiraling as it emerged from the clouds, but differed on the direction of the turn. The most detailed account had it descending at a 20-degree angle in a left turn, rolling right then rolling back to level and pitching up 45 degrees. At that point the outer panel of the left wing broke off.

With such sketchy information, accident investigators can do no more than construct a plausible hypothesis to account for the accident. The first suspicion would be of an instrument failure, but the gyro instruments all seemed to have been turning at the time of the crash. The electric turn-and-bank rotor showed no evidence of arcing on the commutators, which would normally occur if the rotor abruptly stopped turning—as it would on impact—with power on. This might raise the possibility of an electrical failure, at least in the turn-and-bank. A total electrical failure would also have accounted for the lack of a distress call from the pilot; but transponder returns continued after the loss of control. In any case, it was implausible that a pilot would become disoriented solely because of loss of a secondary instrument.

Once instrument failure had been ruled out, spatial disorientation became the most likely diagnosis. The pilot had relatively little instrument experience, and had not flown actual instruments in the last six months (though he had done some hood time recently with a friend acting as a safety pilot). He was a careful, "fussy" pilot who took good care of his airplane, but he was known to shy away from any aspect of flying that could be regarded as "unusual." He did not practice stalls or recoveries from unusual attitudes with his safety pilot, nor had he done anything but a little straight-and-level partial-panel work on his last biennial flight review.

The spatial disorientation hypothesis gains strength from the presence, discovered in the autopsy, of "therapeutic levels" of diazepam components in the pilot's liver. The pilot's family denied that he used this medication, but there it was.

The transponder return track, reconstructed from radar tapes, shows some zigzagging as the pilot climbed; he evidently wanted to fly outbound from the VOR on a heading of 342 degrees, but twice drifted left to the 337-degree radial before correcting. About six miles north of the airport, immediately following the controller's hint, the airplane began a left turn. Two transponder returns are missing here, perhaps because of the banked attitude of the airplane. After 34 seconds—the turn seems to have been made at about twice standard rate—the target reappears heading southward, but continues to turn with a diminishing radius. The last transponder return comes 24 seconds later: The airplane is again heading more or less northward, and the altitude is 5,300 feet.

Possibly the pilot found that he was having difficulty even before the southward turn; the delay in making the turn suggests preoccupation with something else, perhaps the trouble he was having staying on the 342-degree radial. Evidently the pilot became disoriented during the turn and failed to level out. As the bank angle increased, the climb turned into a dive, and when the airplane emerged from the clouds, the pilot, finally able to recognize his attitude, overcontrolled the airplane while trying to recover.

Pilots who have not experienced spatial disorientation (also called vertigo) probably find it hard to believe that a simple climbing left turn can turn into a fatal disaster. Vertigo has to be experienced to be believed, and this pilot had not gone out of his way to experience it. Those who have know how compelling the physical sensation of turning or "leaning" can be, and how difficult it is to heed the attitude indicator in spite of it.

Pilots have become disoriented without the help of diazepam, and plenty of pilots have probably flown after taking Valium or other drugs and have not become disoriented. There is not a necessary connection between drugs and disorientation; the connection is merely statistical. Nor is diazepam a particularly pernicious drug in this respect; several cases of spatial disorientation have been linked to cold remedies, particularly decongestants. But the use of any kind of drug before flying increases—be it greatly or slightly—the risk of a mishap, and unnecessary risk is something to which pilots ought to just say no.

It's usually difficult to make a strong causal link between a drug and an accident, though the veins of deceased pilots are occasionally found to contain something more like Bloody Mary than blood. In the next report, the NTSB made much of the pilot's habitual use of alcohol—but did not establish that the cause of the accident was anything other than one of those slightly mysterious IFR blunders that put so many airplanes on the ground short of a runway.

The Perils of Perseverance
by Nigel Moll

It was a cold, foggy night in March when a Simmons Airlines Bandeirante made a second attempt at the ILS approach to Alpena Phelps-Collins Airport, Michigan. Fourteen minutes after the crew acknowledged that they were established on the localizer, a passing motorist was flagged down by two passengers who had survived the crash of the Bandeirante. It had come down in trees one and a half miles short of the runway threshold and 300 feet to the left of the extended centerline. The first officer and two passengers were killed. The captain and five passengers survived. A minor fire broke out in the left engine, but a passenger quickly extinguished it by throwing snow on the flames. There was a considerable amount of fuel in the wreckage area.

In its report on the accident, the National Transportation Safety Board attempted to find out why a healthy airplane failed to complete a precision approach with the necessary precision. The investigators delved into the crewmembers' pasts, putting particular emphasis on the captain's use of alcohol; they questioned the efficiency of current methods of disseminating weather information; they renewed the old call for cockpit voice recorders in Part 135 multiengine turboprops; and they also recommended that the same airplanes should be equipped with ground-proximity warning systems.

The report is of note perhaps more for the ammunition it contains to support current legislation and crackdowns than for its conclusions about an accident that was, at least for those not involved, relatively unremarkable.

Simmons Flight 1746 departed Detroit Metropolitan at about 8:50 p.m., bound for Sault St. Marie with a stop in Alpena. For the two crewmembers, it had been a day of schedule changes resulting from bad weather that covered Michigan. They had reported for duty at 3:05 that afternoon and, because of a schedule disruption, were assigned to fly a Bandeirante from Detroit to Toledo and back. Under the original schedule, their next trip was to Muskegon and back, but this flight was canceled, and they were reassigned to fly Flight 1746.

The en route portion of the flight was uneventful. At 9:25 p.m. the crew was given the latest Alpena weather by the Wurtsmith controller, who had obtained the conditions from Pellston Flight Service. The weather observation had been made at 8:50 p.m. by a National Weather Service specialist at Alpena, and it reported that the sky was partially obscured, measured ceiling 100 overcast, visibility half a mile, light drizzle and fog. Despite the ceiling of 100 feet (100 feet below the 200-foot minimums), the crew was allowed to attempt the approach because the reported visibility was at minimums—half a mile.

But the airplane was unable to land at Alpena, and it declared a missed approach at 9:42. Unbeknownst to the crew, a special weather observation taken at 9:19 p.m. showed that the visibility at Alpena had dropped to three-eighths of a mile, rendering any further attempts at the ILS illegal. The crew was also unaware of another special observation, taken just four minutes after the miss, reporting that the visibility had further deteriorated to a quarter of a mile.

The captain was flying, and the first officer was talking with Wurtsmith Air Force Base Radar Approach Control—the Alpena Tower was closed. Having declared the miss, the Bandeirante was instructed to climb and maintain 2,800 and fly direct to the outer marker. The airplane's DME was inoperative. There followed some confusion about whether they were to fly to the VOR "or the marker." Once it was established that they were to cross the locator outer marker (LOM), they were cleared for the approach. When they asked for vectors to the procedure turn, the crew was cleared to climb to 4,000 feet for radar identification.

Wurtsmith then asked for the Bandeirante's flight conditions on final, but the controllers were likely not much wiser for the reply: "Okay, we, ah, we picked up the lights but we were, uh, we were in a little bit, uh. But I'm not really sure, uh, what the visibility was and, uh, you know there's just fog and it was really hard to tell."

Vectors to put the Bandeirante on the localizer followed, and it was cleared for the second attempt at the ILS Runway 1. About seven minutes later the airplane was in the trees.

The mystery is why the Bandeirante hit the ground a mile and a half short of the runway threshold while flying a precision approach. If the glideslope guidance had been followed religiously (but illegally) below the decision height, it would at worst have taken the crash to the runway environment, not a mile and a half short of it. At best the airplane would have landed. On a nonprecision approach with no vertical guidance, it is easier to imagine how an airplane could end up crashing short if the pilot were to tempt fate by dropping below the minimum descent altitude for a better look.

The NTSB explored this question and concluded that at the point where the airplane hit the ground, the glideslope deviation had to have been significant. In fact, the point of impact was about 300 feet below the bottom of the glidepath.

The Board then considered what could have caused such a significant deviation. It ruled out any problems with the airplane's structure, systems, or powerplants. The first officer's altimeter was incorrectly set; but the error amounted to only about 30 feet, and the altimeter of the captain (who was flying) was correctly set. Ice accumulation did not contribute to the accident. The ILS, with the exception of the doubtful LOM beacon signal, was found to be functioning properly, and the crew had received accurate guidance to the point of missing the approach the first time. (The Simmons station manager at Alpena heard what he said sounded like Flight 1746 pass directly over the airport a few minutes after he had discussed the airplane's arrival with the crew.)

The board pointed out that if the LOM had been inoperative, then the crew violated the regulations by executing the approach, since the LOM was a critical element of the missed-approach procedure. That they did not request alternative missed-approach instructions suggested to the NTSB that the crew did not know the LOM was out.

Because of the indefinite nature of the data necessary to reconstruct the flight path, the Board was unable to conclude with any certainty where the Bandeirante intercepted the localizer or the glide-slope. But it proposed that if the airplane had intercepted the local-izer inside the LOM it might have been well above the glideslope. Without knowing the distance from the LOM or to the VOR, the cap-tain might have entered a rapid descent to capture the glideslope and, by so doing, allowed the approach to become unstabilized. If the air-plane intercepted the localizer about one mile inside the LOM at the prescribed 2,800 feet, a descent rate of more than 1,000 fpm would have been required to intercept the glideslope, potentially taking the airplane rapidly through and below the glideslope. The touchdown-zone elevation for Runway 1 at Alpena is 685 feet. Unable to prove the point, the Board could only suggest this possibility: The Ban-deirante intercepted the localizer late; the captain then initiated a high rate of descent that continued through the glideslope and decision height to an altitude that was too low to effect a complete recovery. The captain remembered little about the approach.

The Board considered the possibility that the crew had intention-ally ducked down for a better chance of locating the runway's visual indicators, but ruled this out for a couple of reasons. On a precision approach, with vertical guidance to the runway threshold, there was little incentive for the crew to descend below decision height at that distance from the runway; and the captain said he had never felt pres-sured by the company to complete a flight illegally.

Alcohol played a quite prominent role in the report, particularly in regard to the captain but also to a 75-year-old passenger who died. Based on toxicological analysis, the Board decided that she must have been highly intoxicated when she boarded the airplane since no alcohol was served, nor was she seen to consume any on the Ban-deirante. The Board repeated its belief that drunken passengers are a hazard to themselves and their fellow travelers. The airplane did not carry a flight attendant, and it is not known whether the passenger was wearing her lap belt.

The Board spent more time researching the captain's use of alco-hol. By the sheer volume of words devoted to the subject, the NTSB placed significance on the facts that the captain had been seen to consume between eight and 10 beers (quantity of each not estab-lished) at a party and, later, at a club, the night before the accident; that he had been arrested four times for driving while intoxicated (once in 1977, twice in 1978, and once in 1982); that at least one ab-sence-without-notification at a former employer (which fired him) was said to have been alcohol-related; and that he had been de-scribed by people who knew him at Simmons as a heavy drinker while he was off duty. The Board suggested that the captain, even without the presence of alcohol in his system, could still have experienced "hangover effects" from the alcohol consumed the night before, but in the end it admitted that it was unable to determine if his performance on the night of the accident had been affected by alcohol consumption. People who had talked to the captain before the departure of Flight 1746 said that he appeared normal. What's more, he had effectively served as pilot in command in several IMC flights just before the accident, including the execution of a missed approach over the runway at Alpena—all indicating a level of precision flying uncharacteristic of a pilot whose skills were impaired by alcohol. Tests on the first officer revealed no alcohol.

The Board reiterated previous recommendations that turbine aircraft carry cockpit voice recorders and flight-data recorders.

It had a number of recommendations centering on alcohol: support of more alcohol rehabilitation programs; improved screening for drunken passengers; a reexamination of the eight-hour "bottle to throttle" rule; and legislative authority to use the national driver register to identify pilots whose driving licenses have been suspended or revoked for alcohol-related offenses. The captain of Flight 1746 had not met the requirement to show his drunken-driving record on his application for an FAA medical. This subject and the FAA's efforts to expose such pilots have met with much controversy.

The Board also called for better cockpit resource management, another topic that has been receiving more attention. The FAA has just announced an NPRM that would require all multiengine turbo-prop airplanes with 10 or more seats to carry a ground-proximity warning system—another recommendation in this report.

Finally, and perhaps most important in the aftermath of this accident, the Board recommended that all military facilities that are the controlling units for civilian air traffic should be provided with equipment that would allow them to receive updated weather as quickly as FAA facilities can receive it. Simmons has since improved the lines of communication between weather observers, station managers, and flight crews. Had the crew been aware of the special weather observations on that foggy night in Alpena, it probably would not have attempted the approach.

Most human errors are inadvertent; a few, however, are deliberate. Perhaps a deliberate error is not really an error, but something more like a sin. Whatever you call it, deliberately violating an airplane's op-

erating limitations is a mistake. You may get away with it a few times, but sooner or later your luck will run out.

Reverse Psychology
by J. Mac McClellan

On a scale of flying risks, a visual approach to a long runway on a perfectly clear and nearly windless day would rank near the bottom. But on a perfect March day in Detroit a CASA C-212 regional airliner ended up on its back, sliding across the ramp. Both crewmembers were killed, along with seven passengers. It was a miracle that 13 people survived the crash and that nobody on the ramp was injured—the airplane came to rest very near the terminal building. What could have gone wrong under such ideal conditions?

The actual flight path of the CASA was established early in the National Transportation Safety Board's investigation. Several eyewitnesses on the ground, and other pilots deadheading as passengers in the CASA's cabin, reported the same thing: the Spanish-built 22-seat high-wing turboprop was flying higher than normal on short final when it suddenly entered a steep, left, nose-down bank. The airplane then abruptly rolled right to an almost vertical bank and the right wing struck the concrete ramp. The airplane skidded 398 feet across the ramp, striking three ground-support vehicles in front of a terminal gate before bursting into flames.

Early speculation about the cause of the crash centered around engine failure. Witnesses and surviving passengers reported hearing changing sounds from the engines just before the crash. A sudden engine stoppage may have explained the apparent loss of directional control. But examination of the Garrett TPE331 turboprop engines revealed both were operating at the time of impact.

Further examination of the wreckage uncovered maintenance discrepancies with both the engines and propellers. The NTSB discovered that the flight-idle fuel flows were set higher than normal, causing the engines to produce more thrust with the power levers pulled back to the flight-idle stop. The other potentially significant maintenance problem was that incorrect feathering spring assemblies were installed in both propellers. The CASA was equipped with composite blade props that required a double feathering-spring assembly to quickly push the lightweight blades out of prop reverse on landing rollout. The NTSB found that only the single feathering springs used on metal-blade props were installed.

But what would a slightly higher flight-idle setting and a slightly delayed return from prop reverse to normal operation have to do with loss of control under perfect flying conditions? After all, the same airplane had made 402 uneventful landings since the props with the wrong springs had been installed. The NTSB discovered that props on other CASAs also had the wrong feathering springs, but pilots reported no problems. In fact, the airline had flown its CASA fleet through 148,927 landings with only a few isolated instances in which pilots reported problems with a prop sticking in or out of reverse when the power levers were moved to the reverse position. And in those few instances no maintenance problem could be found, and the problem could not be duplicated.

These seemingly minor problems with the props and idle fuel flows took on greater significance when the NTSB interviewed other pilots who had flown with the ill-fated captain. He was a veteran of 17 years with the company and had 17,953 total flying hours, 3,144 of which were flown in the CASA 212. His peers had many positive things to say about his flying skills, but according to the NTSB report, most also said he "handled the CASA 'sportier' than others." Other pilots who had flown with the captain said he was considered a "cowboy" and never used his shoulder harness. He reportedly used steeper descent angles and descent rates on visual approaches, and he frequently flew at or below VREF approach speed to see if he could use the least amount of runway. And he always tried to turn off at the first taxiway. But the most revealing comments came from three first officers who had flown with him. They said he had on occasion retarded the power levers to the "beta" position in flight.

Propellers on turboprop engines operate in a flight range and a beta mode. Within the normal flight range a governor adjusts prop pitch to maintain constant rpm as power and aerodynamic loads change. When the pilot moves the power levers back past the flight-idle stop and into the beta mode, the governor is locked out of the loop, and prop-blade pitch is directly controlled by the power levers. Beta mode ranges from a nearly flat ground-idle pitch to actual reverse prop-blade pitch, which is used to decelerate after landing. Beta mode is *never* to be used in flight.

An NTSB re-creation of the left traffic pattern visual approach flown by the CASA determined that the captain was flying very high and very fast. About five miles from the runway threshold the CASA was flying at 180 knots—descending at about 1,000 fpm—but was still almost 800 feet above the glideslope. At 2.1 nm from the threshold the airplane was 550 feet above glideslope and flying at 150 knots. The NTSB calculates that the power levers were brought back to flight idle at that point and the airplane continued at 150 knots until it was about three-quarters of a mile from the runway. Then, the CASA suddenly slowed to less than 100 knots and went out of control. The NTSB calculates from performance tests flown in another CASA that the airplane could have slowed so suddenly only with 3,000 pounds of negative thrust. The Board concludes that the only possible explanation for such sudden deceleration is that the captain moved the power levers into the beta reverse position and left them there for 15 to 20 seconds.

It's almost unbelievable that a highly experienced pilot would blatantly ignore approved operating procedures and use reverse thrust in flight. But the evidence adds up. Survivors in the cabin and witnesses on the ground reported hearing strange, surging noises from the engines shortly before control was lost. When the NTSB test pilots experimented with beta mode in flight, they heard similar sounds. And there is no other explanation for the sudden deceleration of the CASA on short final.

Use of beta mode is forbidden in flight for a host of reasons, not the least of which is the incredible sink rate that would develop with the props in reverse. With the power levers back to flight idle and the props in a flat pitch, drag is very high and the CASA will develop a sink rate of between 1,500 and 2,000 fpm. You can imagine the sink rate that would result from actual beta reverse. But the most potentially lethal problem of using beta in flight is the one that the NTSB determined caused the crash—the props asymmetrically came out of beta when the captain brought the power levers up. With the airplane slowing at an incredible rate, the tremendous asymmetric thrust of having one engine in normal flight mode and the other still in beta would have been too much for the airplane or the captain to handle.

The NTSB examined the triggers under each power lever knob that lock the levers out of beta mode until they are raised by the pilot, and speculated that it may be possible to inadvertently enter beta mode. But in the end, the Board concluded that the captain's use of beta mode in flight was intentional and consistent with his habits of flying unstabilized approaches.

There is, unfortunately, nothing new to learn from this accident. When the NTSB began its investigation, it was difficult to understand how an airplane could come to grief under such benign flying conditions. But the Board determined that it was human actions—the captain's disregard for operating limitations—that mattered most. The Board makes no attempt to explain why the captain chose to ignore the limitation that prohibited use of beta mode in flight, and neither will I. Instead, I leave it to you to wonder why we break rules, at least on occasion, and for any without sin to cast the first stone.

The final accident in this chapter was particularly gruesome and unnecessary. Because the victims were a rock band, there were inevitably rumors after the crash that the inflight fire had been started by some kind of incendiary drug use, like freebasing cocaine. The NTSB found that the explanation was more mundane.

Falling Stars
by Peter Garrison

Readers who allowed their children to tow them to the film *La Bamba* are aware that in 1959 a singer named Richie Valens died, along with Buddy Holly, and the self-styled Big Bopper, in an airplane crash (it was a chartered Bonanza). The unhappy event was something of a milestone in the history of rock n' roll and was subsequently memorialized in a long, maudlin hit song called "American Pie." Chartered airplanes have in fact dispatched more rock singers than just about anything else except accidental overdoses. Jim Croce and Otis Redding died in airplane crashes; so, more recently, did Eric Hilliard Nelson, whom paleologists of television will remember as the crewcut younger brother, Ricky, in the series *Ozzie and Harriet.*

Nelson, his fiancée, and all five members of his Stone Canyon Band died when their DC-3, en route from Guntersville, Alabama, to Dallas, caught fire in flight. The airplane made a successful emergency landing in a field near DeKalb, Texas, but only the pilot and copilot survived.

The accident sequence, as described by controllers and witnesses on the ground, is simple. The flight left Guntersville at one p.m. CST. At 5:08, one of the crewmembers radioed to Fort Worth Center, with understatement characteristic of pilots in dire emergencies, "I think I'd like to turn around, head for Texarkana here, I've got a little problem."

Several transmissions regarding headings and distances to various possible landing places followed. At 5:11 came the last transmission received from the airplane: ". . . smoke in the cockpit, have smoke in the cockpit." At 5:12, radar showed the DC-3 600 feet above the ground. Radar contact was lost two minutes later.

Witnesses saw the airplane line up with a farm field out of a descending left turn. It was trailing smoke, and bits of falling debris ignited small grass fires in its wake. It struck and severed power lines before landing, gear down, in the field, where it plowed through some trees before coming to rest. Both pilots escaped, seriously injured, through the cockpit windows; but none of the passengers got out. Fire, initially confined to the right side of the cabin, eventually consumed most of the airplane.

National Transportation Safety Board investigators were able to determine from examination of the debris that dropped from the airplane during its landing approach and of the charred fuselage itself that the fire most likely started in the right rear portion of the cabin, where the gasoline-fired cabin heater was located. The heater itself was too badly damaged, however, to reveal a source of ignition. Investigators therefore relied on the testimony of the pilots to piece together the sequence of events that preceded the accident.

The two pilots' accounts of the flight, though given under oath, were notably divergent. According to the captain, he went back to the cabin at one point during the flight to attend to the passengers and noticed smoke in the area occupied by Nelson and his fiancée. He checked the cabin heater and found its fire shield cool to the touch. Seeing no evidence of smoke or fire coming from the heater, he nevertheless activated one of its two built-in fire extinguishers and then opened the fresh-air inlets on his way back through the cabin. When he returned to the cockpit, the copilot was already discussing landing places with center. The captain opened his cockpit window and the smoke increased. "Things rapidly got worse . . . I started a slow descending turn . . . and the window was open, and from there, things went completely blacked out. The smoke came through the cabin . . . it stained the windows, the cockpit glass, everything . . ."

He leaned through the open window to land. After the airplane had stopped, the captain said, he climbed out of the cockpit window and opened the airstair door. He could see into the smoky interior, he said. There was a small fire in the area where he had originally seen smoke, but no one answered his calls; so he left to search for the passengers.

The copilot testified differently. After takeoff, the cabin heater began to "act up," showing an overheat light in the cockpit despite repeated resettings. After a number of unsuccessful attempts to make the heater work properly from the cockpit, the captain went to the passenger cabin several times to try to solve the problem. "He signaled for me to turn it on or he . . . came up front and told me to turn it on or whatever. This happened several times. One of the times I refused to turn it on. I was getting nervous. I didn't think we should be messing with that heater en route. I had discussed this with [the captain] on previous flights . . . he turned it on again . . . Once, again, it either shut off or the overheat light came on, [it] went through the same cycle . . . The last time [the captain] went aft to the tail, he was aft for not very long, came out, and signaled me to turn it on again, which I did. Several minutes after that, [a passenger] . . . came forward to me and said, "There is smoke back here in the cabin.'"

After the emergency landing, the copilot climbed out through the right cockpit window and fell to the ground. There was no fire on the outside of the right side of the airplane, but "the cabin of the aircraft through the windows appeared to be an inferno. Flames and smoke was all that one could see." Fearing an explosion, the copilot moved away from the airplane. He encountered the captain. "Don't tell anyone about the heater," the captain said. "Don't tell anyone about the heater . . ."

The NTSB concluded that, though it was impossible to pinpoint the source of the fire from material evidence, the copilot's testimony suggested that the captain's attempts to troubleshoot the cabin heater in flight had "apparently resulted in a fire" in or near the heater. The Board admitted that other sources of ignition were possible, including "careless smoking or other activity" in the cabin. It did not specify what "other activity" it had in mind.

The Board noted, however, that whatever the source of ignition might have been, the captain had failed to follow recommended emergency procedures for an inflight fire. These included closing the fresh-air vents rather than opening them; instructing the passengers to begin using supplemental oxygen (which was available); and fighting the fire with the fire extinguisher that was in the cockpit. Since it was most likely smoke inhalation that killed or incapacitated the passengers, using oxygen might have enabled some to escape.

The captain's testimony that after he opened the cockpit window "things rapidly got worse" is worth remembering. In general, areas of expanding cross section and curvature on a fuselage are subject to low pressure. Internal spaces are usually at a pressure equal to or higher than ambient. Open cockpit windows therefore pull air out of the cockpit rather than allowing fresh air in. The air that enters the cockpit to replace that which is drawn out usually comes from the after part of the fuselage. Thus, opening the cockpit windows on the DC-3 was most likely responsible for the cockpit filling rapidly with smoke. Ventilating the fuselage probably made conditions in the passenger cabin worse.

Inflight fire is terrifying but uncommon. When it occurs, there is little time to take action. Since it's difficult to think clearly in a cockpit full of smoke, pilots must consider their reactions to a fire in advance. The steps outlined in the emergency procedures section of the flight manual should be memorized. There is valuable insight and experience contained in actions that may appear counterintuitive, such as closing the air vents when smoke is detected.

Above all, time is of the essence. At the first suspicion of fire or smoke the pilot should begin a descent *before doing anything else*. If fire breaks out, every second will count. If it turns out to be a false alarm, he can console himself with the reflection that regaining lost altitude is a minor inconvenience compared with being burned alive.

7

Mixed Bags

The final group of articles in this collection resist classification because several accidents, usually of different types, were included in a single column. The first set consists of three mishaps that were more or less explicitly foreseen, but that even foresight failed to prevent.

Waiting to Happen
by Peter Garrison

We who are still on this side of an accident like to imagine that they come more or less as bolts from the blue. If accidents were preceded by warnings, who would let them happen?

Yet many accidents *are* preceded by warnings of one kind or another. It's not easy to separate the valid warnings from the frivolous ones. Do you cancel if your aunt has a premonition? If a 20,000-hour captain standing beside you looks up at the clouds and says, "I don't like the look of it"? Or if everyone agrees that some place or situation toward which you are heading is "an accident waiting to happen"?

Here is a little bouquet of accidents that were waiting to happen, and did.

The scene of the first is Unalaska, Alaska, a.k.a. Dutch Harbor, a 100-foot-wide, 3,900-foot-long compacted-gravel strip at the eastern end of the Aleutian Islands. The runway, elevation 10 feet, has the Pacific Ocean at both ends and a 600-foot cliff all of 56 feet from, and parallel to, its approach end. It's one of those places where windsocks point accusing fingers at each other from opposite ends of the field.

Many pilots would hesitate to take a Cessna into this airport, but commercial 737 flights use it. Authorization to use 737s for the scheduled Unalaska flights was secured with a restriction on takeoff and landing weights to about 15,000 pounds below normal limits; by Boeing computation, the airplane required 3,700 feet of dry runway for Part 121 landing at the lowered weight.

At the time of the accident, some of the threshold markers had been washed away by the tides, which occasionally flooded the runway and left it covered with debris. The VASI system had also been destroyed by a storm five years earlier; bureaucratic snarls over funding had delayed its replacement.

Some people in the airports divisions at both the federal and state levels said from the outset that it was unsafe to operate 737s at Dutch Harbor, and on a videotape made during the initial approval flight for commercial operations an FAA principal operations inspector was heard to say, "If a pilot's not mighty careful, he'll land short of the runway."

Guess what.

A 737 arrived from Anchorage at Dutch Harbor on a blustery postfrontal afternoon. The flight had been canceled earlier, then reinstated after rains cleared out—but not before they had left three inches of standing water on the approach end of the runway. There was a sigmet in effect calling for moderate to severe turbulence and low-level wind shear.

The airline's operating rules precluded dispatching the flight when there was standing water on the runway, but it was dispatched anyway. During the approach the airplane encountered a 15.7-knot wind shear at 570 feet agl—just within limits in the airplane flight manual, which recommends discontinuing the approach if the indicated airspeed varies by 15 knots or more below 500 feet.

The 15,000-hour captain, who had made only nine previous landings at Dutch Harbor, was flying the airplane. He was uncomfortable with the situation but did not abort the approach. The airplane passed through a downdraft, settling and then leveling out; on short final, it hit another, and did not recover in time.

It hit 72 feet short of the runway in an area cluttered with flotsam and large rocks and logs, bounced, shed its left main gear and left engine, and came to rest, like an airplane making a STOL landing in a Polish joke, about 1,200 feet down the runway. The crew and 17 passengers evacuated the airplane, and there were no serious injuries.

While investigating the accident the National Transportation Safety Board contacted at least 14 737-rated pilots who were familiar with Dutch Harbor. All agreed that, without VASI or some other kind of glideslope guidance, the airport was unsafe. The NTSB recommended that the FAA withdraw its authorization for 737 operations, but the FAA rejected the recommendation.

The second accident took place at Erie, Pennsylvania. It was snowing, and ceilings and visibilities were around minimums but variable; some improvement was forecast. There was wet snow on the runway; braking action was poor.

A DC-9 inbound from Toronto arrived in the area a little before eight a.m. and found the runway visual range (RVR) for the active runway, Runway 6, well below the minimum required for the approach. The crew elected to hold at 10,000 feet, hoping for improvement; but the company dispatcher on the ground advised the flight to overfly Erie and continue to its final destination, Pittsburgh.

In the course of a radio conversation with the operations office, the crew reported that the wind was from 330 degrees at nine knots. It wasn't, and the crew later couldn't remember what had given them the idea that it was. On the basis of this information they requested an ILS approach to Runway 24, whose minimum visibility was equal to the current visibility.

As tower cleared the flight for the approach, it reported the wind as variable from 350 to 020 at nine knots. The weather was indefinite ceiling 200, sky obscured, visibility one-half in light snow and fog. Shortly, tower instructed the flight to hold at 5,000 feet because of an ILS malfunction.

While the ILS was not working, the captain decided to proceed to Pittsburgh. Six minutes later, on being informed that the ILS approach for Runway 24 was available, the captain elected to return to Erie and try the approach. The wind and weather were unchanged.

When the flight contacted tower, the wind was 010 at 10, and there was a report of poor braking action. A few seconds later the tower reported the wind picking up: 010 to 020 at 15.

The jet had a 10-knot tailwind component on a landing on a slushy runway. The airline ops manual explicitly prohibited landings on this runway when it was wet, but the crew either overlooked the prohibition or misunderstood the wind reports.

To complicate matters, the approach was fast. At 500 feet, the first officer called airspeed at 10 knots above reference speed; the flight-data recorder showed that the air-speed actually varied from 13 to 18 knots above V$_{REF}$ throughout the final approach. The DC-9 leveled out at decision height and remained there for eight seconds before continuing its descent; it touched down 2,000 feet beyond the displaced threshold.

You didn't have to be Nostradamus to see what was liable to happen. But the airplane could still have landed safely had the captain used correct technique: Touch down firmly, immediately lower the nose, and apply reverse thrust. Instead, after the airplane touched down the autospoilers failed to deploy because the main-wheel tires, presumably hydroplaning, failed to spin up. Nose-strut compression deploys the autospoilers regardless of wheel spin-up; but the nosewheel did not touch the runway until seven seconds after main-gear contact, and the captain took the time to deploy the spoilers manually before lowering the nose, actuating reverse thrust, and applying the brakes.

The jet went off the end of the runway at about 44 knots and, after striking a chain link fence, came to rest 180 feet beyond and 20 feet below the tarmac. As with the first accident, no one was seriously hurt.

The third accident wasn't so merciful.

Four months after the accident at Dutch Harbor and thousands of miles away, a pilot and 16 parachutists died when a Cessna 208 Caravan lost power after takeoff and crashed during an attempted return to the runway. NTSB investigators found the fuel system contaminated with a "dark, stringy foreign material" resembling algae; and more than a third of the milky liquid recovered from the engine fuel control was water.

Two weeks earlier the airplane had been fueled from contaminated drums and the engine had quit during the takeoff roll with the owner at the controls. At that time, all of the fuel was drained from the airplane and replaced with clean fuel.

Four days later, the owner flew the airplane to a repair facility. The mechanic who worked on it noted various discrepancies in the fuel system: water, discoloration and trash particles in the fuel, a "syrup-like black/brown material" in the header tank. He had drained four gallons of fuel from the system before it finally ran clear.

The mechanic advised the owner to purge the fuel system, but the owner declined, saying that he had already drained it.

A week after that, the airplane was used for a training flight in preparation for a Part 135 check ride. Both pilots noted that the fuel-filter bypass indicator, which is triggered by a blocked fuel filter, went on during the flight. The indicator was reset, but no other action was taken.

Two days later, just before the scheduled check ride, a check of the airplane's fuel revealed it to be "highly contaminated" with water, dirt, and unidentified stuff. The check ride was canceled and the owner of the airplane informed. Again, he described what had been done to correct the problem—namely, that the fuel had been drained almost two weeks earlier—and said that he thought this a sufficient precaution. Later that day the owner flew the airplane away, after being advised not to.

The next day, the Caravan flew parachute operations without incident. A parachutist reported later that he had seen the owner check fuel from the fueling drums and that it had an amber color at first, "like rust from the bottom of the drum," but soon became clear.

It was on the day after this that the accident occurred.

All of these accidents share a common element: They were more or less foreseeable. The short landing at Dutch Harbor had been explicitly predicted. The overshoot at Erie occurred in spite of a company rule forbidding landing on that runway under those conditions. The crash of the Caravan came in the wake of repeated warnings about a clearly identified mechanical problem.

Commercial pilots occasionally find themselves making life-and-death decisions on behalf of a lot of other people. When they make a wrong decision, it is usually because they are in an area of uncertainty—conditions are neither bad enough to force one course of action nor good enough to permit another. In the gray area between, the will is unstable and apt to be set by an obscure impulse.

Once a decision is made, it is hard to unmake. The pilot of the 737 behaved as though it were his destiny to attempt the landing. The pilot of the DC-9 seems to have vacillated about going into Erie at all; but once he determined to try it, he became obstinate, in spite of unfavorable winds and a badly executed approach.

The Caravan's owner, on the other hand, simply did not take due care. Failure to exercise caution is arguably the prerogative of people whose actions affect only themselves, but it is a luxury denied those who act on others' behalf. Would the pilot and all of the parachutists in the Caravan have chosen to make the flight if they had known the airplane's history of fuel contamination?

We can answer with certainty for only one of them. The owner of the airplane was one of the parachutists killed in the crash.

It's rare that accidents are preceded by as much forewarning as those three, but many are just as inevitable, given the incredible recklessness that leads up to them. The next collection unites pilots who seem to have one trait in common: an imprudent single-mindedness.

Exploring the Down-to-Earth
by J. Mac McClellan

Few of the accident reports issued by the National Transportation Safety Board come to profound conclusions or involve unusual circumstances, so most of them tend to pile up on my shelf while I search the files for more meaningful wrecks to analyze. But that may be reverse logic. If most pilots come to a predictable grief, maybe it's time to review the prosaic. Here are three accidents so obviously waiting to happen, I would have been surprised if the pilots hadn't crashed.

In mid-afternoon on an autumn day, a Piper Seneca pilot was briefed for an IFR flight from Springfield, Missouri, to Dothan, Alabama. A cold front was in the Springfield area and forecast to move southeastward, with showers and thunderstorms along and ahead of the front. Terminal forecasts along the route called for broken clouds, showers, and a chance of low-ceiling conditions in thunderstorms.

He was a commercial pilot with an instrument rating and at least 770 hours in the Seneca, but his total flight hours are not known. He filed an IFR flight plan and made a routine departure from Springfield less than 30 minutes after his weather briefing at Springfield Flight Service Station.

About 45 minutes later, as the Seneca was cruising at 11,000 feet, the Memphis Center controller broadcast a convective sigmet. A 30-mile-wide line of thunderstorms with tops to 45,000 feet was on radar. The Seneca pilot's route would cross the northern edge of the reported line of storms. The pilot never asked the controller for advice on how to deviate around the storms. Not surprising; the Seneca was equipped with weather radar, and the line of cells detailed in the sigmet was still far ahead.

The first indication of trouble came when the controller noticed that the Seneca had climbed above its assigned altitude. The controller asked the pilot to report his altitude to be certain that his Mode C radar report was accurate.

"We're in a cell here, and ah, we're going back to one-one-zero," the Seneca pilot responded. "I'm going through one-one-two hundred now." He made no request for a turn to exit the cell. He didn't ask how other pilots in the area were doing. He didn't even ask for a block altitude in which to ride out the turbulence.

In fact, he never made another transmission. A few seconds after the pilot reported returning to 11,000 feet, the controller saw his Mode C report descend to 10,300 feet and then go into "track coast," which means that the radar was no longer receiving a reliable return. A nearby pilot flying VFR at 8,500 feet reported no problems with thunderstorms or with turbulence.

No witnesses saw the Seneca emerge from the clouds, but the sheriff thought he heard an exploding sound following a normal crack of thunder. The airplane broke apart in flight and the wreckage was scattered over several acres of farmland. The pilot was the only person on board.

Analysis of National Weather Service radar of the area revealed that the Seneca was about three miles south of a level-four "very strong" weather echo and flying in an area of moderate rain. The weather service also reported that moderate to severe turbulence, and updrafts and downdrafts, probably occurred in the thunderstorm.

Why did this pilot fly into a strong thunderstorm that everybody seemed to know was there? Nobody knows. Toxicological tests revealed he had a blood alcohol level of .0336 percent. In most states .1 percent is the level that is necessary to be considered a drunken driver, but maybe a little booze dulls a pilot's natural terror of thunderstorms.

A Beech Baron 58 pilot and his passenger planned to fly their airplane from Leesburg, Virginia, to Hot Springs, Virginia, early in the morning. At Hot Springs the pilot planned to pick up two passengers for a charter flight to Florida. When the Baron departed for the short flight, no weather reporting was available at Hot Springs, an airport serving a posh resort area located deep in the Virginia mountains.

The Baron's pilot had at least 10,000 hours' total flying experience. He left Leesburg in IFR conditions: low clouds, light rain, fog, and drizzle. Hot Springs issues weather reports only when the airport is attended, and at no time during the flight did the pilot have a valid report of conditions at the destination.

The flight proceeded normally and the Baron pilot was cleared—after the controller reminded him that no weather reporting was available—to intercept and track the localizer to Runway 24 at Hot Springs. The pilot replied, "That's what I'm doing." But he wasn't doing it very well. The controller told the Baron pilot that he was three miles south of the localizer and issued a vector of 270 degrees to rejoin.

That's when the pilot told the controller he wasn't receiving the localizer and asked to confirm the frequency. The frequency was correct, and the Baron pilot reported he still hadn't picked up the localizer and continued the approach.

There were no notams or other reports of problems with the Hot Springs ILS equipment, so the controller issued the Baron pilot an ILS approach clearance and terminated radar service. The pilot accepted the clearance from ATC and continued, though he still wasn't receiving the localizer signal.

It seems that the Baron pilot attempted to fly the ILS using only the ADF outer marker signal for lateral guidance. As he flew inbound from the outer marker, still in the clouds and no longer sure of his position, he called the controller and asked if he was still on radar. The controller told him that he was two miles northeast of the airport.

Finally, the Baron pilot told the controller, "[I] missed it. I never did get the localizer and I can't do it [fly the approach] with the ADF." The controller instructed the pilot to climb to 6,000 feet and never heard from him again.

The actual weather conditions at Hot Springs were indefinite ceiling 100 feet, sky obscured, one-eighth of a mile visibility in fog. Because the airport was unattended, minimums for the ILS approach were 630 feet above the runway and two miles visibility. The Hot Springs NDB approach, which is based on the outer marker, has a minimum descent altitude of 629 feet above the runway; but a straight-in approach is not authorized without a local altimeter setting (when the airport is unattended, the Roanoke altimeter setting must be used, and circling minimums for the approach are 1,508 feet agl and three miles visibility).

The Baron crashed about 200 feet below the airport elevation. The outer marker transmitter is located about 1,800 feet below the runway, with terrain rising away from it toward the runway threshold. When the Hot Springs airport manager arrived in his office, around the time of the crash, he instantly saw that the localizer transmitter had been tripped off the air by its automatic internal monitors.

The system is designed to detect possible problems with the ILS transmitters and shut them off to prevent false signals from being broadcast. The theory is that pilots will not attempt an approach without receiving a valid, identified signal. The localizer, glideslope, and outer marker each had independent automatic monitors. Only the localizer had been tripped off.

A reconstruction of the radar track shows that the Baron pilot flew almost directly over the outer marker at the appropriate altitude. The airplane then continued down the correct approach path, descending on the electronic glideslope. Everything appeared reasonably normal on radar until the airplane reached descent minimums, at which point the Baron's airspeed and rate of descent increased and the airplane wandered slightly left of course. It struck rugged terrain below and short of the runway, with the landing gear and flaps up, suggesting that the pilot had begun a missed approach.

It's apparent from his comments to the controller that the pilot tried to fly an ILS using only the outer marker ADF signal for lateral guidance. Even in his last transmission, shortly before impact, he reported that he had never received the localizer.

A pilot busting the minimums at a fog-bound airport in the mountains defies reason. But trying to fly an ILS without any localizer guidance defies imagination.

A Bell 47D helicopter pilot and his friend moved the helicopter out of the hangar on a warm, late-winter day in southern Missouri. The mission: a short pleasure flight around the local area. The weather was perfect for the outing.

As the two maneuvered the helicopter on its ground-handling wheels, the right wheel and skid slipped off the concrete helipad and got stuck in the mud. After much effort the pilot and his friend were unable to pull the Bell back onto the pad. The pilot told his friend to stand clear; he would fly the helicopter out.

That may sound reasonable to an airplane pilot who's blasted the throttle to taxi through soft sod, but in a helicopter it's a sure prescription for disaster because of a phenomenon, peculiar to helicopters, known as dynamic rollover.

There are several possible takeoff and landing situations that can lead to dynamic rollover, but a stuck skid is the classic example. Every helicopter pilot learns that during basic instruction.

To understand dynamic rollover, you must understand that a helicopter pilot is flying the rotor disc, not the airframe, as one does in an airplane. During normal maneuvering a rotor disc assumes many different angles relative to the fuselage. For example, in forward flight the rotor disc is tilted forward, pulling the helicopter along.

In a turn the rotor disc banks into the turn and the fuselage follows. When landing on a slope the rotor disc remains level relative to the horizon while the fuselage settles on its landing gear at an angle.

But there are limits to the relationship between rotor disc angle and the fuselage that cannot be exceeded. When one skid is stuck to the ground, the helicopter pivots laterally around it, banking toward the stuck skid, which acts as a fulcrum. The helicopter begins to rise, but let's say the right skid is firmly planted. The pilot senses the helicopter rolling to the right, so he moves the cyclic left, which levels the rotor disc parallel to the ground. But as the helicopter continues to rise the fuselage continues to roll right, toward the stuck skid, very slowly, and the pilot continues to move the cyclic left to counteract the roll. At some point the pilot has the cyclic full left and the rotor disc can no longer be flown level with the ground. When that happens the rotor disc begins to roll with the fuselage and its thrust (instead of lifting straight up) is now a vector pointed right.

It's over in a split second. The thrust of the tilted main rotor shoves the helicopter over on its side, and it thrashes to pieces.

An eyewitness said the left skid of the Bell 47 lifted off the ground several times before the helicopter suddenly rolled over and caught fire. The witness said a piece of one main rotor blade flew off just before the Bell 47 rolled over, but the NTSB blamed the accident on dynamic rollover caused by the pilot's poor judgment in trying to take off with a stuck skid. Dynamic rollover happens so quickly and from such an apparently small bank angle that the witness could have seen the rotor piece depart as the blades were striking the ground.

It's hard enough to understand how a helicopter pilot could be ignorant of dynamic rollover, but there's more. The helicopter was more than two and a half years out of annual, had been built from scavenged parts, and had not complied with three airworthiness directives issued against it. Worse yet, the landing gear skids had been moved inboard about 11 inches on each side so that the helicopter would fit on a trailer. There was no supplemental type certificate or any other authorization for the landing-gear modification.

Such a cavalier attitude toward safety may also make a pilot believe he's immune to dynamic rollover.

The two pilots in the next article have nothing in common other than that they both flew Bonanzas and both crashed in fog. One paid the price of his recklessness. What the other may have been paying for we don't know; perhaps just one small mistake.

Twice-Told Tale
by J. Mac McClellan

Two Bonanzas crashed on dark winter nights at opposite ends of the country. One fits a high-risk scenario perfectly, while the other has no apparent cause.

In Hamilton, Alabama, a VFR-only pilot was seen flying his Bonanza A36 at low altitude near the Marion County Airport in fog and drizzle. There was no weather reporting available, but witnesses estimated visibility at one-half to three-quarters of a mile.

In California, an experienced IFR pilot was flying an ILS into Sacramento Metro Airport in weather that was officially, but only marginally, IFR. For reasons unknown, the pilot declared a missed approach and crashed about 1.5 nm west of the ILS Runway 16.

The two pilots apparently had different attitudes and capabilities. The pilot in California was reportedly a careful and qualified IFR pilot flying in weather that was easily within his and the airplane's capabilities. According to others who knew him, the other pilot ignored the rules, and continued VFR flight into low instrument conditions. While the cause of the IFR pilot's crash remains a mystery, the VFR pilot was done in by a combination of circumstances, including poor judgment.

The NTSB was unable to determine the total flight hours or recent flying experience of the A36 pilot in Alabama, but he was well known at his home airport. "Everybody around here sort of expected [him] to crash in weather, but not so far away from the field," his home-base airport manager and sometimes instructor told the National Transportation Safety Board. "[He] was a good VFR pilot, but it is my impression, as well as other pilots who flew with him, that he was scared to hand-fly in instrument meteorological conditions. However, I flew with him a few months back, and he could control the airplane with the autopilot off in IMC, but he did believe in his RNAV and autopilot."

The airport manager described how the A36 pilot used an RNAV-based semi-IFR procedure to find his way back to Haleyville Airport, his home airport, when the weather was bad. Even though the crash occurred 17 nm southwest of his home base, the pilot had told the airport manager he would be returning that night. Before departing Jackson, Mississippi, he told the Jackson controllers he was "trying to make up his mind—I'm either going into Birmingham or Haleyville, and I'm going to leave out of here at 3,500 feet."

Routine radar advisories were issued in the Jackson TRSA, and the Bonanza pilot was cleared from the frequency and told to squawk 1200. The NTSB provides no information on the progress of the flight over the approximately 150 nm from Jackson to Hamilton. There were marginal VFR weather conditions in the area, with Muscle Shoals, the closest weather observation point 40 nm to the northeast, reporting a 2,000-foot broken ceiling with three miles visibility in fog. Because Hamilton lies almost on a direct course from Jackson to the pilot's home airport of Haleyville, one might assume he was trying to make it home when he was seen maneuvering near Hamilton.

Maybe he had flown in weather this bad before and had made it home. Or maybe the weather closed in quickly and he became disoriented in the fog, which can happen quickly at night. Evidence of a vacuum-pump failure found in the wreckage is most revealing. The autopilot was found in the heading mode, and the NTSB determined that the vacuum-pump shaft had sheared before the engine was stopped by the crash.

Such clues clarify the picture. The pilot knew his turf well and was reportedly experienced as a scud runner who relied on his RNAV for guidance and on the autopilot to control the airplane. When the vacuum pump failed, both his attitude and directional gyros would have spun down, giving erroneous information to the autopilot, which could have followed the misleading gyro commands into the ground.

But the vacuum pump, gyros, or autopilot cannot be blamed entirely for this crash. The pilot was VFR rated only, flying in deteriorating weather on a dark night. His turn-and-bank indicator was inoperative, as were the altitude-hold and pitch functions of the autopilot. Why a pilot who reportedly placed faith and trust in his autopilot failed to maintain his only hope is unimaginable. Had the pump—which had 730 hours in service—not failed at that exact moment, pilot and passenger would have survived. Or, more reasonably, had the pilot decided not to take off into marginal conditions, or had he earned an IFR rating and maintained instrument proficiency, he would still be among us.

No such pat-and-tidy conclusion can be made about the Sacramento crash. This Bonanza pilot had an instrument rating, more than 3,000 hours of flight time and had reportedly flown 60 hours in the past six months. He demonstrated a cautious attitude toward flying when talking with the FSS briefer. He had planned to fly his F33A from Riverside, California, to Bend, Oregon, that night but was concerned about a storm brewing over the northern sections of the route. He told the briefer he would fly to Sacramento and wait to complete the trip the next day.

The pilot departed Riverside VFR and contacted Sacramento FSS for a weather report. Conditions at Sacramento Metro were sky partially obscured, estimated 1,100 broken, 5,000 overcast, visibility three miles in fog—no problem for an IFR pilot and an airport served by an ILS approach.

When the pilot called Sacramento Approach Control and requested an IFR clearance into the airport, he was immediately issued the clearance, weather, and vectors for the approach. Everything was routine, but the Bonanza was not descending quickly enough, so the pilot said he would extend the landing gear to increase his rate of descent. The controller vectored the Bonanza pilot across the localizer to allow additional time for descent and then turned him back on an intercept heading and cleared him for the ILS approach with instructions to call the tower.

The pilot reported passing the outer marker to Sacramento tower and was cleared to land. The controller read off RVR visibility of 5,500 feet at touchdown, greater than 6,000 feet at midfield and 5,000 at the roll-out end. Minimums for the ILS approach were 1,800 feet RVR.

Nothing about the approach seemed unusual to the Sacramento controllers until, two minutes and 36 seconds after passing the outer marker, the Bonanza pilot told the tower, "I better make a missed, a missed." That was the last transmission from the pilot. The last radar fix was a quarter mile north of the runway at 100 feet agl.

A missed approach at night in bad weather can be a challenging maneuver, admittedly, but the weather was not bad enough to cause an accident. The captain of a PSA BAe 146 jet on final behind the Bonanza reported that he had the runway clearly in sight from outside the outer marker. He reported the weather to be clear with "a lot of ground fog."

The PSA captain said he became concerned when he heard the Bonanza pilot report the missed approach, wondering why that pilot could not see the runway when he could see it clearly from several miles out: "In retrospect, I think he may not have been able to see the runway if he were significantly below the glideslope. As I said, there was a lot of ground fog in the area, and if he were low, he might have gotten into it."

The NTSB sheds no light on the actual cause of the crash. "IFR procedure—not followed—pilot-in-command" is the official probable cause, which is as useful as saying the crash was caused by the airplane striking the ground.

What else is there to say? Investigators determined that the vacuum pump and instruments were operating normally; the engine was developing power; the pilot was experienced and certified; and the runway could be seen for miles. We can learn how to avoid the mistakes of the scud-running pilot in Alabama, but the Sacramento crash remains a mystery.

The NTSB publishes hundreds of brief summaries of aircraft accidents every year—summaries too lacking in detail for a full Aftermath column. Every once in a while, though, we can make a full meal out of leftovers.

The Good, Bad and Ugly
by Peter Garrison

In the Middle Ages people who couldn't find a fortune teller would obtain advice by opening a copy of Virgil's *Aeneid* at random and poking a finger at the page; they would read the lines upon which their finger fell as advice for the future. Sentences picked at random from the NTSB's narratives also often seemed laden with a more general kind of significance for a future that is now past:

"While on a corporate flt thru a canyon in marginal wx . . ."

"During a pleasure flight, the pilot intentionally shut down the engine . . ."

"During a solo flight, the student pilot attempted a landing in a neighbor's cow pasture . . ."

Others seem a bit comical, if it is permissible to chuckle over the misfortunes of others:

"The acft struck three cows . . ."

". . . the right wing dropped off . . ,"

". . . landed on a grass strip adjacent to the paved rwy, to 'save the tires' . . ."

In these narratives one encounters the extremes of human fortune, good and bad. In Sparta, Illinois, an airplane landed uneventfully after a skydiver's parachute deployed while he was still in the airplane. The jumper hit the stabilizer after the billowing parachute dragged him out. Miraculously, he landed uneventfully as well.

A Piper and a Cessna collided at 6,000 feet. Both landed safely. A Piper and a homebuilt collided in the traffic pattern; they, too, landed safely. Accidents like this restore your faith in midair collisions.

Bad luck and good luck often go hand in hand. The pilot of a Mooney lost control of the airplane while flying "over a black cloud at 8,500 ft." It was, he said, as if an "invisible tornado had reached out" and grabbed the airplane, which went into a spin—all the way to the ground. The airplane's wings were torn off by trees and it struck the ground inverted. Yet both the pilot and his passenger survived.

In the "Enough, already!" department: The pilot of a Cessna 337 bound for Hawaii was about 10 hours out of Oakland when the rear engine overheated. He shut it down, feathered the prop, bumped up the power a bit on the front engine, and crossed his fingers. An hour later the front engine overheated. He reduced power on the front engine and restarted the rear, but it soon ran so roughly that he caged it again. He was giving a position report to a Coast Guard C-130 when the front engine quit completely. He ditched in the ocean and was eventually picked up. So much for twin-engine safety.

Hours are no guarantee, either. A 10,000-hour pilot became so engrossed in conversation with a passenger during takeoff that he allowed the airplane to settle back onto the runway after he had retracted the landing gear. A 15,000-hour pilot lost power in IMC; he broke out 300 feet above the ground with one mile visibility and bellied into a field. Luckily he was in Indiana, not Utah. Total fuel aboard: one cup.

Some accidents don't seem to be accidents at all, but statements. An 8,000-hour professional pilot argued with his wife about his drinking, then left the house at nine p.m., announcing (correctly, as it turned out) that this might be the last time he flew. He hit the ground at a 75-degree angle with .21 percent alcohol in his blood—almost three times the legal criterion for drunken driving in many states.

The number of accidents in which alcohol plays a role would astound the majority of pilots, who wouldn't think of flying shortly after drinking. In one case, the pilot of a Taylorcraft crashed on the median of an interstate highway while on a seven-mile flight. He had been visiting friends and had enhanced the effect of the libations that he shared with them with an antidepressant drug. His spirits thus buoyed, he continued drinking as he flew the airplane down the highway at 1:30 a.m. Not surprisingly, he did not remember how he had got onto the median. His blood alcohol level was a relatively modest .15 percent.

Some pilots evidently haven't been reading Aftermath, because they keep making the same horrible errors of judgment that we've been writing about for years. One with 122 hours in his logbook set off with a friend at night in marginal weather—1,200 overcast and five miles—over the sparsely lighted wastes of east Texas. They ended up snagging some inconveniently tall trees. The pilot blamed the accident on an altimeter malfunction; but investigators tested the altimeter and found that in spite of not having been serviced in 17 years, it still worked fine.

A 61-hour pilot and his wife took off in a 152 to photograph the beautiful fall colors. They flew into a box canyon where the density altitude was 10,400 feet. That's the end of that story.

A 500-hour pilot tried to take off in predawn darkness just as heavy fog rolled over the airport. Witnesses preflighting their own airplane (they decided not to go because of the deteriorating weather) couldn't see the other airplane, but they heard it run up and then take off. Shortly the engine sound changed to a high-pitched scream. Then came a thump. Then silence. The wreckage was found on the airport. The late pilot had received 2.8 hours of instrument dual seven years earlier.

A 100-hour pilot tried to cross a portion of the Colorado Rockies in a Cessna 150 in darkness, high winds, and blowing snow. You guessed it. The wreckage was pointed straight down.

An instrument-rated businessman-pilot with 4,000 hours flew his Bonanza into clouds and rain. No contact with center; just a controlled descent from 9,500 to 5,500—and a mountain—on a straight line from the starting point to the destination. Loran has made perfectly positioned accidents possible for everyone.

Quite a few airplanes lose power on takeoff. Since many of these balky engines run fine after the accident, carb ice and fuel contamination are the usual suspects. Many power losses occur, it would seem, because of problems brought on in one way or another by autogas—or perhaps this recurrent finding merely betrays a prejudice against autogas on the part of accident investigators.

Pilots continue to take off with frost on their wings. They continue to try to land at night on unlighted runways. They forget to check their oil caps and lose their oil after takeoff. And with uncanny regularity pilots crash with fuel in one tank and the selector pointing to the other.

Negligent maintenance crops up from time to time. In one sad case, a Beech 18 flying night cargo went out of control when the right wing's deice boot partially tore loose and spoiled lift on that wing. The boots had not been maintained in 10 years, and the pilot's wife reported that he had previously been pressured to fly in airplanes with discrepancies—not an uncommon occurrence with carriers operating on a shoestring.

I can hear Peter, Paul, and Mary now: *When will they ever learn?* It's small wonder that Part 91 operations have a far worse safety record than Part 121 operations. Whereas all aviation is subject to the hazards of mechanical failure and weather, Part 121 operations are generally (though not absolutely) free of those of pilot inexperience, ineptitude, and gross disregard for the warning signs that in the wake of an accident are often clearly seen to have preceded it. (They are also, of course, free of the hazards attendant upon aerial application, bush flying, external load work, and so on, all of which is chalked up to the account of Part 91 flying.)

A more rigorous flight training syllabus might eliminate some of the many accidents that involve undershooting, overrunning, and veering off the side of the runway. A little more fear and caution might be salubrious for some pilots. But probably the government could make the biggest dent in the accident stats just by mailing a volume or two of these accident briefs to every student pilot on his birthday.

Other Bestsellers of Related Interest

THE ILLUSTRATED GUIDE TO AERODYNAMICS
2nd Edition
H. C. "Skip" Smith
Avoiding technical jargon and scientific explanations, this guide demonstrates how aerodynamic principles affect every aircraft in terms of lift, thrust, drag, in-air performance, take-off velocities, load and velocity-load factors, hypersonic flight, area rules, laminar flow airfoils, planform shapes, computer-aided design, and high-performance lightplanes.
#157748-3   Hardcover $28.95

STICK AND RUDDER: An Explanation of the Art of Flying
Wolfgang Langewiesche
Students, certificated pilots, and instructors alike have praised this book as "the most useful guide to flying ever written." The book explains the important phases of the art of flying, in a way the learner can use. It shows precisely what the pilot does when he flies, just how he does it, and why.
#036240-8   Hardcover $19.95

THE PILOT'S AIR TRAFFIC CONTROL HANDBOOK
2nd Edition
Paul E. Illman
Keep up with the most recent changes in rules and regulations and gain an understanding of why air traffic control is essential for both safe and legal flight with this handbook. It familiarizes you with the national airspace system, the federal facilities that comprise the ATC system, and the operating procedures required to use the system properly—including a close-up look at the new airspace designations currently being implemented.
#031769-0   Paperback $18.95
#031768-2   Hardcover $28.95

STANDARD AIRCRAFT HANDBOOK

5th Edition

Edited by Larry Reithmaier, originally compiled and edited by Stuart Leavell and Stanley Bungay

Now updated to cover the latest in aircraft parts, equipment, and construction techniques, this classic reference provides practical information on FAA-approved metal airplane hardware. Techniques are presented in step-by-step fashion and explained in shop terms without unnecessary theory and background. All data on materials and procedures is derived from current reports by the nation's largest aircraft manufacturers.

#157642-8   Paperback $11.95

THE PILOT'S RADIO COMMUNICATIONS HANDBOOK

4th Edition

Paul E. Illman

"If you own or are responsible for maintaining a panel, [this book] should have a spot on your bookshelf right next to the airplane's service manual."

—*Private Pilot*
on the previous edition

Learn to use your radio correctly with this book. Increase your flight safety with correctly worded communications and gain the knowledge of radio communications and ground facilities you need to go beyond the local airport. Additions to this edition include new airspace classifications, emergency procedures, hazardous inflight weather advisories, the 30-mile Mode C veil, new requirements for Mode C transponders in Class B airspace and more.

#0317740-4   Hardcover $29.95

SEPARATED BY WAR: An Oral History by Desert Storm Fliers & Their Families

Ed Herlik

"I highly recommend these stories to you."   **—*Colonel Steve Ritchie*,** USAF,
the only Air Force Pilot Ace
from the Vietnam War

Here are the intensely personal, extremely moving stories of 15 American and British pilots who fought in the Persian Gulf War and the families they left behind. From the controlled chaos of the cockpit to loneliness and uncertainty on the homefront, this book records the harsh reality of modern air combat as well as the emotions of the loved ones waiting for news from the war.

#028362-1   Hardcover $24.95

How to Order

Call 1-800-822-8158
24 hours a day,
7 days a week
in U.S. and Canada

Mail this coupon to:
McGraw-Hill, Inc.
P.O. Box 182067,
Columbus, OH 43218-2607

Fax your order to:
614-759-3644

EMAIL
70007.1531@COMPUSERVE.COM
COMPUSERVE: GO MH

Shipping and Handling Charges

Order Amount	Within U.S.	Outside U.S.
Less than $15	$3.50	$5.50
$15.00 - $24.99	$4.00	$6.00
$25.00 - $49.99	$5.00	$7.00
$50.00 - $74.49	$6.00	$8.00
$75.00 - and up	$7.00	$9.00

EASY ORDER FORM—
SATISFACTION GUARANTEED

Ship to:

Name _____

Address _____

City/State/Zip _____

Daytime Telephone No. _____

Thank you for your order!

ITEM NO.	QUANTITY	AMT.

Method of Payment:

☐ Check or money order
enclosed (payable to
McGraw-Hill)

☐ *VISA*   ☐ DISCOVER

☐ AMERICAN EXPRESS Cards   ☐ MasterCard

Shipping & Handling charge from chart below	
Subtotal	
Please add applicable state & local sales tax	
TOTAL	

Account No. ☐☐☐☐☐☐☐☐☐☐☐☐☐☐☐☐☐

Signature _____ Exp. Date _____
Order invalid without signature

**In a hurry? Call 1-800-822-8158 anytime,
day or night, or visit your local bookstore.**

Code = BC15ZZA